Critiques of Capital in Modern Britain and America

Critiques of Capital in Modern Britain and America

Transatlantic Exchanges 1800 to the Present Day

Edited by

Mark Bevir
Associate Professor
Department of Political Science
University of California, Berkeley

and

Frank Trentmann
Senior Lecturer
School of History, Classics and Archaeology
Birkbeck College
London

First published 2002 by
PALGRAVE MACMILLAN
Houndmills, Basingstoke, Hampshire RG21 6XS and
175 Fifth Avenue, New York, N.Y. 10010
Companies and representatives throughout the world.

PALGRAVE MACMILLAN is the global academic imprint of the Palgrave
Macmillan division of St Martin's Press, LLC and of Palgrave Macmillan Ltd.
Macmillan® is a registered trademark in the United States, United Kingdom
and other countries. Palgrave is a registered trademark in the European
Union and other countries.

ISBN 978-0-333-98081-1 hardback

This book is printed on paper suitable for recycling and made from fully
managed and sustained forest sources. Logging, pulping and manufacturing
processes are expected to conform to the environmental regulations of the
country of origin.

A catalogue record for this book is available
from the British Library.

Library of Congress Cataloging-in-Publication Data
Critiques of capital in modern Britain and America : transatlantic exchanges
1800 to the present day / edited by Mark Bevir and Frank Trentmann.
        p.cm.
    Includes bibliographical references and index.
    ISBN 0–333–98081–6 (cloth)
        1. Capital. I. Bevir, Mark. II. Trentmann, Frank.
HB501 .C796 2002
330.12'2–dc21   2002075964

10   9   8   7   6   5   4   3   2   1
11 10 09 08 07 06 05 04 03 02

Contents

Notes on the Contributors

Christopher Beauchamp is a doctoral student in history at the University of Cambridge. He is completing a PhD on the politics of the telephone industry in the United States and Britain.

Mark Bevir is Associate Professor in the Department of Political Science at the University of California, Berkeley. He has also held permanent posts at the University of Newcastle, and a Leverhulme Studentship at the University of Madras. He is the author of *The Logic of the History of Ideas* (1999).

Jamie L. Bronstein is Associate Professor of History at New Mexico State University. She is the author of *Land Reform and Working-Class Experience in Britain and the United States* (1999), which won the Samuel Beer Prize of the American Political Science Association. She is currently researching the social and cultural history of accidents in the nineteenth-century transatlantic workplace.

Simon Caney is Senior Lecturer in the Department of Politics at the University of Newcastle. He has published articles in philosophy and politics journals on liberalism, cosmopolitanism, intervention and human rights. He is the editor, with Peter Jones, of *Human Rights and Global Diversity* (2001), and is completing a book to be entitled *Global Political Theory* (forthcoming)

Sandra den Otter is Associate Professor of History at Queen's University Canada. She is the author of *British Idealism and Social Explanation* (1996).

Kevin Grant is an Assistant Professor in the History Department at Hamilton College. He received his PhD from the University of California at Berkeley and has worked on the history of the British Empire. He is presently completing a book entitled *A Civilised Savagery: Britain and the New Slaveries in Africa, 1884–1926.*

Colin Hay is Professor of Political Analysis in the Department of Political Science and International Studies at the University of Birmingham (UK). He is the author of a number of books, including most recently, *Political Analysis* (2002), *British Politics Today* (2002) and *Demystifying Globalization* (2000, with D. Marsh). He is an editor of the new international journal *Comparative European Politics.*

Axel R. Schäfer teaches US History at Keele University. He received his PhD from the University of Washington. His main research interests are in nineteenth and twentieth-century US social thought and social policy. He is currently working on a cultural history of the US welfare state.

Frank Trentmann is Senior Lecturer in History at Birkbeck College, London, and Director of Cultures of Consumption, an ESRC/AHRB research programme. He has also taught at Princeton University and the Universität Bielefeld. He has written on consumption, citizenship, and political culture, and is the editor of *Paradoxes of Civil Society* (2000).

1
Critique within Capitalism: Historiographical Problems, Theoretical Perspectives

Mark Bevir and Frank Trentmann

The collapse of the Berlin Wall in 1989 marked the end of a historical constellation dominated by a divide between socialism and capitalism.[1] The decade after 1989 was prone to celebrations of the triumph of the latter over the former. 'Real socialism' has indeed effectively ceased to exist – almost no country today pursues a socialist path of development. However, rather than seeing the historical failure of real socialism as justifying a neoliberal triumphalism in which global capitalism has swept all before it, we can use it as an opportunity to retrieve alternative critiques of capitalism, for 1989 inevitably also eroded the conceptual pairing of socialism and capitalism. This volume offers new histories of capitalism and social justice; it reappraises diverse critiques of capitalism, their historical and transnational genealogies, their theoretical workings, their impact on political economy, and their continuing legacy and relevance today.

As the first industrial nation, Britain offers a uniquely rich field for our revisionist project. The dialogue between intellectual traditions, social practices and modern capitalism first took shape in Britain in the eighteenth century, and Britain's pioneering role often made the British case the ideal or critical model for debate and developments elsewhere. Nonetheless, the imperial and transnational dimensions of Britain's power and cultural influence ensured that its experience was never insular or self-contained. On the one hand, although other countries faced different problems and conceived these from within different traditions, they often did so in a context in which the British experience and British debates provided constant points of reference. On the other hand, British debates often drew on ideas and images associated with other parts of the globe, especially those over which it exercised, or had exercised, imperial power.

If the end of the false dichotomy between socialism and capitalism makes it possible to tell new histories, related developments in philosophy and history have changed the ways that these can be told. Historical studies have followed a range of linguistic, cultural and postmodern turns promoting greater sensitivity to the languages and beliefs of the past.

1

Historians no longer reduce meanings to 'real' socioeconomic developments; they have moved beyond the restricted focus on nation-states; and they have consequently become more sensitive to diverse critiques of capitalism. The pioneering role of British social historians in the international development of social history as a professional subject and political commitment meant that the arrival of the linguistic turn provoked particularly explosive debates therein.[2] Once again, then, the British case, itself placed within an Atlantic and global context, offers a convenient entry point into larger methodological and theoretical arguments.

Our theoretical approach and historical questions sit comfortably alongside many themes associated with the linguistic turn. We locate diverse critiques in languages or traditions rather than returning to the reductionism implicit in orthodoxy. Equally, however, we tie languages to traditions and practices, and the ways these develop in response to dilemmas, so as to encourage new ways of conceiving of the interaction of economy and culture. Traditions here refer to social complexes of belief that embed individuals, giving them their initial beliefs and influencing their later reasoning. By practices we mean the complexes of actions, often stable over time, that arise from the intersubjective beliefs and understandings of individuals. Our notions of tradition and practice thus embrace social movements and institutions conceived as the more or less stable emergent entities that arise out of diverse sets of beliefs and actions. If the old social history suffered from a materialist account of culture, the new preoccupation with language has often led to an unfortunate divorce of ideas and culture from the changing material world of political economy. By contrast, our invocation of traditions and practices captures the relationship between belief and action or praxis, between the interaction of ethical, social and political efforts to reform or transcend capitalism and the development of commercial and industrial societies. Retrieving alternative critiques of capitalist society is also, therefore, an opportunity for reintegrating the historical study of ideas, society and political economy.

The chapters in this volume unpack diverse critiques of capitalism by exploring how different accounts of capitalism are constructed from within wider webs of beliefs often embedded in distinct social and political practices. They then explain these beliefs and practices by reference to the traditions that informed them, and the dilemmas in response to which people modified the relevant traditions, where the development of these traditions and dilemmas takes place in a series of transnational exchanges. Our opening chapter provides a pathway through the principal historiographical and theoretical undergrowth of this revisionist project. A brief discussion of the intellectual and political challenges to orthodoxy points to continuity, transnationalism and populism as prominent themes in new narratives of capitalism and its critiques. We then highlight methodological and theoretical blind spots in these new narratives, especially the twin problems of explaining change and of situating languages in beliefs and practices. New, more persuasive narratives, we believe, will arise once we exchange a problematic view of language as a quasi-structure that provides individuals with beliefs with one in which individuals are influenced by traditions but are nonetheless creative actors capable of modifying the beliefs they thus inherit. The latter view opens up fresh questions and perspectives on the evolving relationship between modern capitalism and ideas of social justice. Greater attention needs to be given to the pluralistic and evolving nature of traditions, and to how individuals and groups respond to dilemmas by changing their beliefs. Critique and capitalism are not opposites but interwoven processes, deeply implicated in the evolution of each other.

Historiographical issues: class and language

The linguistic turn has transformed an orthodox historiography that emerged in the late nineteenth century alongside the socialist movement, and then remained largely unchallenged within social history until the 1970s.[3] Orthodoxy attracted Marxists, labourists, and some progressives, ranging from G. D. H. Cole to the Hammonds, and E. P. Thompson to Eric Hobsbawm. These historians generally told a unified and linear story about capitalism and its critics. Capitalism, they argued, possessed an innate, largely natural trajectory that was defined by its inner laws. Initial opposition to capitalism took the form of Luddite resistance, which was soon exposed as naïve.[4] Social critics had to learn to come to terms with a capitalist society generated independently of their beliefs and their actions. Once the workers caught up with this reality – once they acquired greater class-consciousness around 1832 – they then began increasingly to aim at class cohesion as a means of acquiring political power.[5] Their class-consciousness appeared and grew in Chartism, the trades union movement, the Labour Party, and the welfare state. Orthodox historiography thus defined a clear research agenda around the topics of class, production, the rise of trades unions, the Labour Party, and the state as the agents of socioeconomic transformation.

Orthodox historiography sometimes drew on a materialism and determinism associated with Marxist theory. Equally important, however, it easily fitted into general accounts of the nineteenth century as a time of unprecedented growth and modernization. The Industrial Revolution, most historians were convinced, resembled a sudden, rapid 'take off' to modernity in the early nineteenth century: it marked a decisive break with 'traditional society', producing factories, the bourgeoisie, political reform, and also an organized working class, and consequently class conflict and accommodation.[6] Even when social historians, led by E. P. Thompson, emphasized human agency against the crude, reifying Marxism of the

Stalin era, they still studied the way agents had made this modern world. When Thompson studied 'the poor stockinger, the Luddite cropper, the obsolete hand-loom weaver, the utopian artisan', he did so not only to rescue them 'from the enormous condescension of posterity', but also to show how they had made a modern, organized and politically conscious working class.[7] Although Thompson emphasized the part played by English radical protestantism, agency was fundamentally taken to rest on more or less pure experiences of socioeconomic reality. Moreover, because the nature and transparency of this socioeconomic reality was not questioned, the turn to agency left the orthodox historiography intact even as it broadened the research agenda to encompass more subjective aspects of the past.

The challenges to orthodoxy that arose in the late 1970s and the 1980s reflected the failings and the successes of Thompson's intervention as well as a changing political and social landscape marked by the rise of the new conservatism, deindustrialization, identity politics and new social movements. These challenges propelled, on the one hand, a reconsideration of the apparent failure of the working-class and, on the other, a greater appreciation of non-class-based identities and the construction and frailty of the nation-state. Together, they prompted recognition of the gulf between language and material reality. Marxist historians had long appealed to various alibis to explain the embarrassing failure of the working-class to fulfil its revolutionary role. The rise of Thatcherism posed a broader dilemma for orthodoxy as a whole: the march of labour from the factory through class consciousness and political organization to the welfare state had ended in a way that raised questions about its efficacy as the dominant story of modernity.[8] Historians sometimes attempted to deal with such embarrassments by appealing to theories about the peculiar natures of the British bourgeoisie and workforce or to theories about hegemony and social control.[9] Thompson, in contrast, associated his turn to agency with an influential repudiation of theorizing in favour of a focus on the experience of the people of the past.[10]

Gareth Stedman Jones was one who defended theory in the wake of Thompson.[11] While his early work still appealed to social control as a way of explaining the 'failure' of the working class,[12] his later study of Chartism treated the language of protest as relatively autonomous from the external development of capitalism.[13] The language of Chartism revealed a political movement as much as a social one, and a movement that was less the inauguration of a modern working-class looking forward to the twentieth century than the end of a popular radicalism reaching back to the eighteenth century. While his argument can be read as a response to the orthodox concern with the workers' failure to perform their allotted role, it also undermined the foundations of orthodox historiography. On the one hand, the absence of the working-class meant it no longer needed an alibi for its failings. On the other, its very absence, and the gap between social reality and language, shattered the orthodox narrative of classes arising inexorably out of the industrial revolution.

Ironically, parallel challenges to orthodoxy also arose out of the very success of Thompson's intervention. Thompson's conviction of the moral importance of conferring voice and agency on hidden figures of the past inspired numerous historians. Whereas Thompson held an idealized view of a robust masculine working-class engaged in public bodies and didactic self-improvement, a view that echoed a long-standing cultural bias among socialists in favour of production over consumption, other historians, engaging with the popular culture of the 1960s and 1970s, began to unpack the rather different voices and agency of workers interested in the music hall, football and private leisure activities.[14] This interest in consumption also began to recast the study of cultural and political identities so as to challenge the privileging of production and the state within orthodox historiography.[15] The new social movements reinforced the shift in research from the factory floor to the household, the department store and the imperial museum. Feminist and postcolonial theories gave voice and agency to women, gays, minorities and other subalterns. Their inclusion in the historical record pointed to frequent contrasts and tensions between such people and the workers. Joan Scott explicitly argued, for example, that the Victorian working class was a masculine construction defined in contrast to a middle class that had a correspondingly feminine identity.[16] Similarly, a new generation of imperial historians highlighted the racist elements of many of the social and political reform movements in nineteenth-century Britain.[17] A greater awareness of issues of gender, sexuality, ethnicity and consumption cut through the comfortable unifying thread of the orthodox narrative in which the working class, as the natural champion of people's rights and interests, walked toward the telos of industrial modernity and social democracy.

The turn to non-class-based social categories, like gender and ethnicity, was accompanied by a theoretical shift that widened the gap between language and social reality further still. Scott criticized Stedman Jones for adopting too conservative a conception of language. Appealing to French poststructuralists such as Michel Foucault, she urged historians to pay attention to the way in which language constructed individuals and their worlds. Patrick Joyce made much the same point while arguing that class was one identity among many – one, moreover, that had little relevance in the nineteenth century when a discourse of 'the people' dominated.[18] Class thus became reduced to one possible linguistic construct among others.

The shift away from the orthodox concept of 'class' forms part of a general rethinking of the relationship between the domains of politics, society and economy. Accounts of the creation and reordering of these domains as webs of belief or systems of knowledge now challenge the older account of the linear evolution of modern 'society' and 'economy' as given and self-explanatory spheres. Instead of conceiving of the economy as an essential domain that impinged directly on the lives of historical actors, recent studies have shown how the understanding of social and economic processes remained embedded in larger religious, moral and political webs of belief. It was only in the Victorian period that political economists and social analysts came to define the 'economy' as a separate secular sphere composed of self-regulating individuals – a sphere from which 'social' problems could be read off. Even after the Victorian era, moreover, popular debates continued to locate topics such as 'consumption' in normative understandings of civil society and citizenship.[19] In short, the orthodox narrative of modernity operated with key categories of 'society' and 'self', structure and agency, which were themselves historically specific categories of the era in question falsely masquerading as universal analytic ones. Orthodoxy was itself implicated in a concept of 'society' that many post-modernists, following Michel Foucault, held responsible for modern 'disciplinary individualism'. As a result, the emancipatory project of orthodox social history became increasingly problematic.

Continuity, transnationalism and populism

The various challenges to orthodoxy point to the outlines of an alternative narrative in which three themes dominate: continuity, transnationalism and populism. We want broadly to endorse these themes, while pointing to problems within them, problems to which this volume hopes to provide theoretical and historiographical resolutions.

Continuity has emerged as a leading theme as the chasm between the eighteenth and nineteenth centuries has been bridged from both ends. For the eighteenth century, J. G. A. Pocock, Donald Winch and other intellectual historians have explored the diverse, complex languages within which social theorists and economists responded to the rise of capitalism, commercialism and market society.[20] For the nineteenth century, Stedman Jones, Eugenio Biagini, Greg Claeys and others have traced the persistence of these same languages among the Painites, Owenites, Chartists and liberal radicals.[21] Indeed, popular radicalism continued to have a definite presence in the late nineteenth-century 'socialist revival' and even the Labour Party.[22] Although we should be careful not to neglect the transformation wrought on political languages by the Enlightenment, evangelicalism and romanticism,[23] it now seems clear that early critics of capitalism often expressed a popular radicalism that resembled eighteenth-century republicanism at least as much as it does twentieth-century socialism.

The growing concern with continuity sits alongside the revival of interest in 'civil society', itself a response to suspicions of totalizing ideologies and the state.[24] Whereas orthodoxy asked questions about class formation, class conflict and the relationship between class-based parties and the state, 'civil society' has been invoked as a relatively autonomous space outside formal politics, characterized by toleration, difference and a culture of voluntary association. The turn to civil society further emphasized the importance of pre-socialist ideas for the analysis of modern society.[25] Social historians retrieved the continued significance of voluntary associations.[26] Instead of looking at the politics of social movements primarily in relation to the state, the turn to civil society took seriously the idea that many groups directed their collective action towards self-governance and the reform of society from within. In contrast to a simple divide between capitalism and its critics, we now have a richer understanding of the reform aspirations of groups like cooperators and radicals who embraced policies such as Free Trade in the hope of strengthening their autonomy within civil society and against commercial capitalism.[27]

The emphasis on continuity overlaps with the second theme of the emerging historiography – transnationalism. We now have several studies, in particular, of the rich transatlantic networks through which republican and radical traditions circulated. It is no coincidence that the scholar most responsible for drawing attention to the longevity of republicanism, J. G. A. Pocock, also issued a clarion call for a new British history that would move beyond England to take seriously the interaction between the different components of the British Isles and their role within the Atlantic archipelago.[28] This Atlanticist turn has born a variety of fruits. American historians have given renewed attention to the Anglicization of the American colonies and explored the 'empire of goods' that made for a genuinely transatlantic consumer revolution.[29] Irish historians have located Ireland within a mid-Atlantic system.[30] Radical historians have written on the 'black Atlantic'.[31] Other historians have taken a fresh look at older subjects, such as Anglo–American radicalism, the influence of Lockean ideas on the American Revolution, and the role of parliamentary ideas and practices.[32]

Populism is a third theme in many of the works challenging the orthodox historiography. In contrast to the orthodox preoccupation with class as the defining identity of modern society, interest today has shifted to other identities, with class being diffused, even dissolved. At times, class is reinterpreted as just one identity that exists only in tandem with others, such as gender. Historians have discussed, for example, the ways in which the making of the middle and working classes was intertwined with the making of a patriarchal domestic ideology: patriarchy cut across and reinforced class distinctions, with both working-class and middle-class women being excluded from the public sphere, but with the former experiencing this principally in labour markets while the latter did so in the household.[33] What is more, historians have not limited themselves here to the categories associated with identity politics – gender, ethnicity and sexuality. In defiance of the orthodox denigration of primitive rebellions, they have paid increasing attention to the impact of religious, aesthetic, moral and patriotic beliefs on radical politics.[34] Finally, historians of the populist turn have argued that 'the people' or 'demos', not class, acted as the main frame of collective identity for workers in the nineteenth century.[35]

The new focus on continuity, transnationalism and populism has a symbiotic relationship to studies of the long and ambivalent nature of the industrial revolution.[36] Industrialization, it now appears, was a gradual process with uneven regional dynamics in which older trades and socioeconomic relations continued to flourish well into the nineteenth century and played as important a role in economic growth and development as did the new trades of cotton, iron and steel. Workshops dominated much of the country, with factories, and the industrial relations that came with them, being of relatively little significance until the second half of the nineteenth century. Historical estimates of economic growth rates have been downscaled. Finance and trade, as well as older trades like wool, are now recognized as having been just as important to growth and development as were the new industries. This emphasis on continuity has also been reinforced by the tracing back of many 'modern' dynamics to the eighteenth century, such as the creation of the 'fiscal–military state' and its contribution to imperial, financial and administrative expansion, on the one hand, and the rise of the 'middling sort' and the expansion of consumer culture, on the other.[37]

The reappraisal of domestic trades, shopping, and imperial and transnational contexts has inspired research into non-class identities underlying the turn to populism. Historians have emphasized the crucial role of women engaged in business, workshops and especially domestic production.[38] As attention has shifted to commerce and trade, so the role of imperial subjects and transnational relationships have become increasingly prominent.[39] Conversely, the sociological dialectic of an industrial bourgeoisie as the dynamo of economic modernity to which the working class reacted has been superseded by studies that have shown the divided nature of the middle classes and emphasized the crucial contribution played by Whig aristocrats, evangelical thinkers and, ultimately, popular radicals themselves in the creation of a political economy based on Free Trade.[40] Together, these studies have effectively severed the direct link between politicoeconomic development and the sociology of class.

Although we would endorse a greater recognition of continuity, transnationalism and populism, the new historiography is not free of unresolved problems. Two principal questions stand out. How should we explain ideational or linguistic change? And how can we situate populist discourse so as to recognize its diverse forms and possibilities within and beyond the nation-state? If postmodernists and other exponents of the new historiography have not ignored change and diversity altogether, the tendency has been to neglect these problems or to answer them from outside their own theories.

The new historiography on continuity has problems dealing adequately with change because of its theoretical assumptions. Inevitably, the relative autonomy given to language in relation to the development of capitalism renders problematic any direct appeal to experience as a source of cultural change. Within postmodern theory, indeed, the rejection of the real appears to preclude all attempts to invoke a world outside of discourse as a source of change, no matter how indirect. In addition, the frequent emphasis on language as constitutive of all subjectivity renders problematic any appeal to agency – if individuals merely construct their selves in terms given to them by a social discourse, they must lack the capacity to modify or transform such discourses. All too often, therefore, the new historiography invokes languages or discourses as quasi-structures. In so far as these quasi-structures produce both the social and agency, without in turn being produced by either of these, it is hard to grasp how and why they come to change. Without an analytical space for agents and agency, it becomes difficult to link languages of social justice and radical reform projects to the changing nature of political economy and the changing ways in which capitalism is understood, contested and reformed.

The second and related problem in the new historiography stems from its neglect of the diversity of populist discourse or its confusion of such diversity with difference. The concern with language as a quasi-structure has encouraged historians to look for a common set of meanings or conventions as opposed to the diverse beliefs that agents express in speech and action. Populism often acts as little more than a broadening out of the concept of class from a narrow Marxist notion to one that covers how workers and artisans used 'class' – and yet few people in Britain described their beliefs as populist, whereas many invoked class in just this way. Surely, however, we ought to pay more attention to diverse beliefs about 'the people' and 'class' rather than deploying the former as an amorphous category. When exponents of the new historiography do unpack diversity, however, they generally do so in terms of the different connotations given to binary concepts by an overarching quasi-structural language: women are defined as other than men, or the east as other than the west, within a discourse. Much less attention is paid to the diverse beliefs that agents hold, for reasons of their own, about women or the east.

Many of the beliefs people held developed as traditions within transnational exchanges – they were not insular constructions of one nationality or state. These transnational exchanges continued to develop, moreover, long after the eighteenth century, the period on which most attention has been focused since the Atlanticist turn. Historians of the nineteenth and twentieth centuries have invoked transnationalism mainly along an imperial axis, emphasizing how European societies were shaped by imperial experiences as much as colonial societies were shaped by European politics.[41] Although they are surely right to do so, we would argue that attention also should be paid to the many diverse transnational networks that connected British debates with traditions beyond the Empire. To date, these networks have rarely been explored apart from the anti-slavery and suffrage movements.[42] One reason for this neglect of transnationalism, we believe, is the widespread assumption that during the nineteenth century the nation-state grew in strength and so cut across early modern networks of cultural exchange, effectively 'caging' national societies.[43] Another reason for the neglect of transnationalism lies in the way in which imperial history – whether old or new – focuses attention on imperial exchanges without situating these equally firmly within broader transnational relations.

The significance of broader transnational relations, even for imperial concerns, has been illustrated by the seminal work of those American scholars, led by James Kloppenberg and Daniel T. Rodgers, who have unravelled the important transatlantic dialogues that shaped the development of progressive thought and social policy in the late-nineteenth and early-twentieth centuries. This volume offers a series of case studies in transnational exchanges beyond empire that adopt the Atlantic as a common focus. The reader should not assume, however, that this focus implies a commitment to the Atlantic as the only place where important examples of such exchanges can be found. The aim of this volume, to avoid misunderstanding, is neither to suggest that traditions always follow a North Atlantic route, nor to assert a special Anglo–American relationship. It is, rather, to adopt a particular geopolitical focus on the Atlantic nexus in order to reconstruct the dynamics, tensions and possibilities of transnational exchanges for the history of diverse critiques of capitalism in the nineteenth and twentieth centuries.

Theoretical resolutions

While the new historiography provides welcome departures from orthodoxy, the underdevelopment of its theoretical assumptions creates blind-spots within it.[44] To address the two blind-spots we have just highlighted – explaining change and situating languages – we need to rethink some of these theories.[45] Rather than rejecting the new historiography, therefore, our aim is to propel it forward by resolving key methodological shortcomings and opening up new historical questions.

Let us begin with the problem of situating language. Earlier we suggested that the new historiography does not sufficiently situate languages: it typically takes discourses to be quasi-structures that generate conceptual pairings irrespective of the reasoning of the speakers. This problem can be resolved once discourses are conceived instead as the products of individual agents using languages to express their beliefs. The shift of perspective here is from a concern with discourse as quasi-structure to a conception of discourse as an abstraction based on people's beliefs. Whereas the former view presents discourse as a quasi-structural framework that gives individuals what they can believe as well as the words through which they express their beliefs, the latter reclaims individuals as agents who can adopt beliefs for reasons of their own within any given language.[46] By conceiving of discourse as an abstraction based on people's beliefs, historians are able to think about who precisely held the relevant beliefs, and thus to situate the relevant meanings more precisely within the social and cultural environment of the time. What is more, by unpacking discourses in relation to the beliefs of particular individuals, we open up the possibility that individuals held very different beliefs even if they did so through much the same words, concepts or language – we encourage a sensitivity to diversity as well as difference. To what varied webs of beliefs have critiques of capitalism been tied?

To shift attention from language as a quasi-structure to the beliefs of specific individuals and groups, it must be stressed, need not entail a naïve return to an autonomous subjectivity. Unfortunately much of the energy in the internal debate about the future of social history has gone into constructing a false dichotomy between a postmodern notion of discourse and an older view of autonomous actors, where theory favours structure and an interest in agency is seen to favour empiricism, a methodological dogmatism that has prevented theoretical dialogue and tended to create tunnel-vision on both sides.[47] The concept of tradition offers a way out of this false dichotomy by capturing the socially embedded nature of agency. Historical actors do not have neutral experiences or unmediated knowledge of capitalism as a given reality. They encounter various forms of capitalism through diverse traditions that are socially constituted and disseminated.

To prevent traditions becoming disembodied in much the way that languages often are, we must avoid reifying them. They are not given objects that we can define by reference to allegedly core ideas prior to locating individuals within them in so far as the individuals held these core views. Traditions are, rather, contingent and changing objects that individuals produce through their particular utterances and actions. We can unpack the content of a tradition and trace its development only by following the processes through which its exponents inherited, applied and modified a loose collection of changing themes. While traditions are thus the products of human agency, it remains the case that agency always occurs within the context of a social inheritance. Individuals experience the world only through their existing beliefs, and they initially inherit these beliefs from their community. To avoid reducing beliefs or discourses prematurely to experience, therefore, historians need to locate beliefs within the context of traditions. How have varied critiques of capitalism continued to embody traditional legacies and when and how have they transformed traditions?

While the concept of tradition helps to forestall a premature reductionism, it should not be taken simply as a tool of high intellectual history – far from it. Traditions are prevalent throughout society, where they are embedded within social practices and political movements. Just as our individual beliefs inform and respond to our actions, so traditions inform and respond to collective practices. We can unpack beliefs and traditions, then, not only by looking at written texts but also by exploring the meanings embedded in social practices. Similarly, we might unpack beliefs and traditions not for their own sake but in order to grasp better the nature of social practices. By rethinking language as beliefs embedded in traditions and practices, it thus becomes possible to connect the new intellectual history to social and political history, and to bridge the gulf between languages of social justice and the development of capitalist society. What practices have critiques of capitalism given rise to? And how have capitalism, the state and society been influenced by alternative beliefs, traditions and practices?

The shift from conceiving of discourse as quasi-structural to conceiving of it as an abstraction based on individual beliefs embedded in traditions also points to a resolution of the second blind-spot of the new historiography: how to explain change. The concept of tradition has the advantage over that of language or discourse that it clearly allows for agency as well as the socially embedded nature of the subject. It acknowledges that the relevant social structure is one into which individuals are born, and which then acts as the background to their later beliefs and actions, while also allowing for the possibility of their modifying and developing much of this structure for reasons of their own. Change can thus be explored in relation to processes of local reasoning, that is, agency in the context of tradition. Here traditions, and so practices, change as people respond to dilemmas. Whenever people adopt a new belief or action, they have to find a way of accommodating it within their existing beliefs or practices. A dilemma arises for individuals or groups whenever they adopt a new belief or action, no matter how strongly or consciously, that stands in opposition to their old beliefs and thus puts these into question. In this way dilemmas can explain change without postulating a teleological process or a universal rationality immanent in subjectivity. Dilemmas do not have correct, let alone historically necessary, solutions. Indeed, because traditions cannot fix their own criteria of application, when people confront new circumstances or new beliefs, they necessarily change traditions in a creative process.[48] In short, to explore change, historians should trace contingent processes of local reasoning. What dilemmas prompted people to modify the traditions and practices in which various critiques of capitalism arose, and under what circumstances were these dilemmas generated?

By associating dilemmas with new beliefs, we have precluded a straightforward identification of dilemmas with social or economic pressures in the 'real' world. People modify their beliefs and actions in response to new beliefs irrespective of whether or not these new beliefs reflect material changes in the world and irrespective of whether or not they arise from changing social knowledge about forms of capitalism or from theoretical and moral debate. Nonetheless, it is useful to recall that people do have experiences of the world, including capitalism, and that their interpreted experiences often constitute the dilemmas to which they respond. Just as we hope to explore the genealogy of different beliefs, traditions and practices, so we want to problematize these genealogies in relation to changes in the political economy of societies. Despite the statist ambition of caging communities into national societies in the nineteenth and twentieth centuries, the transnational exchanges of traditions and practices continued to operate. Instead of portraying traditions and practices as lurking in a detached linguistic realm, this volume inquires into their development and revision in response to historical dilemmas that were often composed of interpreted experiences of markets, capitalism and relations of production. How did different traditions and practices inspire diverse ways of comprehending and responding to changes in political economy? And how did transnational flows influence the development of traditions and practices?

If it is wrong to presume that people have unmediated experiences of markets, it is equally unhelpful to think that critiques of capitalism exist in an intellectual vacuum unrelated to the changing socioeconomic and political landscapes inhabited by actors over time. The main questions should be about how these landscapes are interpreted or mediated in different traditions, and how they change as a result of people's contingent responses to the dilemmas they help to generate. It would be misleading to picture the relationship as a one-way street, as if thinkers and social movements merely 'respond' to the prior workings of capitalism. The idea of capitalism as a distinct system of relations with its own rules arose as a historical product of classical and neo-classical economics. We need to recover the awareness of the social and political contexts of capitalism, found in thinkers of the eighteenth century, including Adam Smith, as well as later historical economists.[49] Equally, we need to recognize the extent to which various forms of capitalism helped to shape the contingent outcome of politics. Here too our exploration of change in relation to dilemmas and interpreted experience helps to connect the new intellectual history to social, economic and political history. What economic changes inform the dilemmas in response to which people transform traditions and practices? And, finally, how do people's responses to dilemmas transform the social and political contexts of different forms of capitalism?

Emerging questions

The conceptual shift towards the dynamics of change and the ways in which languages are situated in beliefs and practices opens up new perspectives on the relationship between capitalism and its critiques. A focus on the way languages are situated in beliefs and practices prompts us to explore, first, the transnational dynamics underlying ideas of social justice, and, second, the diversity of critiques of capitalism. Likewise, a focus on the way change arises out of dilemmas – which themselves often derive from interpreted experiences of the social – prompts us to explore, first, the relationship between cultural critique and social change, and, second, the impact of critique on the political economy of capitalism. The following chapters take up these four problems.

The concept of tradition opens up a space for thinking about relationships between beliefs and practices in Britain, its colonies and other transnational exchanges. A concept of language as a quasi-structure mistakenly prompts a concern with the way that quasi-structure of itself sets up certain oppositions – the east is other than the west. A concern with traditions, in contrast, encourages an inquiry into the transnational, interactive nature of many critiques of capitalism. By undoing the functionalist link between a specific material or linguistic environment and a particular set of beliefs, we open the way for a less insular study of the beliefs and practices connected to capitalism and a greater sensitivity to the interplay as well as relative autonomy of diverse traditions. Sandra den Otter explores such interplay in her chapter on Henry Maine's attempt to bring to mid-nineteenth-century India capitalist ideas of contract in agrarian relations and a market economy in labour. As a linchpin of modern political economy, freedom of contract was closely tied to broader notions of progress and civilization in nineteenth-century Britain and America. Yet far from documenting a simple hegemonic, top-down application of British ideas to Indian practices, den Otter shows how British traditions changed in response to a series of dilemmas thrown up by India. Maine's Indian experiences severed the utilitarian equation of capitalism with modernity and custom with backwardness.[50] Den Otter further shows how American scholars, like Francis Walker, writing in a different context, used Maine's critique of deductive economic reasoning to highlight the imperfections of competition.

Belief in the exceptionalism of Britain and America has obscured the transatlantic exchanges informing traditions, especially with respect to critiques of capitalism. A concern with transatlantic connections is now part and parcel of eighteenth-century studies, but for the postrevolutionary period such concerns are all too rare. Instead, Werner Sombart's question 'Why is there no socialism in America', and widespread assumptions about the peculiarity of the British labour movement continue to prop up exceptionalist lines of inquiry that preclude explorations of transatlantic exchanges.[51] The chapters by Mark Bevir and Axel Schäfer, in contrast, retrieve dynamics of exchange in the development of socialist and progressive critiques of capitalism. Bevir traces one strand of the distinctive ethical dimension of British socialism in the late-nineteenth century back to American romanticism with its immanentist belief in a God omnipresent throughout the world. The ethical socialism of Thomas Davidson, Edward Carpenter and John Trevor derived not from a material analysis of capitalist conditions peculiar to Britain, but from American romantics such as Emerson, Thoreau and Whitman, with their faith in the moralizing effect of a simple life, and their religious vision of community and democracy.[52] Axel Schäfer explores the reverse transatlantic reception of progressive and social democratic ideas in America. The decades before World War I, as Dan Rodgers has argued, marked a new phase in the cultural perception and political uses of Europe within America: the old contrast between a republican, modern America and a despotic, feudal Europe gave way to a fresh emphasis on the similar challenges and learning experiences of industrial societies.[53] Progressives in the United States, as Schäfer shows, drew on European, and especially British, social thought to articulate a critique of nineteenth-century liberalism and to promote a democratic vision that looked towards an enlarged public sphere and social welfare.[54] Yet the distinctive institutions and traditions of America led progressives to receive British social thought in a manner that ultimately sustained racism and legitimated expert rule and bureaucracy at the expense of democratic accountability and participation.

The emphasis on the relative autonomy of beliefs and traditions encourages new inquiries into the pluralistic nature of transatlantic critiques of the market. Building on recent explorations of non-class-based forms of collective identity, several chapters in this volume ask how different groups understood, and hoped to order, their economic environment. In the new historiography, there is no analytic reason why we should associate critique with socialism or the working class any more than with other social groups. Thus, our interests move beyond varieties of social democracy to include radical, utopian, cooperative and liberal traditions in their own right, not just as part of an alternative grand narrative that connects radicalism to social democracy by means of a liberal embrace.[55] Likewise, we rethink the evolution of capitalism to portray it as always shaped by diverse non-socialist and socialist critiques.[56] Free Trade, for example, drew support from individuals and groups who understood it to be a source of social and international ethics that would help supersede an acquisitive market-oriented society – a diverse set of radical, liberal and social-democratic beliefs thus propped up a politicoeconomic regime, which, with hindsight, we can recognize assisted the global expansion of market society.[57]

An awareness of the diversity of critiques of capitalism informs the chapters in this collection. Jamie Bronstein takes seriously the appeal of land reform visions in both Britain and America. Her chapter shows how land reform politics in these countries developed differently not simply because of their different institutional and economic settings, but also because of diverse traditions: Jeffersonian republicanism in America favoured ideals of self-sufficiency and the myth of the independent farmer, whereas in Britain the diversity of liberal and conservative views of industrial society meant land reform came to be viewed as an anachronistic nostalgia.[58] Chris Beauchamp explores the changing place and meaning of consumption in twentieth-century debates about social democracy and political economy. Here too the turn away from class and production helps to bring into focus neglected beliefs and traditions as well as revealing the operation of transnational exchanges.[59] Beauchamp shows how American beliefs and practices helped to inspire a shift in Britain from a radical Free Trade tradition of the 'citizen-consumer' to the politics of consumer protection as championed by Political and Economic Planning (PEP) and later the Consumer Association. His argument too moves beyond the simple dichotomy between capitalism and its critics by usefully complicating the narrative in which consumer protection appears as an unmediated response to the expansion of mass consumer society in the 1950s. As he shows, consumer protection developed out of a redefinition of an older radical tradition that was already under way in the inter-war years.[60]

The concepts of dilemma and interpreted experience open up a space in which to reimagine the relationship of economic change to social critique in a way that avoids the older action–reaction model. Social critiques and movements constitute integral elements of the clusters of actions, practices and institutions that shape the very development of capitalist society. Once we recognize this, we overturn a social-democratic nostalgia that narrows attention to the historical high-points of radical ambition. The power of critique to transform capitalism exists even when economic liberalism appears to hold the whip-hand. Colin Hay's chapter unravels the ways in which a belief in globalization as an allegedly non-negotiable external constraint came to define Labour's view of political economy and legitimate its increasingly modest understanding of its role as an agent of reform.[61] Far from being a political response to global material pressures, the growing popularity of the globalization thesis since the 1970s is here understood in terms of transnationalism, interpreted experience and agency – even conscious deception. Globalization appears as a concept with which Labour politicians have sought to resolve – or at least to give the appearance of resolving – the dilemmas of the 1970s and 1980s, such as governmental 'overload'. The 'Third Way', with its transatlantic roots revealed, stands as a self-fulling prophecy that helps to liberalize political economy in the globalizing direction to which it is said to be a response.

Two chapters in this volume explicitly discuss British and American traditions of international government and transnational relations. It is, perhaps, not surprising that the orthodox framing of social history, with its focus on class, production and the welfare state, privileged the nation-state as a terrain of inquiry. International history and social history rarely combined to explore the transnational dimensions of wealth, justice and welfare.[62] In spite of the recent resurgence of interest in 'globalization' and 'global civil society', the historical study of diverse transnational traditions of social justice, human rights and international governance is still in its infancy. Kevin Grant and Simon Caney offer contributions to such a history. Grant traces the emergence of the international organizations established during and after World War II by unravelling various imperial traditions of 'trust' in Britain and America. His chapter may make uncomfortable reading to those who prefer a clear ethical dichotomy between 'good' international organization and 'bad' imperial government, but it alerts us to the ways in which the expansion of capitalism and debates about its social implications have, for better or worse, been informed by imperial and international traditions of justice, such as trusteeship.[63] Turning to the latter half of the twentieth century, Simon Caney's chapter explores the emergence of contemporary cosmopolitanism. As Caney emphasizes, 'the English school' of international relations, and the Kantian tradition of John Rawls in America alike eschewed global principles of justice on the grounds that a genuine society of states requires acceptance of the principle of non-intervention. Current ideas about cosmopolitanism – whether theories of transnational distributive justice or defences of transnational democratic organizations – arose out of reflections on the dilemmas that confronted these traditions.[64]

As a collection, these chapters show that much can be gained by being sensitive to the place of critique within capitalism, to the diversity of critique, and to the traditions, dilemmas and transnational exchanges that inform critique. If they depart from an older heroic picture of social actors preparing for the overthrow of capitalism in the long run, they also provide a warning against a fashionable neo-liberal fatalism. Critique should not be understood as engaged in a win or loose battle with capitalism. It is, rather, part and parcel of the way capitalism operates and develops. The workings of capitalism have been affected by various policies and collective actions that grew out of critiques of it. Thus, we cannot properly discuss the scope of capitalism and its operation without picturing it as part of a continuous, dynamic relationship intertwined with traditions and their projects of reform. Interpreted experiences of capitalism and arguments for reform can generate dilemmas even for those who do not seek to overthrow the system. In grappling with these dilemmas, actors rethink, and so reconstitute, capitalism in ways that effect its development. Critical and historically informed reflection on this process remains an essential part of evaluating projects for social justice today.

Notes

1. Earlier versions of some chapters in this volume appeared in a special issue of the journal *European Legacy* 6/2 (2001). We thank the journal editors for permission to reuse some of this material.
2. See the exchange between Patrick Joyce, Lawrence Stone and Gabrielle M. Spiegel in *Past and Present* 133 (1991), 204–9 and 135 (1992), 189–208; David

Mayfield and Susan Thorne, 'Social History and Its Discontents: Gareth Stedman Jones and the Politics of Language', *Social History* XVII (1992), 167–88; Jon Lawrence and Miles Taylor, 'The Poverty of Protest: Gareth Stedman Jones and the Politics of Language – A Reply', *Social History* XVIII (1993), 1–15; Patrick Joyce, 'The Imaginary Discontents of Social History: A Note of Response to Mayfield and Thorne, and Lawrence and Taylor', *Social History* XVIII (1993), 81–5; James Vernon, 'Who's Afraid of the "Linguistic Turn"? The Politics of Social History and its Discontents', *Social History* XIX (1994), 81–97; Patrick Joyce, 'The End of Social History?', *Social History* XX (1995), 73–91; Geoff Eley and Keith Nield, 'Starting Over: The Present, the Post-modern and the Moment of Social History', *Social History* XX (1995), 355–64; David Cannadine, 'British History: Past, Present and–Future?', *Past and Present* 116 (1987), 169–91; Gareth Stedman Jones, 'The Determinist Fix: Some Obstacles to the Further Development of the Linguistic Approach to History in the 1990s', *History Workshop* 42 (1996), 19–35. For the reception of the linguistic turn in a country with a different tradition of histories of society, such as German Gesellschaftsgeschichte, see eg, Thomas Mergel and Thomas Wellskopp, eds, *Geschichte zwischen Kultur und Gesellschaft* (Munich: Beck, 1997).

3. See Mark Bevir, 'Republicanism, Socialism, and Democracy in Britain: The Origins of the Radical Left', *Journal of Social History* 34 (2000), 89–107. For non-Marxist traditions of social history, see Miles Taylor, 'The Beginnings of Modern British Social History', *History Workshop* 43 (1997), 155–76.

4. Eric Hobsbawm, *Primitive Rebels* (Manchester: Manchester University Press, 1959).

5. E. P. Thompson, *The Making of the English Working Class* (London: Harmondsworth, 1981; 1st edn 1963).

6. W. W. Rostow, *The Stages of Economic Growth: a Non-Communist Manifesto* (Cambridge: Cambridge University Press, 1971); Asa Briggs, *The Age of Improvement, 1783–1867* (London: Longman, 1959) G. Kitson Clark, *The Making of Victorian England* (Cambridge, MA: Harvard University Press, 1962); Harold Perkin, *Origins of Modern English Society, 1780–1880* (London: Routledge, 1969); and G. M. Young, *Victorian England: Portrait of an Age* (London: Oxford University Press, 1936).

7. Thompson, *Making of English Working Class*, p. 12.

8. For an orthodox attempt to deal with this difficulty see Eric Hobsbawm *et al.*, *The Forward March of Labour Halted* (London: New Left Books, 1981).

9. See Eric Hobsbawm, 'The Labour Aristocracy in Nineteenth-Century Britain', in *Labouring Men* (London: Weidenfeld and Nicolson, 1964), pp. 272–315; Tom Nairn, 'The Fateful Meridian', *New Left Review* 60 (1970), 3–35; Stuart Hall, 'The Great Moving Right Show', in Stuart Hall and Martin Jacques, eds, *The Politics of Thatcherism* (London: Lawrence and Wishart, 1980).

10. E. P. Thompson, 'The Poverty of Theory', in *The Poverty of Theory and Other Essays* (London: Merlin Press, 1978). The conflation of a concern for agency with a dismissal of theory has left an unfortunate legacy on British history. A commitment to theory has characteristically come to mean an eschewal of agency, as among most followers of linguistic, cultural and postmodern turns who conceive of language as quasi-structure, see n. 2 above, and p. 11.

11. Gareth Stedman Jones, 'The Pathology of English History', *New Left Review* 46 (1967), 29–45; and Gareth Stedman Jones, 'From Historical Sociology to Theoretical History', *British Journal of Sociology* 27 (1976), 295–305.

12. Gareth Stedman Jones, *Outcast London: A Study in the Relationship Between Classes in Victorian Society* (Oxford: Oxford University Press, 1971).
13. Gareth Stedman Jones, 'Rethinking Chartism', in *Languages of Class: Studies in English Working-class History, 1832–1982* (Cambridge: Cambridge University Press, 1983), pp. 90–178.
14. For example, Peter Bailey, *Leisure and Class in Victorian England: Rational Recreation and the Contest for Control, 1830–1885* (London: Routledge and Kegan Paul, 1978); Peter Bailey, *Popular Culture and Performance in the Victorian City* (Cambridge: Cambridge University Press, 1998); Ross McKibbin, 'Working-Class Gambling in Britain, 1880–1939', *Past and Present* 82 (1979), repr. in Ross McKibbin, *The Ideologies of Class* (Oxford: Clarendon Press, 1990), pp. 101–38 ; Chris Waters, *British Socialists and the Politics of Popular Culture* (Manchester: Manchester University Press, 1990); and Gary Cross, *Time and Money: The Making of Consumer Culture* (London: Routledge, 1993). Note, both Gareth Stedman Jones and Patrick Joyce have done work on the music hall.
15. For example, Judith Walkowitz, *City of Dreadful Delight* (Chicago: Chicago University Press, 1992); Ellen Ross, *Love and Toil* (Oxford: Oxford University Press, 1993); Victoria deGrazia, ed., *The Sex of Things* (Berkeley: University of California Press, 1996); and most recently, Erika Rappaport, *Shopping for Pleasure: Women in the Making of London's West End* (Princeton, NJ : Princeton University Press, 2000); and Frank Trentmann, 'Bread, Milk, and Democracy: Consumption and Citizenship in Twentieth-Century Britain', in Martin Daunton and Matthew Hilton, eds, *The Politics of Consumption* (Oxford: Berg, 2001), pp. 129–63.
16. Joan Scott, *Gender and the Politics of History* (New York: Columbia University Press, 1988). Cf. Anna Clark, *The Struggle for the Breeches: Gender and the Making of the British Working Class* (Berkeley: University of California Press, 1995). For an argument about the political construction of the middle class, see Dror Wahrman, *Imagining the Middle Class: The Political Representation of Class in Britain, c. 1780–1840* (Cambridge: Cambridge University Press, 1995).
17. Catherine Hall, *White, Male and Middle Class: Explorations in Feminism and History* (Cambridge: Polity Press, 1992); Antoinette Burton, *Burdens of History: British Feminists, Indian Women, and Imperial Culture, 1865–1915* (Chapel Hill: University of North Carolina Press, 1994); and Anne McClintock, *Imperial Leather: Race, Gender and Sexuality in the Colonial Context* (New York: Routledge, 1995).
18. Patrick Joyce, *Visions of the People: Industrial England and the Question of Class, 1840–1914* (Cambridge: Cambridge University Press, 1991). See also James Vernon, *Politics and the People: A Study in English Political Culture, c. 1815–1867* (Cambridge: Cambridge University Press, 1993).
19. Mary Poovey, *Making a Social Body: British Cultural Formation, 1830–1864* (Chicago: University of Chicago Press, 1995); Patrick Joyce, 'End of the Social?'; Patrick Joyce, *Democratic Subjects: The Self and the Social in Nineteenth-Century England* (Cambridge: Cambridge University Press, 1994); Boyd Hilton, *The Age of Atonement: The Influence of Evangelicalism on Social and Economic Thought, 1795–1865* (Oxford: Clarendon, 1988); Frank Trentmann, 'Civil Society, Commerce, and the "Citizen-Consumer"', in Frank Trentmann, ed., *Paradoxes of Civil Society: New Perspectives on Modern German and British History* (Oxford: Berghahn Books, 2000), pp. 283–305; and Frank Trentmann, 'National Identity and Consumer Politics: Free Trade and Tariff Reform', in Patrick O'Brien and

20   *Critique within Capitalism*

Donald Winch, eds, *The Political Economy of British Historical Experience, 1688–1914* (Oxford: Oxford University Press, 2002), pp. 187–214.

20. J. G. A. Pocock, *Virtue, Commerce and History* (Cambridge: Cambridge University Press, 1985); and Donald Winch, *Adam Smith's Politics* (Cambridge: Cambridge University Press, 1978). For an extreme revisionist emphasis on institutional and social, as well as intellectual, continuities between the eighteenth and nineteenth centuries, see Richard Price, *British Society, 1688–1880: Dynamism, Containment and Change* (Cambridge; Cambridge University Press, 1999).

21. Greg Claeys, *Citizens and Saints: Politics and Anti-Politics in Early British Socialism* (Cambridge: Cambridge University Press, 1989); Greg Claeys, *Thomas Paine: Social and Political Thought* (London: Unwin Hyman, 1989); Greg Claeys, 'The Origins of the Rights of Labour: Republicanism, Commerce, and the Construction of Modern Social Theory in Britain, 1796–1805', *Journal of Modern History* 66 (1994), 249–90; and Stedman Jones, 'Rethinking Chartism'; James A. Jaffe, 'Commerce, Character and Civil Society', *The European Legacy* 6 (2001), 251–64. On the persistence of the language of moral economy see also Joyce, *Visions of the People*, pp. 87–113.

22. Jon Lawrence, 'Popular Radicalism and the Socialist Revival in Britain', *Journal of British Studies* 31 (1992), 163–86; Eugenio Biagini and Alastair Reid, eds, *Currents of Radicalism: Popular Radicalism, Organised Labour, and Party Politics in Britain, 1850–1914* (Cambridge: Cambridge University Press, 1991); Duncan Tanner, 'The Development of British Socialism, 1900–1918', *Parliamentary History* 16 (1997), 48–66; and Mark Bevir, 'The British Social Democratic Federation 1880–1885: From O'Brienism to Marxism', *International Review of Social History* 37 (1992), 207–29.

23. Boyd Hilton, *Age of Atonement*; and Mark Bevir, 'English Political Thought in the Nineteenth Century', *History of Political Thought* 17 (1996), 114–27.

24. John Keane, ed., *Civil Society and the State: New European Perspectives* (London: Verso, 1988); Andrew Arato and Jean L. Cohen, *Civil Society and Political Theory* (Cambridge, MA: MIT Press, 1992); John Hall, ed., *Civil Society: Theory, History, Comparison* (Cambridge: Polity, 1995); Trentmann, ed., *Paradoxes of Civil Society*; Sudipta Kaviraj and Sunil Khilnani, eds, *Civil Society* (Cambridge: Cambridge University Press, 2001); and Helmut Anheier, Marlies Glasius and Mary Kaldor, eds, *Global Civil Society 2001* (Oxford: Oxford University Press, 2001).

25. John Keane, 'Despotism and Democracy: The Origins and Development of the Distinction between Civil Society and the State 1750–1850', in Keane, ed., *Civil Society*, pp. 35–71. See also, Istvan Hont and Michael Ignatieff, eds, *Wealth and Virtue: The Shaping of Political Economy in the Scottish Enlightenment* (Cambridge: Cambridge University Press, 1983). For the role of association in British socialist thought, see Paul Hirst, *The Pluralist Theory of the State: Selected Writings of G. D. H. Cole, J. N. Figgis and H. J. Laski* (London: Routledge, 1989). The idea and praxis of civil society, concerned with ideals of tolerance and the ability to disagree, ought to be distinguished from the concepts of community and public sphere that have made their way into some of the historiographical literature on radical continuities, eg, Eugenio Biagini, ed., *Citizenship and Community: Liberals, Radicals and Collective Identities in the British Isles, 1865–1931* (Cambridge: Cambridge University Press, 1996).

26. R. J. Morris, 'Clubs, Societies and Association', in F. M. L. Thompson, ed., *The Cambridge Social History of Britain, 1750–1950*, III, (Cambridge: Cambridge University Press, 1990), pp. 395–443.

27. Trentmann, 'Civil Society, Commerce, and the "Citizen-Consumer"'.

28. J. G. A. Pocock, 'British History: A Plea for a New Subject', *Journal of Modern History* 47 (1975), 601–28; and J. G. A. Pocock, 'History and Sovereignty: The Historiographic Response to Europeanization in Two British Cultures', *Journal of British Studies* 31 (1991), 361–4, 380–9. See also the recent assessments by David Armitage, Jane Ohlmeyer, Ned Landsman, Eliga Gould and Pocock himself in 'AHR Forum: The New British History in Atlantic Perspective', *American Historical Review* 104 (1999), 426–500.

29. T. H. Breen, '"Baubles of Britain": The American and Consumer Revolutions of the Eighteenth Century', *Past and Present* 119 (1988), 73–104; T. H. Breen, 'An Empire of Goods: The Anglicization of Colonial America, 1690–1776', *Journal of British Studies* 25 (1986), 467–99; John Clive and Bernard Bailyn, 'England's Cultural Provinces: Scotland and America', *William and Mary Quarterly* 11 (1954), 200–15; and David Armitage, 'Making the Empire British: Scotland in the Atlantic World, 1542–1707', *Past and Present* 155 (1997), 34–63. See also, Jack P. Greene and J. R. Pole, eds, *Colonial British America: Essays in the New History of the Early Modern Era* (Baltimore: Johns Hopkins University Press, 1984).

30. Nicholas Canny, *Kingdom and Colony: Ireland in the Atlantic World, 1560–1800* (Baltimore: Johns Hopkins University Press, 1988); and Brendan Bradshaw and John Morrill, eds, *The British Problem: State-Formation in the Atlantic Archipelago, c. 1534–1707* (Basingstoke: Macmillan (now Palgrave Macmillan), 1996).

31. Paul Gilroy, *The Black Atlantic: Modernity and Double Consciousness* (London: Verso, 1993).

32. J. C. D. Clark, *The Language of Liberty, 1660–1832: Political Discourse* (Cambridge: Cambridge University Press, 1995); and Margaret C. Jacob and James R. Jacob, eds, *The Origins of Anglo-American Radicalism* (London: George Allen & Unwin, 1984). See also Lois G. Schwoerer, *The Declaration of Rights, 1689* (Baltimore: Johns Hopkins University Press, 1981); and Pauline Maier, *American Scripture: Making the Declaration of Independence* (New York: Knopf, 1997).

33. Leonore Davidoff and Catherine Hall, *Family Fortunes: Men and Women of the English Middle Class, 1780–1850* (London: Hutchinson, 1987); Catherine Hall, 'The Early Formation of Victorian Domestic Ideology', in Sandra Burman, ed., *Fit Work for Women* (New York: St Martin's now Palgrave Macmillan, 1979), pp. 15–31; Anna Clark, *Struggle for the Breeches*; and Dror Wahrman, '"Middle Class" Domesticity Goes Public: Gender, Class, and Politics from Queen Caroline to Queen Victoria', *Journal of British Studies* 32 (1993), 396–432. Cf John Tosh, *A Man's Place: Masculinity and the Middle-Class Home in Victorian England* (New Haven, CT: Yale University Press, 1999).

34. Steven Yeo, 'A New Life: The Religion of Socialism in Britain 1883–1896', *History Workshop* 4 (1977), 5–56; Miles Taylor, 'Patriotism, History and the Left in Twentieth-Century Britain', *Historical Journal* 33 (1990), 971–87; Raphael Samuel, ed., *Patriotism: The Making and Unmaking of British National Identity*, 3 vols. (London: Routledge, 1989); Paul Ward, *Red Flag and Union Jack: Englishness, Patriotism and the British Left, 1881–1924* (Woodbridge: Royal Historical Society, 1998); Greg Claeys, 'The Lion and the Unicorn: Patriotism and Orwell's Politics', *Review of Politics* 57 (1985), 186–211; Graham Johnson, 'British Social Democracy and Religion, 1881–1911', *Journal of Ecclesiastical History* 51 (2000), 94–115; Michael Kenny, 'Socialism and the Romantic "Self": The Case of Edward Thompson', *Journal of Political Ideologies* 5 (2000), 105–27; and Meredith Veldman, *Fantasy, the Bomb and the Greening of Britain: Romantic Protest, 1945–1980* (Cambridge: Cambridge University Press, 1989). See also our own

work on this problematic, Mark Bevir, 'Annie Besant's Quest for Truth: Christianity, Secularism, and New Age Thought', *Journal of Ecclesiastical History* 50 (1999), 62–93; Mark Bevir, 'The Labour Church Movement, 1891–1902', *Journal of British Studies* 38 (1999), 217–45; and Frank Trentmann, 'Wealth versus Welfare: The British Left between Free Trade and National Political Economy before the First World War', *Historical Research* (1997), 70–98.

35. Joyce, *Visions of the People*; Joyce, *Democratic Subjects*; Vernon, *Politics and the People*; John Belchem, 'Republicanism, Popular Constitutionialism and the Radical Platform in Early Nineteenth Century England', *Social History* 6 (1981), 1–32; and Stedman Jones, *Languages of Class*. See also James Epstein, 'The Populist Turn', *Journal of British Studies* 32 (1993), 179–89.

36. N. F. R. Crafts, *British Economic Growth During the Industrial Revolution* (Oxford: Clarendon, 1985); Maxine Berg, *The Age of Manufactures, 1700–1820* (London: Fontana, 1985); Peter Kriedte, Hans Medick, and Jürgen Schlumbohm, *Industrialization before Industrialisation: Rural Industry in the Genesis of Capitalism* (Cambridge: Cambridge University Press, 1982); Sidney Pollard, *Peaceful Conquest: The Industrialisation of Europe, 1760–1970* (Oxford: Oxford University Press, 1981); Martin Daunton, *Progress and Poverty: An Economic and Social History of Britain, 1700–1850* (Oxford: Oxford University Press, 1995); James A. Jaffe, *Striking a Bargain: Work and Industrial Relations in England, 1815–1865* (Manchester: University of Manchester Press, 2000); Raphael Samuel, 'The Workshop of the World: Steam-power and Hand-technology in Mid-Victorian Britain', *History Workshop* 3 (1977), 6–72; Jonathan Zeitlin and Charles Sabel, 'Historical Alternatives to Mass Production: Politics, Markets and Technology in Nineteenth Century Industrialisation', *Past and Present* 108 (1985), 133–76; and David Cannadine, 'The Past and the Present in the English Industrial Revolution, 1880–1980', *Past and Present* 103 (1984), 131–72.

37. Patrick K. O'Brien, 'The Political Economy of British Taxation, 1600–1815', *Economic History Review* 41 (1988), 1–32; John Brewer, *Sinews of Power: War, Money and the English State, 1688–1783* (London: Unwin Hyman, 1989); Neil McKendrick, John Brewer and J. H. Plumb, eds, *The Birth of a Consumer Society: The Commercialisation of Eighteenth-Century England* (Bloomington: Indiana University Press, 1982); John Brewer and Roy Porter, eds, *Consumption and the World of Goods* (London: Routledge, 1993); John Brewer, *The Pleasures of the Imagination: English Culture in the Eighteenth Century* (New York: Farrar, Straus, Giroux, 1997); and Paul Langford, *A Polite and Commercial People: England 1727–1783* (Oxford: Clarendon, 1989); Maxine Berg and Helen Clifford, eds, *Consumers and Luxury* (Manchester: Manchester University Press, 1999). See also the debate about 'gentlemanly capitalism' between P. J. Cain and A. G. Hopkins, 'Gentlemanly Capitalism and British Overseas Expansion', *Economic History Review*, 2nd ser XXXIX and XL (1986, 1987), 501–25, 1–26 and Martin Daunton, '"Gentlemanly Capitalism" and British Industry, 1820–1914', *Past and Present* 122 (1989), 119–58.

38. Maxine Berg, 'What Difference did Women's Work Make to the Industrial Revolution?' *History Workshop* 35 (1993), 22–44.

39. C. A. Bayly, *Imperial Meridian: The British Empire and the World, 1780–1830* (London: Longman, 1989); Kathleen Wilson, *The Sense of the People: Politics, Culture, and Imperialism in England, 1715–1785* (Cambridge: Cambridge University Press, 1995); Patrick K. O'Brien, 'The Costs and Benefits of British Imperialism 1846–1914', *Past and Present* 120 (1988), 163–200; Hall, *White, Male,*

and Middle Class; Burton, *Burdens of History*; Gyan Prakash, ed., *After Colonialism: Imperial Histories and Postcolonial Displacements* (Princeton: Princeton University Press, 1995); and Gyan Prakash, *Another Reason: Science and the Imagination of Modern India* (Princeton: Princeton University Press, 1999).

40. Boyd Hilton, *Corn, Cash, Commerce: The Economic Policies of the Tory Government, 1815–1830* (Oxford: Oxford University Press, 1980); Hilton, *Age of Atonement*; Peter Mandler, *Aristocratic Government in the Age of Reform: Whigs and Liberals, 1830–1852* (Oxford: Clarendon Press, 1990); Peter Mandler, 'The Making of the Poor Law Redivivus', *Past and Present* 117 (1987), 131–57; A. C. Howe, *Free Trade and Liberal England, 1846–1946* (Oxford: Clarendon, 1998); and Frank Trentmann, 'Political Culture and Political Economy', *Review of International Political Economy* 5 (1998), 217–51.

41. Frederick Cooper and Ann Laura Stoler, eds, *Tensions of Empire: Colonial Cultures in a Bourgeois World* (Berkeley: University of California Press, 1997); Martin Daunton and Rick Halpern, eds, *Empire and Others: British Encounters With Indigenous Peoples, 1600–1850* (Philadelphia: University of Pennsylvania Press, 1999); Catherine Hall, Keith McClelland and Jane Rendall, *Defining the Victorian Nation* (Cambridge: Cambridge University Press, 2000); Catherine Hall, ed., *Cultures of Empire: A Reader* (Manchester: Manchester University Press, 2000); Antoinette Burton, ed., *Gender, Sexuality and Colonial Modernities* (London: Routledge, 1999); and Prakash, *Another Reason*.

42. Christine Bolt, *Feminist Ferment: The 'Woman Question' in the USA and England, 1870–1940* (London: UCL Press, 1995); Christine Bolt, *The Women's Movement in the United States and Britain from the 1790s to the 1920s* (London: Harvester Wheatsheaf, 1993); Jane Rendall, *The Origins of Modern Feminism: Women in Britain, France and the United States, 1780–1860* (Basingstoke: Macmillan now Palgrave Macmillan, 1985); Kathryn Kish Sklar, '"Women Who Speak for an Entire Nation": American and British Women at the World Anti-Slavery Convention, London, 1840, in Jean Fagan Yellin and John C. Van Horne, eds, *The Abolitionist Sisterhood* (Ithaca, NY: Cornell University Press, 1994), pp. 301–34; L. J. Rupp, *Worlds of Women: the Making of an International Women's Movement* (Princeton, NJ: Princeton University Press, 1997); and Ian Fletcher, Philippa Levine and Laura Mayhall, eds, *Women's Suffrage in the British Empire* (London: Routledge, 2000). Suggestive perspectives on other forms of exchange, including media, sport, royalty and finance, can be found in Fred M. Leventhal and Roland Quinault, eds, *Anglo-American Attitudes: From Revolution to Partnership* (Aldershot: Ashgate, 2000) and Martin H. Geyer and Johannes Paulmann, eds, *The Mechanics of Internationalism* (Oxford: Oxford University Press, 2001). See now also A. G. Hopkins, ed., *Globalization. World History* (London: Pimlico, 2002).

43. Michael Mann, *The Sources of Social Power*, II (Cambridge: Cambridge University Press, 1993). Cf the idea of a century of territoriality, between 1860 and 1970, in Charles S. Maier, '"Consigning the Twentieth Century to History": Alternative Narratives for the Modern Era', *American Historical Review* 105 (2000), 807–31.

44. This has been recognized by some leading authors of the new historiography, notably Stedman Jones, 'Determinist Fix'.

45. Throughout this section, we draw on Mark Bevir, *The Logic of the History of Ideas* (Cambridge: Cambridge University Press, 1999).

46. Whereas Joyce contrasts an orthodox faith in 'preconstituted subjects' who construct meanings with his conviction that 'meanings construct subjects' – Joyce,

Democratic Subjects, p. 11 – we want to recognize that subjects do indeed construct meanings though they only ever do so within the context of a tradition that gives them their starting point.

47. See for instance the tone as well as content of the recent debates in *Social History*, cited in n. 2 above.
48. The inability of traditions to fix their own application arises by analogy from Wittgenstein's analysis of rule-following, see Ludwig Wittgenstein, *Philosophical Investigations*, trans. G. Anscombe (Oxford: Basil Blackwell, 1972), pp. 143–242.
49. Winch, *Adam Smith's Politics*; Werner Sombart, *Der Moderne Kapitalismus* (Munich: Duncker und Humblot, 1922, 5th edn); Friedrich Lenger, *Werner Sombart, 1863–1941: Eine Biographie* (Munich: Beck, 1994); Alon Kadish, *Historians, Economists and Economic History* (London: Routledge, 1989); and Charles S. Maier, *In Search of Stability: Explorations in Historical Political Economy* (Cambridge: Cambridge University Press, 1987).
50. In this volume, pp. 49–72 below.
51. Werner Sombart, *Why is There No Socialism in the United States?* (1st German edn 1906, London: Macmillan now Palgrave Macmillan, 1976). See also, Ross McKibbin, 'Why was there no Marxism in Great Britain?', in Ross McKibbin, *Ideologies of Class* (Oxford: Clarendon Press, 1990), pp.1–41. For parallels between the German and British labour movements, see Stefan Berger, *The British Labour Party and the German Social Democrats, 1900–1931* (Oxford: Clarendon Press, 1994).
52. See below, pp. 73–97.
53. Daniel Rodgers, *Atlantic Crossings: Progressive Politics in a Social Age* (Cambridge, MA: Harvard University Press, 1998). See also E. P. Hennock, *British Social Reforms and German Precedents* (Oxford: Clarendon, 1987).
54. See below, pp. 98–126. See also James T. Kloppenberg, *Uncertain Victory: Social Democracy and Progressivism in European and American Thought, 1870–1920* (Oxford: Oxford University Press, 1986).
55. For the latter, see Eugenio Biagini, *Liberty, Retrenchment and Reform: Popular Liberalism in the Age of Gladstone, 1860–1880* (Cambridge: Cambridge University Press, 1992); Biagini and Reid, eds, *Currents of Radicalism*; and Peter Gurney, *Co-operative Culture and the Politics of Consumption in England, 1870–1930* (Manchester; Manchester University Press, 1996). It is worth noticing how the emphasis on an amorphous populism – one that does not situate that discourse with respect to particular agents – encourages such a replication of the Victorian Liberal attempt to embrace radicalism.
56. See José Harris, 'Political Thought and the Welfare State, 1870–1940: An Intellectual Framework for Social Policy', *Past and Present* 135 (1992), 116–41; Mark Bevir, 'Sidney Webb: Utilitarianism, Positivism, and Social Democracy', *Journal of Modern History* (forthcoming); Mark Bevir, 'Socialism, Civil Society, and the State in Modern Britain', in Trentmann, ed., *Paradoxes of Civil Society*, pp. 332–51; and, more generally, Donald Sassoon, *One Hundred Years of Socialism: The West European Left in the Twentieth Century* (London: I. B. Taurus, 1996).
57. See Frank Trentmann, 'Civil Society, Commerce, and the "Citizen-Consumer"'; Trentmann, 'National Identity and Consumer Politics'; and on the location of such beliefs within Labourite, socialist, and Fabian traditions, Trentmann, 'Wealth versus Welfare'.
58. In this volume, pp. 26–48. For the transatlantic nexus of social reform in this period, see Rodgers, *Atlantic Crossings*.

59. Daunton and Hilton, eds, *Politics of Consumption*; Victoria deGrazia, ed., *The Sex of Things* (Berkeley: University of California Press, 1996); and Susan Strasser, Charles McGovern and Matthias Judt, eds, *Getting and Spending* (New York: Cambridge University Press, 1998).
60. See below, pp. 127–50.
61. In this volume, pp. 195–219. For earlier examples of the way in which perceptions of supposedly given external constraints and narratives of crisis and decline shaped social and economic critiques, see Aaron Friedberg, *The Weary Titan: Britain and the Experience of Relative Decline, 1895–1905* (Princeton: Princeton University Press, 1988); Trentmann, 'Political Culture and Political Economy'; Susan Pedersen, 'From National Crisis to National Crisis: British Politics, 1914–1931', *Journal of British Studies* 33 (1994), 322–35; and Richard English and Michael Kenny, eds, *Rethinking British Decline* (New York: St Martin's Press now Palgrave Macmillan, 2000).
62. For such a combination, see Mark Mazower, *Dark Continent: Europe's Twentieth Century* (New York: Knopf, 1998); Eric Hobsbawm, *The Age of Extremes: A History of The World, 1914–1991* (London: Michael Joseph and Pelham Books, 1994); and the essays in Maier, *In Search of Stability*.
63. In this volume, pp. 151–73.
64. In this volume, pp. 174–94.

2
Land Reform and Political Traditions in Nineteenth-Century Britain and the United States

Jamie L. Bronstein

By the 1840s, capitalism had taken on a much different colouration in Britain than it had in the United States. The Lowell mills may have captured the imagination of the American public, but the nation's main economic focus was still primarily agricultural, with much of that agriculture pursued under slavery. What manufacturing did occur still took place overwhelmingly within the small shop. While journeymen in major American cities had begun to complain about restrictions on upward mobility, opportunities for advancement existed. Much American discourse since the Revolution celebrated the virtues of labour, and class boundaries had recently been made more permeable by the expansion of the electorate to include unpropertied white men. In Britain, in contrast, the scale of work was becoming larger and more complicated in industries including textiles, metalworking, mining and the railroads. The problems of amassing sufficient capital and education, and overcoming social prejudices, made it much more difficult for workers to rise to new levels of earning power and social station.

While the life chances of British and American workers were thus different, representatives of both groups in the 1840s sought the solution to their perceived economic problems in broader land-ownership. They sought to slip the bonds of the 'geographic discipline' of industrial capitalism that, like the time-discipline, limited their choices.[1] The main advocates for working-class land reform, the Chartist Co-operative Land Company and the American National Reform Association, had much in common.[2] Both sets of reformers saw land monopoly as the original injustice, which laid the foundation for all other injustices:

> From the exclusion of man from the soil flow all servitude and slavery, all poverty and ignorance, all crime and misery, that can proceed from so fundamental and violent a breach in the system of Nature and God. The people are cast out from the earth and made pensioners on the bounty of the great monopolists who wield their power by the force of legal wrong.[3]

Their intellectual heritage invoked the same predecessors: Thomas Jefferson and James Harrington, Charles Hall and William Ogilvie, Thomas Paine and Thomas Spence, all of whom argued that the state of being alive presupposed that every person had a right to as much land as they needed to support themselves.[4] Their rhetoric invoked the same fears of overcrowding in the cities, and optimism about a life on the land. Their organizational strategies were similar, and they even shared personnel and newspapers.[5]

Like their predecessors writing in the republican tradition, the working-class land reformers associated land-ownership with personal independence, public virtue, and with human improvement.[6] While many British land reformers supported a constitutional monarchy, the desire of both the British and the Americans for land was the physical embodiment of the struggle between virtue and corruption that Pocock described in the context of the American revolution.[7] For nineteenth-century working Americans, the opening of the safety-valve to the land promised a second revolution, enabling them to slip the shackles of the cities, with their dirt, noise, crowding and oppressive wage relationships. They were going to move beyond the compromised and commercial civilization of America in the Early Republic to areas that were still uncontaminated. Land-company Chartists viewed the possession of land as an important vehicle for achieving the Charter and its political reforms, but land reform was also republican in another way. For Chartists, as for the Owenites, settlement on the land was an attempt to constitute, within a liberal and commercial state, a community with alternative values.[8] In contrast with the Owenites, for both the Chartists and the American National Reformers, economic independence and political reform were intertwined.[9]

The land reformers were idealistic, but they were not sanguine about the upward progress of humanity. Rather, they combined optimism about the transformative power of land-ownership with pessimism about the shape that their societies were taking as they moved toward industrialization. Classes were becoming fixed, and even in the United States, land monopoly was importing social distinctions. In the United States as in Britain, the land reformers' rhetoric invoked the same fears of overcrowding, poverty and low wages in the cities, and summoned up the same celebrations of pastoral beauty and landed independence. Even in the United States, however, the land reformers did not completely shun manufactures, hoping instead that removal of some workers to the land would create a safety-valve to raise the wages of the rest. Their shared vision was not backward-looking; rather, in the words of John Ashworth, they looked to a commercialized and pre-capitalist future.[10]

The republican tradition informed the working-class land-reformers' organizational strategies as well as their goals and rhetoric.[11] They were convinced that the 1840s marked a tipping point. Civilization was still malleable, but if firm steps toward a broader distribution of land were not taken, both Britain and the United States were headed for rampant inequality and widespread servility. Their belief that mankind could be appealed to on the basis of good rather than simply self-interest led them to tour Britain and the United States giving speeches, to fill newspaper columns with their reasoned arguments, and to try to convince their governments of the justice of their plans. Sharing personnel and newspapers, they considered themselves participants in an international movement for the improvement of working people's lives.[12]

While I have argued elsewhere that the central difference between the Chartist Co-operative Land Company and the National Reform movement was the reception given each movement by its respective state, the scale of each movement was also quite different. In Britain, Feargus O'Connor and his close allies purchased land, then used a lottery system in order to distribute 2–4 acre parcels. They provided each parcel with a cottage, and hoped to see Chartists create small, spade-cultivated farms. In contrast, workingman and printer George Henry Evans and his fellow National Reformers lobbied the US Congress and state legislatures to pass legislation which would grant free homesteads of a quarter-section each, or 160 acres, to those who agreed to settle on it and farm it.

Why were the land reformers' visions so different? Of course, the availability of land played a role in determining the scope of their desires. In the United States, at least in theory, all of the lands between those already settled and the Pacific lay open to hopeful farmers' ambitions, whereas the Chartist Land Reformers could choose only among colonial lands, 'waste lands' or lands that came on the market for purchase. But, as this chapter will demonstrate, political traditions were also primary determinants of the land reformers' plans. In the United States, the political tradition was to wax lyrical about the independent farmer and to follow previous systems of land allotment in ways that shaped the desire for land into a plan for 160-acre farms. Furthermore, American land reformers strove to differentiate their society from Britain, invoking the existence of land monopoly in Britain and Ireland precisely to call for a broader land distribution in the United States. In contrast with the situation in Britain, the land reform tradition in the United States celebrated the American worker's ability to adapt and change from an urban to an agricultural environment.

In Britain, in contrast, the translation of the Chartists' vision into reality was constrained not only by the cost and scarcity of available land, but also by political traditions. Emigration to colonial lands was rejected both for the effect that it would have on individual lives and for the effect it would have on gaining the charter. Opponents of land reform made it difficult for British workers to seek farms by claiming that working people lacked the skills or intelligence to make the transition from urban labourers to rural landholders. Even though, as in America, British land reformers spoke of the land as conferring a beneficial patriotism in its recipients, it was thought unwise to confer enough land on uneducated artisans to allow them to escape the status into which they had been born. Thus, in contrast with the large independent farms sought by American homesteaders, Chartist allotments resembled the small garden plots that philanthropists rented to British workers in order to supplement their diets and improve their leisure time in the 1830s and 1840s.

Political traditions continued to condition the acceptability of land reform proposals throughout the nineteenth century, although the association of land reform with republican continuity was short-lived. In the United States, the widespread availability of small farms after 1862 did nothing to stem urbanization and industrialization. By the end of the century, even though Populist farmers found themselves joining together with workers to bemoan their lack of power against railroads and corporations, Henry George's ideas had a limited resonance. For British radicals, republican critiques of power became much less relevant by the mid-1880s, after two expansions of the electorate had failed to produce an end to social inequality.[13] America, once a beacon, had become for British radicals a disagreeable test case, illustrating that no matter what form of politics prevailed, the presence of capitalism was linked to exploitation.[14] Land monopoly was symptomatic of social inequality but it was not its only source. Thus, British socialists were both attracted to Henry George's prescriptions, and repelled by George's totalizing (yet non-Marxist) explanations of society's ills.

The independent American farmer

For Americans, landholding was of no use if it did not confer self-sufficiency. The independent yeoman farmer was an integral part of the myth of the state, memorialized by such philosophers of the American condition as Hector St John de Crèvecoeur and Thomas Jefferson.[15] As Jefferson wrote:

> Whenever there are in any country uncultivated lands and unemployed poor, it is clear that the laws of property have been so far extended as to violate natural right. The earth is given as a common stock for man to labor and live on ... it is not too soon to provide by every possible means that as few as possible shall be without a little portion of land. The small landholders are the most precious part of the state.[16]

The fact that such an icon of Republicanism as Jefferson had descanted on the moral superiority of the American farmer was powerful ammunition for those who, like the National Reformers, would make the public lands available for free to 'actual settlers'.[17]

Using the public lands to promote this ideal of self-sufficiency was discussed long before the National Reformers had begun to lobby for free homesteads, but that in itself does not explain how a quarter-section of land, or 160 acres, became their goal. In fact, there was some precedent for smaller parcels. In 1820, a bill to reform the procedure for sale of the public lands had designated 80 acres as the minimum tract that one could purchase.[18] In 1828, the Committee on the Public Lands of the House of Representatives recommended free distribution of 80-acre tracts to heads of families who promised to improve and reside on the tracts for five years.

> This proposition has recommended itself to the consideration of your committee by a knowledge of the fact that there are many families who are neither void of industry nor of good moral habits who have met with the usual share of the difficulties always accompanying the settlement of a new country, and who, living very remote from market, never expect to see the day arrive when they will be enabled to save enough, with all their efforts, from their means of support, to purchase a farm and pay for it in cash.[19]

Well before 1862, both state and federal legislation made a quarter-section of land the customary reward for extraordinary service of one kind or another. For example, Arkansas asked in 1830 that settlers locating within 24 miles of the frontier be given 160 acres after 5 years' residence, and Indiana asked for substantially the same thing in 1827, 1830 and 1832.[20] Similarly, in Texas, the Mexican government allowed Stephen Austin to grant enormous tracts of farming and grazing lands to actual settlers, with the hopes of using Anglo-American settlers to buffer Mexico from hostile Indians.[21]

Twenty years before the Homestead Act was passed, Congress recognized the social good of the widest possible land distribution by passing a pre-emption law. The main suggestions for disposition of the public lands up to 1841 had included Henry Clay's plan to sell the public lands to the highest bidder, and John Calhoun's plan to allow those western states that contained public land within their borders to keep that land. Thomas Hart Benton proposed a third way: to allow an occupant who had anticipated the legal sale of the land, and settled on it in violation of law, the first option to purchase or 'pre-empt' it at $1.25 an acre.[22] In 1841, a law to this purpose conferred on a man over 21, a widow, or an alien who had sworn his intention of becoming a US citizen, the right to settle on a 160-acre tract of land. Once the tract came onto the market, the squatter could purchase it free from competitive bids, at the minimum government price.

If the National Reformers had good reason to choose 160-acre tracts on the basis of tradition, they also had good reason to think that land grants to actual settlers were feasible because pioneers were thought to be providing a public service. From 1842 to 1853 a series of acts was passed giving donations of land to settlers to encourage them to protect border settlements from Indian attacks. The recipients of these land grants were not seen as receiving something for nothing. Rather, their willingness to settle on the frontier promoted the cause of civilization. During an 1844 Congressional discussion of a proposal to give 40 acres free to the head of every family settling on the public domain, Mr Ficklin of Illinois waxed poetic: 'Unless the government shall grant head rights, settlement rights, or donations of some kind, these prairies, with their gorgeous growth of flowers, their green carpeting, their lovely lawns and gentle slopes, will for centuries continue to be the home of the "wild deer and wolf"; their still-ness will be undisturbed by the jocund song of the farmer, and their deep and fertile soil unbroken by the ploughshare.'[23]

In 1852, J. L. Dawson made a similar argument on the grounds of national security: The settlement of some of America's uncharted territory 'would place upon a distant frontier a force able and willing to defend us against hostile savages, and thus spare us much of the expense we are now required to defray'.[24] As Horace Greeley noted, whatever the minimum price of the lands, the price to the actual settler was much more, as he did not want to plunge into the wilderness but preferred to stay where there was some sort of neighbourhood, a school and a church.[25] Bringing land under cultivation also enhanced the remainder of the country by providing new markets for Eastern products. Congressman C. Skelton of New Jersey suggested that 'the individual who takes possession of one hundred and sixty acres, does not get his full share of the public lands of the country.' As he saw it, the social value of free homesteads was to bring that land under profitable cultivation, and there was enough to supply every prospective farmer with three quarter-sections for that purpose.[26]

The call for 160-acre homesteads was enhanced by the image of the fron-tier-dwelling American as a hardy pioneer, able to meet any challenge and rise to any task. In general, even urban working people were assumed to have the skills and adaptability needed to meet the challenge of frontier life.[27] 'A Printer' thought urban cellar diggers the perfect candidates:

> The Cellar Digger is the very man to walk straight off to the woods; he has a strong arm; a stout limb; a hard hand, accustomed to the pick axe and spade; his face is already browned with the rays of the sun; he knows the management of the horse and the cart; and there is not one of them, who could not, in two or three years, raise produce enough to support himself and family, and have five hundred dollars worth of exchange for groceries and clothing, and to educate his children.[28]

Pennsylvania's Galusha Grow gave his paean to the hardy pioneer on the floor of Congress, comparing the pioneer settler with the 'plumed warrior'. The pioneer was never safe on the frontier, living as he did in the realm of the Indian. 'Startled at the midnight hour by the war-whoop, he wakes from his dreams to behold his cottage in flames; the sharer of his joys and his sorrows, with perhaps a tender infant, hurled, with rude hands, to the distant council-fire.' Still the pioneer pressed on, doing immeasurable service to his country by 'snatching new areas from the wild beast, and bequeathing them a legacy to civilized man.'[29] Surely a quarter-section was not too much for the pioneer to ask under these circumstances!

George Henry Evans, the leader of the American land-reform movement, at first did not insist that the free homestead take the form of a quarter-section of land. Influenced by wide reading, which included the works of Owen, Fourier and other communitarians, he at first supported a plan to secure 50- to 80-acre homesteads.[30] Later, he envisioned populating western townships with about 1000 people. In addition to quarter-sections granted to farmers, these townships would include a centre square mile with a public square, and about 40 lots of 5 acres each, plus several lots of 12 to 20 acres each, which would be chosen by mechanics or manufacturers.[31] For Evans, who believed in a certain amount of civilization and sociability, there was such a thing as too much land in a homestead; thus, he opposed an 1845 bill in the House of Representatives for the settlement of Oregon, because it would have allocated to each family an area about 2 miles square. With each township to contain about 18 inhabitants, commerce or transit to markets would have become impossible, and Evans predicted that farmers overcome by hardship would soon sell their land to capitalists.[32]

Despite Evans' reservations, the weight of tradition and the necessity of making farmers fully independent led the National Reformers to adopt the traditional call for 160-acre homesteads as they petitioned the legislature. In 1846, they memorialized Congress to create a Homestead Act 'to reverse the present downward tendency of labor, to secure the means of independence to that portion of the people now deprived of them, [and] to prevent the rapid increase of crime and pauperism through the unnatural augmentation of the city population so much dreaded by the far-sighted Jefferson.'[33] Just as National Reform rhetoric pitted the pastoralism of the farm against the corruption of the cities, so it pitted the virtue of the farmer against the corruption of the city-dweller and the politician. 'Who, that values his native dignity and independence as a man, would not prefer to be lord of a few acres of land, with nobody's humor to consult but his own, and nobody to fear but his Maker, to the cringing the fawning and the lying that enter so largely into political, professional, mercantile and mechanical life?'[34]

The National Reformers appealed to the producerist notion that the man who worked with his hands contributed the most to society. They depicted land as not only a natural right of all Americans, but as an entitlement, because labourers had given so much to their society and got so little in return:

Hear then, you, who, though toiling on the land from sun to sun, are not allowed to possess ground enough for a potato patch; you, who work in shops and in factories; you, who go about from city to village begging employment; you, who drudge, indoors and out, for employers perhaps as much harassed by the fear of want as you are; you, who sail the ships and man the guns; you, in short, who produce for others to consume, and who fight the battles for others to reap the fruits of victory; you, from whose ranks the prisons, poor houses and brothels are mainly filled; listen all of you, and all honest men of every class, to a proposition which, in a very short period, would give each of you your proper station in society. *Abolish the monopoly of the land, and you and your posterity will be freemen indeed!*[35]

The concept that widespread land-ownership would enhance the class of 'freemen' could even be stretched to encompass an attack on slavery (although many land reformers had little interest in the status of the chattel slave). Land reformer and abolitionist Gerritt Smith not only invoked Jefferson in his argument in favour of free homesteads, but also went so far as to argue that distributing the public lands in tracts of 50 or 100 acres would lead to the elimination of slavery, by counteracting the plantation system.[36]

While the myth of the independent farmer and previous systems for distributing lands helped shape the National Reformers' desire for land into a desire for quarter-sections, the British counterexample was also a formidable impetus for tracts of land that would confer independence. The most sustained debate on the free homestead question occurred in the US House of Representatives in 1852, when the House resolved into a committee of the whole to address the issue. The arguments put forth in favour of free homesteads covered the map, from invocations of John Locke's theory of land improvement to the 'natural rights' argument that had been advanced by Thomas Spence.[37] But Britain cast a long shadow over the debate. J. L. Dawson damned Britain with statistics, noting that the British population in 1851 numbered 27,619,866, of whom only about 30,000 were landowners. In the United States, in contrast, the 'free white population' (the only subset considered germane to the debate) was 19,630,738, of whom 2,379,483 were either freeholders or owned farms.[38] Galusha Grow summoned up a contrast; 'in England, the proudest and most splendid aristocracy, side by side with the most abject and debased people; vast manors hemmed in by hedges as a sporting-ground for her nobility, while men are dying beside the inclosure for want of land to till.'[39]

Joseph Cable of Ohio, one of the House's most flowery orators, summoned up a parade of skeletal Irish immigrants hounded by land monopoly: 'Look now at the tears, groans – dying groans, misery, wretchedness, famine, destitution, squalid poverty, and prostration of brave, generous, industrious and faithful Ireland! What is the great, the leading, the only cause of all her calamity? Why does now, seemingly, a curse rest upon the once joyous "land of song"? Monopoly of the soil – nothing else!'[40] Cable went on to argue that the United States Treasury already collected too much money. 'If there was no more than half the amount of revenue collected, there would be less corruption, less peculation and speculation, while the administration of the Government might be reduced to one-half of the present expenditures.'[41] Britain was the land of big Government and centralized power; a United States full of yeoman farmers would be its decentralized opposite.

Cable's criticisms were mild in contrast to those of the land reformers themselves. Thomas Devyr, a former Chartist turned National Reformer, was a particularly effective campaigner for land reform, as he could speak firsthand of the evils of land monopoly in England.[42] In a letter sent to the Senate on behalf of the National Reformers of Williamsburgh, Devyr noted that 'We have shaken off the incubus of kings – we scout with contempt and ridicule the idea of a born legislator – but we permit Land Monopoly, the worst part of the three, to grow up and flourish among us.'[43] William Field Young, a land-reformer and editor of the Lowell *Voice of Industry*, wrote:

> Look at England, with her genial climate and productive soil, sufficient to provide millions more than now number her population, with all the comforts nay luxuries of life, with her people ground down to abject servitude under this system of monopolization, which has built up a guilded and rotten hearted throne, and drawn around it a herd of lords, dukes and political gormandizers ...[44]

The petitions that the land reformers printed and sent to Congress and state legislatures emphasized the threat that European-style land monopoly posed to American society. 'The system of Land Traffic imported to this country from Europe is wrong in principle ... now in the infancy of the Republic, we should take effectual measures to eradicate the evil, and establish a principle more in accordance with our republican theory,' read one petition.[45] A petition from Kalamazoo, Michigan not only held Britain up as the counterexample to avoid, but also called for a Homestead Act on the grounds that it would encourage the working people of Great Britain in their own quest for the soil.[46]

The humble allottee

While the American national reformers, with their emphasis on independent farming, cohered well with the beliefs of their larger society, the British land reformers were much more at sea. They too quoted the agrarian republicans at length, but instead of being surrounded by 'free land' were surrounded by manufacturing, finance and an enclosure movement that sought to promote economies of scale rather than the social good of the peasant farmer. Land-reforming Chartists had to struggle, and in the end did not succeed, to make their land-reforming ideas cohere with their liberal national ethos.[47] Nor did the Chartist Co-operative Land Company embrace the radical option. The desire for land for the working-classes had been stated most strongly by Thomas Spence, but O'Connor, unlike some more radical land reformers, was unwilling to cast aside private property. O'Connor was much more of an intellectual opportunist, focusing on small allotments of land because these were widely endorsed in 1830s and 1840s Britain, with advocates as diverse as William Cobbett, the Labourer's Friend Society, Parliament, and urban workers themselves.

Neither O'Connor nor other Chartists involved in the Chartist Co-operative Land Company ever contemplated homesteads on the order of the American National Reformers. Even when British land reformers spoke of grants of land on a vast scale, they supported five-acre rather than 160-acre tracts.[48] 'Ten millions of acres might be divided into two millions of farms of five acres each, upon which two millions of families might be located ... the location of even half the aforesaid number of families upon the land would take the "surplus population" from the artificial labor market, leaving the residue in a position to secure an equitable remuneration for their toil.'[49] Bronterre O'Brien, who although not a supporter of O'Connor's scheme was a supporter of land reform, criticized the Americans for giving away such large tracts. In his view, the Americans might eventually run out of land to grant as a result of their misplaced generosity. O' Brien suggested that the United States charge moderate rents for occupation of the public lands – something that the American National Reformers never even considered.[50]

Of course, the Chartist Land Company could only purchase land when it came on the market. Ideally, this land had to be within a reasonable distance of transportation and market towns. The demand for allotments far outstripped the supply; eventually; of as many as 70,000 shareholders, only 209 families would be settled on allotments before the company folded.[51] Larger tracts were available in other parts of the British Empire and former empire, but to contemplate moving from England just to secure a birthright on the land was too much to ask of many working people.[52] Leeds Chartist Joseph Barker surely reflected the sentiments of most Chartists when he noted, 'I should never encourage people to leave their native country, for countries far away, if they were able to obtain an honest and a comfortable living at home.'[53] Feargus O'Connor felt that landlords and capitalists supported emigration of workers because it was easier to keep colonists in subjection than it would be to keep English freeholders deprived of their rights.[54] Anti-emigrationist sentiment spanned the political spectrum, as conservatives feared that depopulating the country through emigration might lead to military weakness. A correspondent to the anti-Chartist *Bolton Free Press* called it 'ludicrous' to think of sending the 'surplus population' abroad when everything was not worked to its highest capacity at home.[55] The conservative Labourer's Friend Society likened emigration to 'transporting' the working population of the country, as for some crime.[56]

More than just the difficulty of obtaining allotments influenced O'Connor to think on a small scale. He was also influenced by proposals current in the 1830s and 1840s to rent to labourers small plots of land, so that they would be able to improve their spare time and cultivate vegetables for their families.[57] The Labourer's Friend Society on the right, Home Colonization societies of seemingly neutral politics, and benefit societies formed by labourers themselves on the left, looked to small garden plots of land to lift labourers out of abject poverty and to bring into cultivation waste lands that the Victorians could not stand to see lying idle.[58] A Select Committee of the House of Commons endorsed the idea of allotments of land, and major newspapers not known for being pro-Chartist endorsed the Commons' endorsement.[59] By the end of the decade, Freehold Land Societies associated with the Liberal party had become very popular, securing homes for working people while at the same time qualifying them for the franchise. O'Connor publicly supported allotments as a precursor to the small farm system, and there is some evidence that O'Connor thought that if he could produce results on a small scale, the government would be interested in a larger programme to place labourers on small farms.[60]

With the exception of the Freehold Land Societies, which largely post-dated the Chartist Co-operative Land Company, none of the small-allotment plans current in the 1830s and 1840s was Jeffersonian in the sense of contemplating freeing workers from their primary employment or making them self-sufficient on the land.[61] In the case of the Labourer's Friend Society, proponents emphasized just the opposite. A participant at one Labourer's Friend meeting emphasized that 'it was by no means eligible that the labourer should be exalted to the condition of a small farmer.'[62] The primary goal of the Labourer's Friend allotment proposals seems to have been to palliate the consciences of Tory landowners while at the same time professing to inculcate morals and manners in the working poor. As one of the society's poets waxed:

> Her hard-working rustics, her sinews and strength
> have allotments of land to each family cot
> all taking a pride in improving the spot.
> How delightful to see them gain competence, health
> And while they increase agricultural wealth
> improve in their morals; their sovereign obey ...
> their energies roused, they are slothful no more
> They have almost deserted the publican's door.[63]

O'Connor did depart from the Labourer's Friend Society on the question of inculcating landed independence in working people. His desire to make them independent did not, however, preclude settling them on very small farms. Rather, like many other writers on a broader distribution of the land, O'Connor really believed that spade husbandry would be incredibly productive.[64] As early as 1842, he alleged that a hundred acres of ground subdivided into 10 farms would feed 70 people, rather than the 42 that could be supported on the larger piece of land, since horses would be unnecessary on a smaller farm.[65] Spade husbandry was convenient, and cheap, since the purchase of a horse and plough would be out of reach for those who won the Chartist allotments. In addition, O'Connor believed that reliance on horse-drawn ploughs led to a centralization of capital, just as mechanized weaving had led to a concentration of capital in the textile industry.[66]

While five-acre, or even two- or three-acre tracts would not have produced an independent yeomanry on the scale that George Henry Evans envisioned, Feargus O'Connor did tout the increased independence accruing to even the smallest of smallholders. First, the small farmer would be working for himself, in a more healthful environment and without being under the thrall of an employer. Even if a farm produced less cash than a wage-paying job,

> I would rather pay £10 a year for it and a small cottage than work for the best master in the world for £1 a week ... I'd live better, too, and be more independent, and consequently more happy; and I would call no man my master and no man could call me his slave. I'd work when I was able, and as much as I was able, and have the consolation of knowing that every strike of work was for my own benefit.[67]

The Chartist allottees would absorb this message well, even though they were hampered from the beginning not only by their lack of knowledge of farming but also by their lack of start-up capital. As one of the allottees wrote to a relative, 'the Peas and the Beans got the Blight and the Great Part of the Potatoes Got the Disease, the Land is the only Remedy for the working man but it wants A Little Capital to begin.' Nonetheless, he noted, 'With my trade on Strike in London I would not think of Nobing it I would sooner eat Potatos tops.'[68] With economic power might come political power. O'Connor asserted that the Charter would be achieved at a faster rate even if only 1 in 540 Chartists were to possess land.[69]

Even with its allotments on a small scale, the Land Company enabled O'Connor to cast Chartism as a knife-and-fork question. As he argued before an audience of Bolton Chartists in 1843, 'their disease was hunger, and he proposed to remedy it by applying their labour where there was a surplus to the natural resources of the land and giving them the means of applying the produce for their own benefit. There was no disease where there was no distress and poverty.'[70] O'Connor tempted hungry operatives by peppering his tracts on small farms with bounteous descriptions of the foods that could be produced on two or three acres of land.[71] With results like these, larger plots were just unnecessary.

Not every land reformer was as conservative in his aims as was O'Connor. In 1848, Leicester Chartist Thomas Cooper proposed that the government buy up all available land and parcel it out at the parish level, so that each family could participate in centrally controlled agriculture and be able to fulfil its wants.[72] In 1849, Ebeneezer Jones suggested a board of national land managers be appointed, to whom labourers could appeal for a portion of the land if they were feeling too poorly paid at their jobs.[73] Although he had once been Feargus O'Connor's most charismatic publicist for small farms, Ernest Jones came to believe by 1851 in a proposal for land nationalization.[74] Bronterre O'Brien, one of O'Connor's most ardent critics, also supported land nationalization and re-rental to individual tenants. But in the 1840s, none of these progressives could match O'Connor's style or personal popularity.

Anti-emigrationist sentiment and admiration for the allotment schemes then under discussion helped to predispose O'Connor in favour of Chartist allotments much smaller than the quarter-sections favoured by the Americans. O'Connor's restraint, especially in comparison with other land-reforming Chartists, forces a reconsideration of the idea that both the Chartist Land Company, like the Freehold Land Societies associated with the Liberal party, was intended as an attack on the old landed establishment.[75] There is no evidence that breaking the backs of the landed elite was Feargus O'Connor's intention. The Chartist Co-operative Land Company showed complete respect for private property by purchasing available land rather than seeking to limit landholding. During one 1842 lecture in which he outlined his plans for land reform, he acknowledged that with a wider distribution of land, leading to a wider franchise, the aristocracy might lose £200,000,000 a year they made by class legislation. In his opinion, they would be just as happy with the £10,000,000 which, under the small farm system, they would get by their land.[76]

Despite O'Connor's desire to palliate the conservatives, the reaction of opponents to his plan indicates that it was perceived as a threat to the establishment rather than, as in the American case, a buttress for the national mission. O'Connor's Irishness – as a Protestant and a landowner, particularly – was a potent weapon for those hoping to discredit the land plan. O'Connor's enemies alleged that he patterned the idea that Englishmen could live on two-acre farms after his native Ireland:

> There is the same absence of capital, the high rent, the demand for labour on the land at one time far beyond the tenant's means of supply, contrasted with the want of full employment at another, and the total absence of combined labour, and the mechanical aids on which the pro-

ductive power of modern husbandry so depends, which are the sad characteristics of Irish farming. We are convinced that it would never have
entered into the mind of any Englishman, certainly not of one
acquainted with farming and the management of land, to conceive a
plan of improving the condition of the working classes, by placing them
one by one on small patches of land.[77]

O'Connor himself hedged on the extent to which his Irish background
influenced him. He blamed the poverty in Ireland not on the small farm
system, but rather on large farms, which had transformed the labourers
into serfs, and on the colonization of Ireland by the English.[78]

The idea of the hardy pioneer, so crucial in supporting the American
land reform proposals, was absent in Britain. Those who observed the Land
Company from without assumed that the allottees would fail. In a way,
they were doomed to failure by the decision to make the allotments so
small; but, as shown above, every example around him led O'Connor to
this choice. Enemies of the Chartists took particular delight in pointing to
examples of starving Chartist allottees having to apply for relief or having
to toil on the sabbath.[79] During the Select Committee hearings on the
National Land Company, Poor Law Commissioner John Revans testified
not only that he expected the Chartist allottees to fail, but that expected
them to last just long enough in each locality to qualify for the poor rolls.[80]
Upon visiting one of the allotments, he had found the allottees staying
inside on a cold day, having hired local farm labourers to tend their
crops.[81] The ability of the allottees to make a decent living was an important question, since the Land Company needed to mortgage its existing
land to buy new tracts, and no one was likely to buy the land if its tenants
were not capable of paying a reasonable rent.[82]

Just as different political traditions surrounding the importance of land-
ownership in Britain and the United States helped to determine what the
land reformers asked for, so they affected the historical memory of the
land-reform movement. In the United States, the Homestead Act and its
hardy pioneers have become an integral part of the individualist American
tradition. Americans, including scholars of Western history, have lost sight
of the fact that the Homestead Act was a kind of welfare instituted by an
activist federal government.[83]

The land reform movements were even more politically meaningful in
Britain. Long after the Land Company had been wound up, some Chartists
denied that the small farm experiment itself had been a failure.[84] One
British working-class newspaper reminisced, 'the rage for manufactures and
commercial speculation had disinherited man from his birthright, the projection of the Land Company rekindled this ancient flame, reknit the ties
which bound the labourer to his mother earth, and urged him with passionate vehemence to regain a solid position thereon.'[85] Similarly, Phillip

Ford, one of the last original allottees remaining in 1875, said he and his family were 'much more agreeably situated, infinitely happier, and a thousand times more independent than the paid labourers who were subject to every whim and crochet of the farmer. On this point, Phillip Ford had no doubt whatever!' On two acres, he had been producing large bags of potatoes, sound cabbages, turnips and marigolds, fine and luscious pears, and apples that were 'perfect pictures for size, soundness, taste and colour'.[86]

Most of those who remembered the land company did not prize the landed independence of the former labouring poor. Voices like Ford's were overwhelmed by stories of the incompetence of workmen who had tried farming. As late as the 1880s, during a Parliamentary investigation of the land question, witnesses were still telling stories of the inimitable ignorance of the Chartists who had settled on allotments at Minster Lovell:

> One man thought to plant an acre of wheat with one peck of seed, and he would not be persuaded that it was not sufficient, and he planted it with one peck of wheat, and they said it was the most beautiful flower garden that they had seen for a long time, with poppies and all the rest of it, and an ear of wheat here and there. They all came to grief because they knew nothing about agriculture.[87]

Similarly, Charles William Stubbs reported that a friend of his had visited the Minster Lovell Chartist allotment at his request. There he heard that one of the allottees had actually inquired what he was to plant in order to make bread; 'another sowed his turnips as thick as mustard and cress, and refused to thin them because they looked to flourishing; another wished to know how many *bushels* of the same seed to sow to the acre.'[88] Even worse than this reaction, which might have been expected from opponents of Chartism, Chartists themselves blamed the land plan for the downfall of the Chartist movement.[89]

Henry George and the reinvigoration of land reform

Although the 1840s marked the closest convergence between the land-reform movements in Britain and the United States, transatlantic land reform did not die out, but rather was transformed later in the century. In Britain, some plans for smallholdings were mooted, but ideas for peasant proprietorship shifted to the margins, to Ireland and to the Scottish Highlands. These movements, particularly Irish land reform, had support from constituencies in America.[90] In the United States, the achievement of the Homestead Act sent former land reformers in other directions, including the secret labour society The Brotherhood of the Union, Greenbackism, and the Knights of Labor.[91]

The transatlantic land reform movement reunited in the response of both progressive constituencies to the ideas of Henry George. Like the American land reformers of the 1840s, George celebrated all workers as 'producers', used Christian evangelicalism as a rhetorical weapon, and denied any essential disharmony between workers and bosses.[92] He had a faith in the ability of the state to be impartial that harked back to a pre-Civil-War optimism.[93] Unlike the land reformers of the 1840s, he found a way to reconcile landholding with urban, liberal, civilization, by pursuing the virtual, rather than the actual, nationalization and redistribution of landholding. While the root of all inequality was still land monopoly, the answer was no longer small homesteads, but rather the 'single tax', the confiscation of rent.

In the United States, George's ideas about mankind's natural right to the soil brought many older land reformers, including such National Reformers as J. K. Ingalls and Louis Masquerier, out of retirement. The California experiences that impelled George to write *Progress and Poverty* created a whole new generation of antimonopolists.[94] George's travels to Ireland under the aegis of the *Irish World* also made him a hero among Irish-American workers.[95] In Britain, a new constituency learned of George's ideas through local editions of his *Progress and Poverty*, which sold over 66,000 copies.[96] George's ideas harmonized with the calls for land nationalization made by John Stuart Mill's Land Tenure Reform Association, by Alfred Russel Wallace's Land Nationalization Society, and even by an earlier Herbert Spencer (although by this time Spencer had repudiated the radicalism of his *Social Statics*).[97] Many Fabian socialists would credit George with having first sparked their interest in socialism.[98] Not until the late 1880s did he start defining his single-tax plan in a way that caused him to diverge from the existing nationalizers.[99]

Given the enthusiastic welcome that George's ideas received on both sides of the Atlantic, why did his single tax idea fail to fully rejuvenate the transatlantic land reform movement? The ideas that George put forth were at the same time too radical for the general public and too meek for the radicals. George's positions on land nationalization, on protectionism versus free trade, and, ultimately, on the conviction of those arrested during the Haymarket incident all set him apart from the American Knights of Labor, from where he might have garnered strongest support.[100] When his ideas appeared on the ballot, they were rejected as cranky and confiscatory.[101] In Britain, George's ideas, and particularly his enthusiasm, attracted many to Socialism, but George disappointed them through his failure to target industrialists or to specify a collective programme for the expenditure of confiscated rent.[102]

As a result of George's failure to move to the left or to broaden his prescription for society's ills, by 1889 he was more popular among Liberals than he was among Socialists. But George's failure to find a reliable constituency may not have been a bad thing; his presence in Britain enabled reformers of all stripes to use his ideas as a sounding board for their own land-reforming ideas. As Joseph Chamberlain noted, if landowners refused to act to broaden peasant proprietorship, ideas like George's would have even more currency.[103] The British public was aware now more than ever of the lopsided distribution of land in Britain, and a newly enfranchised group of voters was willing to subject landowners to greater financial discipline.[104] After George's death, when British landlords were finally subjected to land value assessment and taxation, it was through the efforts of Lloyd George and the Liberals rather than any of George's earlier allies.[105]

Conclusion

Throughout the nineteenth century, working people and their tribunes repeatedly responded to encroaching capitalism by turning to the land. As the growth of capitalism imposed strictures on political independence, personal mobility, and health, workers in both the United States and Britain saw a lifestyle of landed independence as an accessible option. Their visions were conditioned not only by the existing configuration of land-ownership, but at least as importantly, by diverse traditions espousing different views of the aptitudes of working people, the relationships between property-ownership and political power, and the sanctity of private property in land.

The Chartist Co-Operative Land Company and the American National Reform movement grew from a common set of assumptions about the desirability of a landed lifestyle for working people. Although industrialization had made greater inroads in Britain than it had in the United States, the fear that mechanization would turn American workers into their disadvantaged British counterparts motivated the Americans, just as the reality of their lives motivated the British workers. But shared rhetoric and organization could not overcome the fact that landed independence for working people had become a much greater fixture in American political traditions than it had in British ones. Liberals generally painted agrarianism as anachronistic, while the conservatives, who might have been thought the natural constituency for such plans, were threatened by a plan that promised workers landed independence. Thus, although Feargus O'Connor had responded to a widespread appeal of allotments of land for the poor when he promoted his plan, it was ridiculed as a throwback to some past time, or even to Ireland. Urban workers belonged in factories, not in the fields.

For American land reformers, the vitality of Jeffersonian republicanism, the tradition of land sales, and a belief that the American worker could be a malleable jack-of-all-trades helped to set their goal at a full quarter-section of land, to be granted by the US Congress and held freehold. The tradition of considering small, rented allotments to help the poor, while still maintaining a deferential and paternalistic social order, similarly shaped the

British land reform movement. It became a quest for 2 to 4 acre farms, which would be carved out of land that came on the market and would be rented by the winners of the Chartist land lottery. Whereas the Americans could cling to the stereotype of the hardy pioneer, British urban workers were already considered to be so narrowly trained that any attempt to make happy farmers out of them was doomed to failure.

The political traditions that shaped the land reform movements of the 1840s continued to condition the audience for land reform into the 1880s. In the United States, once the Homestead Act had been achieved, most Americans were resistant to ideas that threatened the sanctity of landholding. The radical roots of the Homestead Act had been largely forgotten. In Britain, where peasant proprietorship as practised by the Chartists was a well-known failure, progressive thinkers were more responsive to those 'virtual' means of land reform that did not rely on transforming the urban working class into hardy pioneers.

Notes

1. I am indebted to Anne Kelly Knowles for this phrase; see 'Struggles Over Spatial Freedom and Fixity in Nineteenth Century Industry', paper presented at the Social Science History Association Conference, 17 November 2001.
2. Basic narratives of the Chartist Land Company are available in W. H. G. Armitage, 'The Chartist Land Colonies, 1846–1848', *Agricultural History* XXXII (1958), 87–96; Joy MacAskill, 'The Chartist Land Plan', in Asa Briggs, ed., *Chartist Studies* (Basingstoke: Macmillan, now Palgrave Macmillan, 1960), pp. 302–41; Malcolm Chase, 'We Wish only to Work for Ourselves: the Chartist Land Plan', in Malcolm Chase and Ian Dyck, eds, *Living and Learning: Essays in Honour of J. F. C. Harrison* (Aldershot: Scolar Press, 1996), pp. 133–48; Mary Alice Hadfield, *The Chartist Land Company* (Newton Abbott: David and Charles, 1970). The American National Reformers are profiled in Helene Zahler, *American Workingmen and National Land Policy* (New York: Columbia University Press, 1941).
3. This excerpt from the musings of 'an agrarian of America' was published in Ernest Jones, *Notes to the People* I (London: Pavey, 1851), p. 339.
4. James Harrington, The Commonwealth of Oceana, ed. J. G. A. Pocock (Cambridge: Cambridge University Press, 1992); Charles Hall, *The Effects of Civilization on the People in European States* (London: Charles Gilpin, 1850); Thomas Hodgskin, *The Natural and Artificial Rights of Property Contrasted* (London: B. Steil, 1832).
5. Jamie Bronstein, *Land Reform and Working-Class Experience in Britain and the United States, 1800–1862* (Stanford: Stanford University Press, 1999), chs 3–4.
6. David M. Post, 'Jeffersonian Revisions of Locke: Education, Property-Rights, and Liberty,' *Journal of the History of Ideas* XLVII, no. 1 (1986), 147–59.
7. On land and its relation to the maintenance of American virtue, see J. G. A. Pocock, *The Machiavellian Moment: Florentine Political Thought and the Atlantic Republican Tradition* (Princeton: Princeton University Press, 1975), pp. 532–40.
8. For Owenism in the 1840s, see Gregory Claeys, *Citizens and Saints* (Cambridge: Cambridge University Press, 1989).

9. Gregory Claeys makes the case that political republicanism in Britain eventually gave way to the social preoccupations as perceptions of the United States changed. See 'The Example of America a Warning to England? The Transformation of America in British Radicalism and Socialism, 1790–1850,' in Malcolm Chase and Ian Dycks, eds, *Living and Learning: Essays in Honor of J. F. C. Harrison* (Aldershot: Scolar Press, 1996), pp. 66–80.

10. John Ashworth, 'The Jeffersonians: Classical Republicans or Liberal Capitalists?' *Journal of American Studies* [Great Britain] XVIII, no. 3 (1984), 425–35.

11. Daniel Rodgers has expressed well-founded scepticism about the coherence of the term 'republicanism' as used by American historians. See 'Republicanism: The Career of a Concept,' *Journal of American History* LXXIX, no. 1 (1992), 11–38. Nonetheless, working-class land reformers were part of an intellectual tradition pitting the virtue and independence of farmers against the corruption of city-dwellers. They were also fundamentally creative in their tactics, in opposition to the caricature of republican belief that Joyce Appleby sketched in her 'Republicanism in Old and New Contexts,' *William and Mary Quarterly* XLIV, no. 1 (1986), 20–34.

12. Bronstein, *Land Reform and Working-Class Experience*, chs 3–4.

13. Mark Bevir, 'Republicanism, Socialism and Democracy in Britain: The Origins of the Radical Left', *Journal of Social History* XXXIV, no. 2 (2000), 351–68.

14. Owenite and Chartist thinkers were beginning to come to this conclusion by the late 1840s. See Claeys, *Citizens and Saints*, p. 156; Jamie L. Bronstein, 'From the Land of Liberty to Land Monopoly: The United States in a Chartist Context,' in Stephen Roberts, Robert Fyson and Owen Ashton, eds, *The Chartist Legacy* (London: Merlin Press, 1999), pp. 147–70.

15. See, for example, J. Hector St John de Crévecoeur, *Letters from an American Farmer* (New York: Penguin Books, 1986), p. 54.

16. Thomas Jefferson, *Writings* (Monticello ed.) XIX, 18, quoted in Benjamin Horace Hibbard, *A History of the Public Land Policies* (New York: P. Smith, 1924), p. 143.

17. As Daniel Feller notes, the dichotomy between actual settlers and 'speculators', so often invoked in public discourse, was a somewhat specious one. Many average Westerners were involved in land speculation, it being one of the surest ways of making money on the frontier. See *The Public Lands in Jacksonian Politics* (Madison: University of Wisconsin Press, 1984), p. 31.

18. Ibid, p. 29.

19. Hibbard, p. 351.

20. Ibid, p. 352.

21. St George L. Sioussat, 'Andrew Johnson and the Early Phases of the Homestead Bill', *Mississippi Valley Historical Review* V (1918), 264.

22. Ibid, 256.

23. Hibbard, p. 355.

24. Speech of J. L. Dawson, 3 March 1852, *Appendix to the Congressional Globe*, 32nd Congress 1st Session, 260.

25. Hibbard, p. 361.

26. Speech of C. Skelton, 30 March 1852, *Appendix to the Congressional Globe*, 32nd Congress 1st Session, 382.

27. Arguments to the contrary were rare, but not nonexistent; see Speech of Timothy Jenkins, 14 April 1852, *Appendix to the Congressional Globe*, 32nd Congress 1st Session, 432.

28. *Working Man's Advocate*, 11 May 1844. See also 8 February 1845.
29. Speech of Galusha Grow, 30 March 1852, *Appendix to the Congressional Globe*, 32nd Congress 1st Session, 428.
30. *Radical, in Continuation of the Working Man's Advocate*, June 1841.
31. *Working Man's Advocate*, 16 March 1844.
32. *Young America!*, 3 January 1846.
33. *National Reform Almanac for 1848* (New York, 1848), 6.
34. *The Landmark*, reprinted in *National Reformer* [Rochester], 22 June 1848.
35. National Reform Association, *Young America* (New York, n. d.).
36. 'American Tract #7', reprinted in *National Reform Almanac for 1848* (New York, 1848).
37. For Spence, see the speech of Joseph Cable, 10 March 1852, *Appendix to the Congressional Globe*, 32nd Congress 1st Session, 297; for Locke, see the speech of C. Skelton, 30 March 1852, *Appendix to the Congressional Globe*, 32nd Congress 1st Session, 380.
38. Speech of J. L. Dawson, 3 March 1852, *Appendix to the Congressional Globe*, 32nd Congress 1st Session, 260.
39. Speech of Galusha Grow, 30 March 1852, *Appendix to the Congressional Globe*, 32nd Congress 1st Session, 427.
40. Speech of Joseph Cable, 10 March 1852, *Appendix to the Congressional Globe*, 32nd Congress 1st Session, 296.
41. Ibid, 298.
42. *Working Man's Advocate*, 6 April 1844.
43. Letter to the Senate, received 3 June 1852, National Archives Sen 32A H20.
44. *Voice of Industry*, 29 May 1845.
45. Petition from Pittsfield, MA, received 4 February 4 1847, National Archives HR 29A G17.2.
46. Petition from Kalamazoo, Michigan, received 9 February 1846, National Archives Sen 29A H2.
47. On the ideas of the Painite generation, many of whom emigrated to the United States, see Michael Durey, 'Thomas Paine's Apostles: Radical Emigrés and the Triumph of Jeffersonian Republicanism', *William and Mary Quarterly* XLI, no. 1 (1987), 661–88.
48. William Ogilvie suggested 40-acre plots be assigned to each adult through an agrarian law, but was willing to tolerate 6 to 8-acre plots should population pressure require it. William Ogilvie. *An Essay on the Right of Property in Land* (London: J. Walter, 1781), pp. 74–5, 151.
49. Petition of 5 May adopted at a public meeting at the South London Chartist Hall, reprinted in *Young America!*, 7 June 1845.
50. *National Reformer*, 10 October 1846.
51. Hadfield, *Chartist Land Company*, appendix III.
52. Emigration societies were formed, but none was as high-profile as the Chartist Co-Operative Land Company. See, for example, *Manchester Examiner and Times*, 18 November 1848; 31 March 1849; 5 December 1848; 10 February 1849; *Northern Star*, 8 June 1844; 13 July 1849. On the Potters' Joint-Stock Emigration Society, see Bronstein, *Land Reform and Working-Class Experience*, pp. 18–21.
53. *Reformer's Almanac and Companion to the Almanacs* (Wortley), January 1849.
54. Feargus O'Connor, *A Practical Work on the Management of Small Farms* (Manchester: Abel Heywood, 1846), p. 108.

55. *Bolton Free Press*, 22 April 1843.
56. Labourer's Friend Society, *Labourers' Friend Magazine* (1833), 285.
57. See, for example, J. C. Loudon, *A Manual of Cottage Gardening, Husbandry and Architecture* (London: A&R Spottiswoode, 1830), 5; *Journal*, 5 September 1846; Labourers' Friend Society, *Facts and Illustrations* (1831), 59.
58. For Conservative promises to secure to workers small allotments of land, see the speech of Buisfeild Ferrand in *Manchester Guardian*, 20 December 1843. On societies for the purchase of small garden plots, see *Evening Star*, 7 November 1842; *Manchester Guardian*, 10 August 1842; *Manchester Examiner and Times*, 27 March 1849. On home colonization societies, see Home Colonization Company, *Prospectus* (London, 1842); William Allen, *Colonies at Home* (London: C. Greene, 1827); *Journal*, 28 August 1846. For parliamentary committees, see Parliamentary Papers, Reports from Committees, House of Lords Select Committee on the Poor Laws I (1830–1), 393.
59. *Manchester Guardian*, 12 July 1843; Parliamentary Papers, Reports from Committees, *Report from the Select Committee on Labouring Poor (Allotments of Land)* VII (1843), iii.
60. *Northern Star*, 16 October 1844; 31 May 1845. See also Feargus O'Connor, *The Employer and the Employed: Chambers' Philosophy Refuted* (London: M'Gowan, 1844), p. 55.
61. As Malcolm Chase has pointed out, despite their emphasis on providing houses and votes rather than small farms, the Freehold Land Societies celebrated pastoralism in the same glowing terms that had been favoured by the Chartists. Chase identifies the Liberal societies and Chartists as partakers in the same strain of radical agrarianism. See Malcolm Chase, 'Out of Radicalism: The Mid-Victorian Freehold Land Movement', *English Historical Review* CVI (1991), 319–43.
62. Labourer's Friend Society, *Labourer's Friend Magazine* (1833), 327.
63. Labourer's Friend Society, *Labourer's Friend Magazine* (1834–5), 122.
64. Feargus O'Connor, *The Remedy for National Poverty and Impending National Ruin* (Leeds: J. Hobson, 1841), p. 11; Feargus O'Connor, *Management of Small Farms*, p. 46. Cf Charles Hall, *Effects of Civilization*, 236–7; John Sillett, *A Practical System of Fork and Spade Husbandry* (London, 1848). On the discourse of spade husbandry in this period, see A. Plummer, 'Spade Husbandry During the Industrial Revolution', *Journal of the South-West Essex Technical College and School of Art* I, no. 2 (1942), 84–96.
65. *Evening Star*, 28 December 1842.
66. O'Connor, *Management of Small Farms*, p. 40. Similarly, but on a different scale, the American land reformers believed that prosperity was still possible even if the government put a limitation on the amount of land that any one person could own. Hugh T. Brooks argued before the 1848 Industrial Congress that 'our system of agriculture in this country is exceedingly defective, and it is so mainly from the attempt to cultivate too much land … we have no conception of the productiveness of the earth, if its resources were properly developed.' *National Reformer* [Rochester], 13 July 1848.
67. *Young America!*, 5 July 1845.
68. Letter from John Nield to Joseph Schofield, reprinted in *Manchester Examiner*, 11 December 1847.
69. *Young America!*, 6 December 1845.
70. *Bolton Free Press*, 28 January 1843.

71. O'Connor, *Management of Small Farms*, p. 158.
72. Thomas Cooper, *The Land for the Labourers, and the Fraternity of Nations* (London: Effingham Wilson, 1848), p. 9.
73. Ebeneezer Jones, *The Land Monopoly: The Suffering and Demoralization Caused by It, and The Justice and Expediency of its Abolition* (London: Charles Fox, 1849), p. 9.
74. Ernest Jones, *Notes to the People*, I (London: Pavey, 1851), p. 55.
75. David Martin, 'Land Reform', in Patricia Hollis, ed., *Pressure from Without* (London: Edward Arnold, 1974), p. 149.
76. Feargus O'Connor, *The Land and its Capabilities, A Lecture by Feargus O'Connor at the Hall of Science, Camp Field, Manchester on Monday, March 7, 1842* (Manchester: Abel Heywood, 1842), p. 30.
77. *Manchester Examiner*, 27 June 1848.
78. O'Connor, *Management of Small Farms*, p. 101.
79. William Waldo Cooper, *Mr. Feargus O'Connor's Land Scheme* (London: Francis & John Rivington, 1848), p. 12.
80. Parliamentary Papers, Reports from Committees, *Fourth Report from the Select Committee on the National Land Company* XIX (1847–8), 23.
81. Ibid, 32.
82. Testimony of John Finlaison, Esq., Parliamentary Papers, Reports from Committees, *Fifth Report from the Select Committee on the National Land Company* XIX (1847–8), 24.
83. Dorothee Kocks makes this point in her book *Dream A Little: Land and Social Justice in Modern America* (Berkeley: University of California Press, 2000), pp. 16–9.
84. See, for example, *Beehive*, 15 February 1868; 29 February 1868; 27 June 1868.
85. *National Union*, October 1858.
86. *Newcastle Daily Chronicle*, 30 January 1875.
87. Parliamentary Papers, Reports from Commissioners, Royal Commission on Agriculture XIV (1882), 251.
88. Charles William Stubbs, *The Land and the Labourers* (London: W. S. Sonnenschein, 1884), p. 181.
89. As W. J. Linton wrote to George Julian Harney, 'Men looked so hard at Snigg's End, that they forgot the Charter', *Red Republican*, 12 October 1850.
90. John Wood, 'Transatlantic Land Reform: America and the Crofters', *Scottish Historical Review* LXIII, no. 1 (1984), 79–104. Thomas Devyr, the old Chartist and land reformer, worked in the service of Irish land reform at the offices of the *Irish World*. See Thomas Devyr, *Odd Book of the Nineteenth Century* (New York: The Author, 1882).
91. See Bronstein, *Land Reform*, ch 7.
92. Michael Perelman, 'Henry George and Nineteenth-Century Economics: The Village Economy Meets the Railroad', *American Journal of Economics and Sociology* LVI, no. 4 (1997), 441–9. Shaker leader Frederick Evans, George Henry Evans' brother, recognized the remarkable similarity between the two men and their programmes and supported Henry George as the possible fulfilment of his brother's legacy. See John E. Murray, 'Henry George and the Shakers', *American Journal of Economics and Sociology* L, no. 2 (1996), 244–56. For a characterization of George as a unique and even postmodern contributor to American sociology, see Robert Peter Siemens, 'Henry George: An Unrecognized Contributor to American Social Theory', *American Journal of Economics and Sociology* LIV, no. 4 (1995), 107–27.

93. J. H. M. Laslett, 'Haymarket, Henry George, and the Labor Upsurge in Britain and America', *International Labor and Working-Class History* XXIX (1986), 68–82.

94. Mark Lause, 'Progress Impoverished: The Origin of Henry George's Single Tax', *The Historian* LII, no. 2 (1990), 394–410; on land speculation in California, see Gerald D. Nash, 'Henry George Re-examined: William S. Chapman's Views on Land Speculation in Nineteenth-Century California', *Agricultural History* XXXIII, no. 3 (1959), 133–7.

95. Robert E. Weir, 'A Fragile Alliance: Henry George and the Knights of Labor', *American Journal of Economics and Sociology* LVI, no. 4 (1977), 422–39.

96. Elwood Lawrence, *Henry George in the British Isles*, (East Lansing: Michigan State University Press, 1957), p. 34.

97. Ursula Vogel, 'The Land-Question: A Liberal Theory of Communal Property', *History Workshop* XXVII (1989), 106–35. On the Land Nationalization Society, see Michael Silagi, 'Henry George and Europe: A Dissident Economist and Path-Breaking Philosopher, He was a Catalyst for British Social Reform', *American Journal of Economics and Sociology* XLVIII, no. 1 (1989), 113–23.

98. Lawrence, Henry George, p. 77; see also Bernard Newton, 'Henry George and Henry M. Hyndman: The Forging of an Untenable Alliance, 1882–1883', *American Journal of Economics and Sociology* XXXV, no. 3 (1976), 311–24.

99. Mason Gaffney, 'Alfred Russel Wallace's Campaign to Nationalize Land: How Darwin's Peer Learned from John Stuart Mill and Became Henry George's Ally', *American Journal of Economics and Sociology* LVI, no. 4 (1997), 609–15; Lawrence, *Henry George*, p. 57.

100. Weir, 'A Fragile Alliance', p. 432; see also Matthew Edel, 'Rent Theory and Working-Class Strategy: Marx, George and the Urban Crisis', *Review of Radical Political Economics* IX, no. 4 (1977), 1–15.

101. Robert C. Woodward, 'W. S. U'Ren and the Single Tax in Oregon', *Oregon Historical Quarterly* LXI, no. 1 (1960), 46–63.

102. Vogel, 'The Land-Question', 106–35. For the conversion of George Bernard Shaw, see Michael Silagi, 'Henry George and Europe: As Dissident Economist', 119.

103. Michael Silagi, 'Henry George and Europe: George and his Followers Awakened the British Conscience and Started a New, Freer, Society', *American Journal of Economics and Sociology* L, no. 2 (1991), 242–55.

104. As Peter Lindert has pointed out, the land census of 1873 revealed that only one in seven or fewer of all households owned any real estate; the median voter was beginning to have fewer misgivings about egalitarian initiatives than had been the case under a more restricted electorate. See 'Who Owned the Land in Victorian England? The Debate over Landed Wealth and Equality', *Agricultural History* LXI, no. 4(1987), 25–51.

105. Harold Schifflin and Pow-Key Sohn, 'Henry George on Two Continents: A Comparative Study in the Diffusion of Ideas', *Comparative Studies in Society and History* II, no. 1 (1959), 85–109.

3
Freedom of Contract, the Market and Imperial Law-making

Sandra den Otter

'A society based on contract is a society of free and independent men, who form ties without favour and obligation, and cooperate without cringing or intrigue. A society based on contract, therefore, gives the utmost room and chance for individual development, and for all the self-reliance and dignity of a free man.'[1] So declaimed William Graham Sumner in 1883. For Sumner, the American republic was the triumph of contract. Constraints on state power, and the energy of competitive markets and the independent entrepreneur had taken America to the pinnacles of progress. About two decades earlier, a similar paean to the moral power of contract had been made in a very different context – the executive council of the imperial government of India. In deliberations over colonial policy, a senior council member defended freedom of contract as indispensable to the imperial mission to civilize India: 'all the modern progress of society seemed to be intimately connected with the completest freedom of contract, and in some ways, was almost mysteriously dependent on it.'[2] Was it not the duty of the colonizing state to introduce this 'modern' conception to a country locked in primitive stagnation? Introducing contract was a kind of 'moral education' that would remedy 'possibly the most moral failing which a people can possess'.[3]

These two instances, drawn from American and British imperial records, were not coincidental. Sumner was echoing the words of a best-selling treatise on ancient law, written by the advocate of contract in India's executive council: H. S. Maine. The resonance of 'contract' as it reverberated throughout the nineteenth century was captured by Maine's *Ancient Law* published in 1861. It was not read by its many British and American admirers to gratify antiquarian curiosity as much as to explain how England had attained such liberty, economic vitality and civilization, and to shed light on current dilemmas of political economy, colonial administration and public policy. Maine's central argument, that societies evolve from status to contract, encapsulated a principal theme in nineteenth-century whig and liberal traditions. This narrative was essentially a moral one, in which contract was the means by which the virtues of independence, honour and self-government could be cultivated. This state of modern enlightenment was juxtaposed to primitive societies and the vestiges of these earlier arrangements that were thought to live on in India, all governed by custom, superstition and often despotic kinship ties. It was largely on the strength of his bold argument about the movement from primitive status to modern contract, and its laudatory reception that Maine was invited to join the imperial government in India and became one of the principal architects of the Indian legal system as it stands today.

This chapter uses one instance of colonial law-making in India to re-examine the calibration between freedom of contract, morality and progress which were seemingly omnipresent in nineteenth-century whig and liberal traditions in Britain and America. It considers the attempt in the mid 1860s to create law that would enforce contracts between indigo planters and cultivators, and so to entrench a particular form of a market economy in labour. Maine was forced to abandon his attempt, and the incident, rather than exemplifying the power of law to introduce contract and redeem a seemingly backward civilization, ruptured the pervasive equation of indigenous customary law with a pre-capitalist primitiveness and law with a capitalist modernity. By looking at this one attempt to implant contract in India, the chapter examines the intersection of law and political economy in the imperial context, and relates this back to metropolitan debate about contract, the market and community.[4] The actual experience of colonial governance combined with the ferment of new anthropological and ethnological investigations of the 1860s and 1870s to spur on a reappraisal of market society. The imperial experience and the new scholarly investigations which were in part stimulated by colonial administration created a catalogue of alternative forms of society which could be used to challenge as well as to confirm the superiority of capitalism. Marx's study of H. S. Maine and the American anthropologist L. H. Morgan exemplified the possibilities for radical traditions, but more widespread were those who integrated this new knowledge into the whig and liberal traditions of Anglo-American political life in a much more ambivalent manner.

The theoretical template: from status to contract

In *Ancient Law* (1861), Maine had argued that 'the movement of progressive societies has hitherto been a movement *from status to contract.'*[5] In primitive societies individuals had few or no rights and duties; the rules that they obeyed derived from the station into which they were born and from the dictates of the rulers of their societies: 'Such a system leaves the very smallest room for Contract.'[6] Although in these kinship systems, families might have contracted with other families or chieftains with other chieftains, Maine asserted that there was not the same sense of obligation to performance that existed in advanced civilizations, for 'the positive duty resulting from one man's reliance on the word of another is among the slowest conquests of advancing civilization.'[7] In contrast, contract governed social relations in progressive societies. By contract, Maine, citing Bentham and Austin, simply meant the disposition to make good a promise and the expectation that promises would be kept by others. The mutuality of agreements was assumed.

Maine took this abstract template to India, and there, at least initially, found empirical evidence for his theoretical account of social evolution. What he encountered in India conformed to his abstract view of social development: 'Authority, Custom, or Chance are in fact the great sources of law in primitive communities as we know them, not Contract.'[8] He found contract to be 'utterly unregulated, except by the small portion of Muhammadan jurisprudence'.[9] He found economic institutions to be quite unlike their British counterparts: ownership tended to be joint rather than by individuals. Maine found nothing resembling a competitive market rate in rents in India since land very rarely sold or rented, and fixity of tenure meant the virtual absence of market standard. Succession of property through wills and testaments was rare, because succession was guided not by individual caprice but by custom. Because trading tended to be within kinship systems, such commercial principles as getting the best price for property or labour did not operate. All of this stood in stark contrast to the axiom of political economists that the practice of the highest obtainable price was the universal measure of price. He observed further that there was no notion of right or duty in Indian village community where 'a person aggrieved complains not of an individual wrong but of the disturbance of the order of the entire little society'.[10]

Most of these conclusions were based on partial and sometimes inaccurate evidence gleaned from Maine's own limited travels in India, his conversations with other colonial administrators, government reports and the writings of orientalist scholars. While Maine tended to be more aware of the complexity of Indian society and the immense local variation than many of his contemporaries – he, for example, was unusual in disputing the way in which caste was understood as an essential category of India – his analysis was overly simplistic and did not account sufficiently for the diversity of social and economic relationships. Individual rights were much more extensive in pre-colonial India than Maine realized.[11] His invocation of the Indian cultivator was simplistic and over-generalized; he repeatedly mentioned the importance of local context so at least was intellectually suspicious of the essentialism of the categories of landlord and cultivator, but nonetheless overstated the ubiquity of the peasant cultivator and the uniformity of this identity. Recent historians, in contrast, have challenged the simplicity of nineteenth-century accounts of agrarian society by indicating the immense variety and changeability of tenant rights and relations.[12] There was much more commercial exchange in property than he realized. Moreover, he himself eventually recognized that there was a sophisticated body of Hindu customary law on succession. Maine's modest expectations of Indian society owed much to the late-eighteenth-century school of Scottish conjectural history; especially the notion that human progress sprang from the energy and vitality of commerce. In Maine's estimation, the apparent torpor of Indian society could be explained not simply by the deadening authority of sacerdotal elites, but by the scarcity of commercial exchange.

Indigo contracts and the labour market

One of the first issues that Maine took up on his arrival in Calcutta in 1862 was the long-standing dilemma of agreements between agricultural labourers and indigo plantation owners and merchants. Since the 1820s, European planters in Bengal and Bihar, to varying degrees of success, had lobbied both the governments in India and London to provide legal means to enforce their agreements with labourers cultivating indigo which was already then an unrenumerative crop. As demand for indigo plummeted in the 1840s and 1850s because of fluctuations in the world market, agricultural labourers had less and less incentive to cultivate indigo instead of the more lucrative crops of sugar and jute. Cash advances to cover the cost of sowing the crop and maintaining the land and its buildings had been the primary incentive to cultivate indigo; plantation owners rarely extracted payment of debts on cash advances since the debt burden tied the labourers to cultivate indigo. By this arrangement, owners were provided with an unpaid or underpaid labour force, for most plantations were worked by raiyats who had some form of ownership of the land they worked and received little payment in return for their labour or that of their families. As Sugata Bose concludes, 'colonial capital preferred a course in which the cost of labour was quite simply "nothing"'.[13] He estimates that in the Nischindapur concern in Nadia, 'out of 865 peasants working 3,300 acres with indigo, a mere 110 acres had no outstanding balances ... unpaid balances mounted over the generations to astronomical figures which no indigo peasant could hope to redeem. Here was a marketing and production mechanism that efficiently and relentlessly attached unpaid labour to indigo cultivation.'[14] But as plantation owners increasingly refused to extend cash advances to indigo cultivators, the most powerful inducement for raiyats to cultivate indigo disappeared and large numbers defaulted on these exploitative contracts.

Immediately on his arrival in Calcutta, Maine was assailed by planters and merchants in Bengal who reported that the relation of employers and employed was disorganized, and that breach of engagement by labourers after advance payment was endemic.[15] In 1860 a 'Blue Mutiny' had spread throughout much of Bengal: cultivators refused 'to honour' agreements to cultivate indigo, attacked indigo factories and pulled out indigo plants. In fear of the disorder of the Blue Mutiny and in response to aggressive lobbying by European planters, factory owners and agency houses, the Indian Government had framed legislation that made breach of contract a criminal offence, punishable by imprisonment and hard labour.[16] This measure was partially modelled on eighteenth-century master and servant legislation making breach of contract in a variety of areas a criminal offence punishable by incarceration in Houses of Correction; this legislation was still in place in England, though by this time, much contested.[17] But Maine, in concert with the Home Government, which vetoed the measure, was opposed to the criminalization of breach of contract, for as he protested: 'half the machinery of modern society seems to me to hinge on the civil nature of contract'.[18] His first act was to urge its withdrawal. However, this left Maine seeking an alternative which would give some teeth to the enforcement of contract. If not punishable as a criminal offence, how might European property owners enforce agreements with the labourers cultivating their lands?

Maine fitted the indigo controversy in the pro-contract framework he had constructed before his arrival in India, and he directly applied this theoretical survey of civilization to colonial policy. He was convinced that it was essential for contracts to be civilly enforced in India and that non-enforcement would be 'especially pernicious in this country. If Europeans are to come to India for the investment of their capital the best relation which can be established between them and the natives is surely one of contract, provided the contracts are fair ones.'[19] Maine warned the Home Government that the 'mercantile community [was] trading without the advantage which is the first condition of success in trade i.e. reasonable security that persons dealing with them will hold to their bargain'.[20] Maine's theoretical vision of the movement from status to contract in India justified the creation of the familiar instruments of commercial exchange which the enhancement of European commercial interests demanded. The ambition to write law for India had from the beginning been closely connected to the project of systematizing market arrangements and enhancing revenue collection. One of the first subjects to which the Law Commissioners, who had been appointed to reform Indian law, turned was promissory notes, bills of exchanges and cheques, a subject, they recognized, 'to which the recent extension of mercantile enterprise in India gives increased importance'.[21] But Maine also appealed to the already pervasive images and contrasts that underwrote the Raj, in which the masculine honour of the British was counterpoised to the duplicity of the Indian character.[22] Maine wrote to Governor General Lawrence: 'What he [the Bengali] has not wit to see is the expediency in the long run of performing a contract even though for a moment it has become comparatively disadvantageous. The Baboo who ... takes you into the High Court if you interfere with him, seems to me the exact counterpart of the ryot who breaks his engagement at the critical moment because the price of jute has risen in comparison with that of indigo, and then calls out against any improvement even of the civil law of contract as a gross oppression.'[23] In the spirit of Burke, Maine's proposals for a civil law of contract bound manners (in this case, keeping one's word) to commercial advantage. Framing legal measures to enforce contract would not only expedite commercial transactions and secure labour arrangements. It would also bring about a change in manners–enforcing contract by law would teach agricultural labourers to honour agreements. This emphasis on manners reflected a more widespread belief among colonial administrators that the establishment of British law in India was 'a moral conquest more striking, more durable, and far more solid, than the physical conquest which renders it possible'.[24] Law had become the repository of utilitarian, whig and liberal aspirations to reform and civilize the sub-continent, and legal reform was one of the legitimating myths of British imperial policy.[25]

Maine proposed legislation on 'specific performance' (that is, actual performance), which would enable courts to order the actual performance of a contract if the contract was fairly entered into by both parties and if the contract clearly stated liquidated damages in case of non-performance. Rather than expecting damages, which almost always raiyots could not hope to pay given the magnitude of their debt burden, legislation would force the actual performance of the contract, the planting and harvesting of indigo.[26] Remedy would be sought in the civil courts; judges would determine whether the disputed contract was equitable; punishment was to be imprisonment at the creditor's expense. Maine's proposal for specific performance soon ran aground. Merchants and planters in Calcutta supported Maine's contract legislation but found that it stopped short of real protection of capitalist interest. One local newspaper wondered 'if anything could be more favourable to the agriculturist, and at the same time less just to the capitalist, than such stringent provisions as these'.[27]

In contrast, the Whig Secretary of State for India, Sir Charles Wood, regarded contracts for indigo cultivation as unfair to the agricultural labourer. He wrote to Maine: 'I cannot help fearing that such a power might be used as an instrument for bullying the ryot awfully. They contract to plough at a certain time, to sow ditto, to weed ditto, reap ditto, deliver & so forth – I do not say that they ought not to do all these things, but look at the way in which contracts were imposed on the ryots who hardly could exercise any free will in the matter.'[28] The Indian Law Commissioners in London, under the direction of the Benthamite Lord Romilly, whose task it was to propose laws and to oversee the drafting of the legal codes, directly contradicted Maine's proposal for specific performance, less because of the oppressiveness of the contracts than its departure from English legal conventions. The Commissioners eventually resigned en masse in opposition to Maine and the Government of India.[29] Maine was not persuaded by their objections, and used the incident to reject the notion that the Indian Law Commissioners could write legislation in London according to abstract principles and to the model of English law. The Viceroy rejected Maine's plan on the grounds that it seemed to champion the interests of the landed classes too strongly and provided insufficient protection to the peasant cultivator: 'nor can they ask the government to legalize their mulcting the labourer's wages. The law is made to save the weak man from oppression by the strong.'[30] Other members of the Viceroy's Council also opposed Maine's solution because determining equity of contract required more sophisticated standards of judgeship than existed at present in the Small Claims Courts and critically, 'the main contracts which ... would be demanded in Bengal are not in themselves equitable contracts ... and I don't view with any favour the legislation that seeks to strengthen the former at the cost of the weaker party'.[31]

Racial considerations became a pivotal element in determining the equity of the proposed entrenchment of contract on the sub-continent. Maine's political masters, both in Calcutta and London, regarded his attempt to strengthen the obligation of agricultural labourers to honour contractual arrangements with landowners as racially divisive: 'it would arm "white" European masters against their "black" servants.' Maine disputed this, asserting that Wood was 'rather too much influenced by general considerations as to the antagonism of races'. Maine wrote to Wood, 'I must in conclusion beg you to believe that I am in no danger of forgetting the reasons for distrusting legislation on behalf of white masters against coloured servants.'[32] But he was not at all convinced by Wood's concern about racial inequality: 'Your language as to the stronger and weaker races might apply to the Spaniards and South American Indians, but leaves out of account the calculating, astute, and wide-a-wake character of the Bengalee, who, whatever his class, knows his interests as well as the keenest Englishman, and is quite as hard a hand at a bargain. Putting aside actual physical constraint, you need never call the Bengalees the weaker race.'[33] But he was forced to concede that racial difference was an obstacle to enforcing agricultural contracts because it would be too difficult to ensure that contracts were equitable. A major difficulty, as Maine himself saw, was that determining equity of contract would require more sophisticated standards of judgeship than he or other members of the Indian Government believed to exist in India.[34]

Constraints on freedom of contract

In the face of opposition from members of the Home and Indian governments and from indigenous groups, Maine abandoned his attempt to strengthen the enforcement of contract between masters and servants. His failed attempt to interject contract into agrarian social relations by legal innovation illustrates how extensively numerous local and metropolitan elements constrained the application of theory to practice. The Rebellions of 1857–8 had vividly shown the fragility of imperial control in Northern India. The confidence of utilitarian reformers like Governor General Dalhousie a decade earlier had given way to much less sanguine expectations of rapid reform. While some colonial administrators and legal reformers might look upon India as a laboratory in which all sorts of legal experiments could be tried, the political reality was very different. More often, proposed legislation changed, often substantially, in response to challenges by diverse parts of Indian society. For example, in response to another attempt by Maine to entrench contract, this time in marriage relations, Shia and Sunni Muslim groups lobbied so effectively that these groups were excluded from legislation. While the whole point of legal codes was to provide a uniform law for all, Maine also framed special legislation to cover marriage and divorce among the Parsi in response to a well-organized campaign by the influential Bombay Parsi community.[35] It was colonized 'subjects' who forced the reframing of utilitarian expectations of a universal and abstract framework for law. Similarly raiyat opposition to the criminalization of breach of contract contributed to Maine's failure to entrench contract in agricultural relationships. Indigenous protests against the oppressive labour relations of indigo cultivation stretched back to the 1830s, to the revolt led by Titu Mir in Barasat in 1831, and the farazi movement in East Bengal throughout the late 1830s and 1840s. The immediate backdrop to Maine's proposal to entrench contract in agricultural labour was the 'blue mutiny' in west and central Bengal: peasant attacks on indigo factories and indigo plants, dramatized in Dinabandhu Mitra's play *Neel Darpan*,[36] effectively pushed the Home Government to force the withdrawal of legislation to criminalize breach of contract.[37] Large scale refusal to cultivate indigo even though cash advances had been made continued to be a powerful form of resistance. The colonial state could not simply set up machinery for accumulation of capital, in this case, to protect the profit margins of indigo merchants and planters by guaranteeing them underpaid family labour. This is not to suggest that imperial policy did not entrench capitalist market society in India; British initiatives from the eighteenth century on inexorably extended existing patterns of commodity exchange and in a deeply inequitable manner.[38] The entire trade in indigo ebbed and waned according to world markets. But as David Washbrook has argued, the need to maintain some legitimacy for the state and the unrestrained ambition to maximize accumulation were to some extent antithetical: 'Capitalist states do not only pass legislation advancing the interests of capitalists. They also pass legislation protecting labour and reducing the opportunities for "maximal" accumulation ... the politico-legal framework within which capitalism developed in India ... [was] by no means designed for "maximal" accumulation.'[39] The disjunction between emergent capitalist structures and a non-capitalist agricultural labour force lingered – agrarian social relations were not transformed swiftly and radically by the commercialization of agriculture.[40]

The pivotal place given to fairness and equity in this political dispute over agricultural contracts is worth noting for several reasons. It points to the diverse ways in which the dominant – though far from hegemonic – political culture of economic liberalism and freedom of contract was challenged. Atiyah, Horowitz and others have depicted the nineteenth century in Britain and the United States as the apotheosis of contract, in which freedom of contract, economic liberalism and the establishment of capitalism more generally were allied.[41] Atiyah has argued that 'will theory' (specifically the notion that individuals freely form contracts with each other and that these contracts shape obligations and determine social relations) exemplified the freedom of individuals to pursue their own interests in a free market. Contract law was the law of the market; its fixed, abstract, rational and universal rules provided a framework for the operation of the market.[42] In this account, equity, justice or fairness were not the primary interest. But the debates over indigo contracts in India show quite a different perspective at work, one in which calculations of justice and fairness were primary, and these calculations expressed a Whig paternalism modulated by considerations of political expediency, more than a desire for economic redistribution. As J. W. Burrow has persuasively argued, there were striking continuities running through eighteenth-century whiggism and nineteenth-century liberal individualism. The debate over indigo contracts reflected a whig liberalism which sought to balance competing interests in indigo cultivation and sought to safeguard equity, more than the primacy of freedom of contract. The protracted deliberations over indigo contracts challenge Atiyah's description of the unrivalled ascendancy of contract in nineteenth-century Britain and America.[43]

The contrast to an earlier debate over indigo contracts, one in which the first law member for India, the liberal utilitarian T. B. Macaulay refused to interfere on behalf of the raiyot, is striking. In a minute on the subject written in 1830, Macaulay maintained, 'If there be any one political truth proved by a vast mass of experience, it is this, that the interference of legislators for the purpose of protecting men of sound mind against the inconveniences which may arise from their own miscalculations or from the natural state of markets is certain to produce infinitely more evil than it can avert... . A ryot consents to bind himself to deliver a certain commodity to the capitalist during several successive seasons. If he has been terrified or deluded into making this agreement, the agreement is of course null. But if he has not been terrified or deluded, on what principle are we to refuse him permission to bring his only commodity, his labour, to market in his own way and to dispose of it on such terms as in the state of the market are the best which he can obtain?'[44] Thirty years later, this position was much less persuasive; legal scholars were beginning to develop a more nuanced understanding of intention in voluntary agreement, and beginning to recognize that freedom of contract could be compromised not only by duress or fraud but by inequitable power relations.[45] The example of indigo contracts vividly demonstrated how difficult it was to measure or adjudicate whether contracts were freely made, when there was such a gulf between the wealth, power and privilege of the contracting parties, and when the contracts perpetuated these inequalities. Classical political economists had not extensively addressed problems of distributive justice, but by the 1870s, political economists were examining the question of equity in contract, and beginning to analyse and challenge freedom of contract which had been so central to classical political economy. W. S. Jevons in particular analysed how unequal and unjust distribution of wealth was replicated in contracts.[46] These arguments were developed later in socialist critiques of contract theory, in which contracts are regarded as giving an illusion of consensual agreement and lending legitimacy to unfairness.

The engagement of whigs and liberals with the equity of contracts opened the window on the expansion of the state. While a state with minimal powers could provide a secure framework for contracts, determining the equity of contract represented an expansion of state responsibility. Hovering on the borders of a much more interventionist liberalism, J. S. Mill asked: 'Is it not part of the duty of governments to enforce contracts? Here the doctrine of non-interference would no doubt be stretched a little, and it would be said that enforcing contracts is not regulating the affairs of individuals at the pleasure of government but giving effect to their own expressed desire ... But governments do not limit their concern with contracts to simple enforcement. They take upon themselves to determine what contracts are fit to be enforced.'[47] The British economist William Thornton who wrote extensively about labour in the 1860s and 1870s, regarded the inviolability of contract as an essential right of labour – the state exists 'to secure the person, property and performance of contract'[48] – but he did not regard the state as responsible for determining the fairness of contracts. That was the province of the trade unions which sought in partnership with capitalist interests to create fair conditions for labour. In the colonial context, Mill's supposition that the state assumed the responsibility to determine which contracts are fit to be enforced, became especially prescient. British claims for dominance in the sub-continent depended on their claims to promulgate justice and equity. As Sudhir Chandra noted, an 'idealized notion of justice promised a thrilling justification to a people whose duty it was to wield power, and wield it without being corrupted by it.'[49] Nonetheless, considerations of equity did not deter the colonial government from administering an extensive system of indentured labour in which contracts to labour on plantations in the Caribbean did not meet the standards of equity set out in the indigo debates. Colonial administrations across the Empire were shot through by contradictions of this sort.

The indigo contracts also point to a curious inconsistency in Maine's social evolutionary theory of the movement from status to contract. While Maine purported to introduce modern contractual relations in indigo cultivation, the ostensibly modern and progressive contracts between planters and cultivators bore parallels to the old status relations. Karen Orren has traced the vestiges of feudal master and servant relations in nineteenth-century America, which she argues was embedded in the American constitution and only reformed by labour agitation towards the end of the nineteenth century. She finds in attempts to enforce performance of contracts evidence of 'how contract concepts did not change master-and-servant relations, but how master-and-servant workplace rules reverberated in the developing abstractions of contract'.[50] While Maine attempted to use the colonial state to assert the potency of contract and thereby climb another rung up the ladder of civilization, the contracts he sought to enforce did not encapsulate free relationships of exchange as much as they embodied much older, semi-feudal status relations.

Reformulating utilitarianism: The force of custom

Maine returned to London after completing his short stint as a colonial legislator with a much greater sense of the power of custom. His experience as a colonial administrator in India had sharpened his sense of how the particularities of time and place shaped law. It would be inaccurate to attribute this wholly to his Indian experiences; even those utilitarians who argued that law was a unified system that ought to transcend the pluralism of local custom had recognized the impact of local environment. Bentham's 'Essay on the Influence of Time and Place in Matters of Legislation' speculated on how English criminal law would have to be modified to suit India.[51] The German historical school, in particular F. K. Savigny, had reached British and American audiences by the mid century,[52] and there mingled with the diverse social evolutionary currents in the writings of Erasmus and Charles Darwin, Auguste Comte, Walter Bagehot and Herbert Spencer.[53] But the practical constraints on legal reform in India highlighted this perspective. Maine disputed the idea that architects of legal codes for India could write legislation in London according to abstract principles and according to the model of English common and statutory law, but with little knowledge of India. Almost all of the illustrations in the draft codes sent out from London were English; they were very few illustrations drawn from Indian examples. Maine mused in a minute on codification a decade after he had returned from India: 'They [Bentham and Austin] sometimes write as if they thought that, although obscured by false theory, false logic, and false statement, there is somewhere, behind all the delusions which they expose, a framework of permanent legal conceptions, which is discoverable by an eye looking through a dry light, and to which a rational code may always be fitted. What I have stated as to the effects upon law of a mere mechanical improvement in land registration is a very impressive warning that this position is certainly doubtful, and possibly not true.'[54]

Maine's experience as a colonial administrator led him to refine a historical–comparative approach to law that departed from the universalism of his roots in the utilitarian tradition.[55] His life-work was devoted to uncovering the origin in antiquity and subsequent evolution of the principal branches of modern commercial society: contract, private property, rent, money and demonstrating that the Western European and American institutions of unrestricted competition in purchase and exchange, and the view of land as a merchantable property have been endorsed in only a small part of the world and have been for a relatively short period of time.[56] Maine used his Indian experience to challenge the assumptions of political economists who are too 'apt to speak of their propositions as true a priori, or from all time; and that they greatly underrate the value, power and interest of that great body of custom and inherited idea'.[57] The 'rule of the market' was not a reflection of an 'original and fundamental tendency of human nature'.[58] Not surprisingly, he maintained that candidates for the civil service should not be taught political economy as a general subject before being sent out to the Empire: the discipline was a positive handicap for colonial administrators because it so often took for granted that private property was an essential and inevitable feature of human societies, when over much of India land was held in common.[59] This historical–comparative approach led not simply to an abstract recognition of difference, but to a normative judgement which circumscribed his endorsement of capitalist social forms: the first step towards a true understanding of political economy, Maine asserted, was to recognize 'the Indian phenomena of ownership, exchange, rent and price as equally natural, equally respectable, equally interesting, equally worthy of scientific observation, with those of Western Europe'.[60] But Maine did not assert that these Indian pre-capitalist forms were equally conducive to the progress of human civilization, and here he parted company with some of his contemporaries who were much more ready to draw more radical conclusions from the comparative study of society.

Anthropology, ethnology and comparative law: Radical, Whig and Liberal interpretations

Maine's study of ancient law was part of a burgeoning of anthropological and ethnological investigations in the 1860s and 1870s which had important implications for the political traditions of late-nineteenth-century Britain and America.[61] These investigations shaped contemporary appraisals of modern commercial society, notably by animating radical traditions that were critical of the market economy. Gregory Claeys has argued that when mid-nineteenth-century radical economists sought alternatives to the market determination of price, they looked to anthropological studies of exchange in primitive societies, primarily to Locke and Smith's accounts of labour in the state of nature.[62] But the more recent study of earlier societies provided Kovalevsky, Marx, Engels and others with a new archive of illustrations of non-competitive social relationships which did not radiate out of contract. Karl Marx devoted the early 1880s to a detailed investigation of Maine, Morgan and McLennan, with the aim of defining early forms of property. Marx's notes on Maine's *Lectures on the Early History of Institutions* (1875) vividly show up the divide between Maine and Marx's interpretation of early society. In his inimitable scrambling of English and German, Marx impatiently derided the conclusion of 'Herr Maine als blockheaded Englishman' ('der sich d. English Private Family after all nicht aus d. kopf schlagen kann'), that pre-capitalist society was grounded in the private, patriarchal family.[63] For Marx, Maine had misinterpreted the early bonds of kinship, had misunderstood the nature of the despotism of these primitive kinship groups. In his 'usual Peckniff unctuosity' he had transported the patriarchal Roman family into the very beginning of time (307, 324), and then wrongly hailed the modern state as the pinnacle of evolutionary progress. The field investigations in Amerindian societies by the American anthropologist L. H. Morgan (1818–81) offered Marx a more satisfactory account of how the 'passion for possession' had led to the institution of private property and the abandonment of primitive communism in which property was held in common, and sexual freedom prevailed.[64] Both Marx and Tonnies found Morgan's investigation of the dominance of matriarchy in primitive societies more persuasive than Maine's assertion of the dominance of patriarchy.[65]

Marx's ethnological writings illustrate how the study of early societies could be harnessed to a far-reaching critique of capitalist society, but the implications of ancient societies for current social and political practice, especially on property, were vigorously and widely contested and debated in the 1870s and 1880s. Some like the colonial legislator and theorist James Fitzjames Stephen, who framed a code for Indian contract law in the early 1870s, dismissed the utility of looking to early or primitive societies for political argument: 'Tribes, families, hordes, small town and village communities like those which the very latest school of historical speculators busy themselves with so much belong to the infancy of the world, and have only a speculative interest. You cannot get much that is worth having out of a village communities.'[66] Clive Dewey has argued that as soon as the radical implications of anthropology became apparent, a conservative reaction set in which denied the usefulness of modelling the modern world on either ancient societies or the vestiges of these societies as they supposedly

lived on in India. At the same time, colonial governments sought to preserve these traditional institutions in order to shore up cohesive and stable
communities in the face of splintering market forces.[67]

It is tempting to conclude that many whigs and liberals in the mid
century were too steeped in the evolutionary thought of the time to regard
primitive communal societies as higher forms than the modern industrial
societies and states that had replaced them, and that their being so mili-
tated against their developing a critique of modern societies. For Maine,
progress moved from status to contract, and a society in which individuals,
unencumbered by the bonds of old status relations freely entered into
mutually advantageous agreements, was the pinnacle of the evolutionary
movement. But evolution was interpreted in many different ways, especially in those decades before Darwinian and Lamarckian positions became
more clearly defined. Private ownership of property was not invariably
regarded as the sole end of social evolution. Herbert Spencer reproduced
Maine's 'from status to contract' paradigm, but instead of placing individual private property at the apex of social evolution, he imagined a Kantian
paradise in which an organic community would arise, characterized by collective ownership and a full and complete individualism.[68] The American
anthropologist Morgan was also much more ready than Maine to use his
anthropological investigations to criticize the centrality of private property:
'A mere property career is not the final destiny of mankind, if progress is to
be the law of the future as it has been of the past... The dissolution of
society bids fair to become the termination of a career of which property is
the end and aim; because such a career contains the elements of self-
destruction. Democracy in government, brotherhood in society, equality in
rights and privileges, and universal education, foreshadow the next higher
plane of society to which experience, intelligence, and knowledge are
steadily tending. It will be a revival, in a higher form, of the liberty, equality and fraternity of the ancient gentes.'[69]

Although Mill was relatively immune from the evolutionary cast charac-
teristic of so many of his contemporaries, he too drew more radical conclusions from Maine's study of ancient law than did Maine. Mill regarded
Maine's *Ancient Law* as 'a most powerful solvent of a large class of conservative prejudices, by pointing out the historical origin not only of institutions but also of ideas, which many believe to be essential elements of the
conception of social order.'[70] But Mill went further: Maine's work had also
demonstrated that modern ideas were as much the product of time and
place as older systems which survived on in so-called primitive societies
like India, and, therefore, they had as little claim for permanence. The
study of Indo-European law and society could be used to justify the moral
right of the British state to turn back the slow conversion of common lands
into private property, held by roughly only three thousand families. Mill
built a case for the transformation of land-holding practices in Britain and

particular in Ireland using Maine's study of Indian village communities. Mill extended this assault on absolute private property in land to India when he castigated post-Mutiny Indian administrators for undermining common ownership of the land through their creation of a land-holding class with inflated rights and interests. This was 'one of the greatest social revolutions ever affected in any country, with the evil peculiarity of being a revolution not in favour of a majority of the people, but against them'.[71] Mill admitted that he did not know whether Maine 'would coincide in the inferences which we ourselves draw' from his historical and jurisprudential work, though he must have known that Maine would have little sympathy for many of them, not least his inclination towards land collectivism.[72] Certainly Maine disagreed with the Irish Land Act of 1881 which contained some of Mill's own proposals for reform of Irish land-holding and carried echoes of Maine's own writings, because it qualified absolute private ownership of land.[73]

In addition to its influence on both radicals and progressive liberals, Maine's comparative legal studies were taken up by historical economists in both Britain and America in the later nineteenth century – notably J.K. Ingram, Cliffe Leslie, W. J. Ashley, L. L. Price, William Cunningham–to challenge the abstract-deductive method of classical economists, and to question their assumptions about universal self-interest.[74] The historical economists collectively broke down the association of economic liberalism with political freedom. The economic historian William Cunningham, for example, censured Alfred Marshall for failing to see alternatives to a dominant economic liberalism. This was epitomized for Cunningham by Marshall's characterization of medieval and Indian economic forms as an illustration of Ricardo's law of rent.[75] Cunningham challenged the primacy of laissez-faire and free trade, and by the 1890s was arguing that national interest lay in tariff protection instead. Ewen Green sees the historical economists W. S. Hewins and W. Cunningham advancing a particular brand of collectivism, which grew out of the moral organicism of the Oxford philosophical idealists but which was opposed to the New Liberal and socialist solutions to the deficiencies of classical liberalism. They maintained that the individualism underlying classical political economy was ill-suited to new trusts and combines, and that organicist theories were more in keeping with these gigantic corporate entities.[76] The neo-mercantalism that they formulated added another layer to diverse political traditions which ran alongside the more social democratic uses which Arnold Toynbee had put to historicist critiques of classical economics.

Maine's historical examination of law and political economy also exercised a long-lasting influence on American scholars who were writing before marginalism began to take root in the 1890s. A generation of economists and social scientists – Henry Adams, Oliver Wendall Holmes, John Fiske, William Graham Sumner – used Maine's comparative study of Indian and European law to bolster claims for American exceptionalism, the belief that America uniquely had experienced the triumphant alliance of the capitalist market, liberal republicanism and general prosperity.[77] For example, Adams argued that the energy of American individualism broke the pattern of stasis that characterized much of the rest of the world,[78] whereas John Fiske argued that the American federation personified both individualism and collective association.[79] William Graham Sumner depended on Maine's comparative study of institutions to explain American exceptionalism and to extol the virtues of the market economy, which had brought America to the apex of social evolution.[80] Francis Walker and Lester Ward, on the other hand, utilized the comparative historical approach to critique classical economics. Like Maine, Francis Walker stopped short of a wide-sweeping attack on the capitalist market economy, but he punctured the Antebellum ideal of unlimited prosperity by arguing that competition was imperfect, that the market was not invariably beneficent, and that capital markets did not naturally balance the interests of capital and labour.[81] He echoed Maine's dismantling of deductive economic reasoning, and disputed the assumption of the universality of the desire for wealth accumulation. Lester Ward was less tentative, and in *Dynamic Sociology* (1883), pointed to the inequities which were wrongly regarded as a natural and necessary feature of modern industrial society, and made an extended plea for the study of social laws so that progressive legislation, which actually does improve the material and moral condition of society, could be formulated.[82] Both Ward and Walker's writings qualify the broad contrast often drawn between mid-Victorian American and British evaluations of the market economy in which British economists and social commentators refashioned classical political economy in response to industrialization and its sometimes harsh effects whereas American writers defend a revitalized raw-boned competitive capitalism.[83] There were many challenges to a laissez-faire political economy in mid- to late-nineteenth-century America, even if convictions about American exceptionalism weakened the forcefulness of the critiques of classical political economy which had been suggested by the historical, comparative study of Indo-European institutions.[84]

The impact of Maine's comparative study of society and law, therefore, was broad reaching and diffuse. It was picked up by writers from diverse traditions and used to develop quite different interpretations of human life. The potential of Maine's study of ancient law and society to buttress diverse perspectives was much more influential than his own distinctive amalgam of whig and liberal principles. At the end of his life, he was writing extensively for both the liberal *Pall Mall Gazette* and the tory *Quarterly Review*, and the battery of obituaries which marked his death illustrated the difficulty of categorizing his own political sympathies:'a pronounced and uncompromising Anti-Radical', opined the *St. James Gazette*.[85] Maine's evacuation of an early communal past, as we have seen, could act as a powerful radical solvent, and yet, in contrast, American writers used Maine's writings to support the liberal individualism of the American republic. Maine himself was not convinced that a society based on freedom of contract was unambiguously desirable. Though Maine fitted his investigation of Indian social forms – hasty, partial and reductionist as it was – into clearly demarcated stages of social evolution, culminating in a society of free contract, he nonetheless repeatedly warned against the blithe confidence that his evolutionary account might engender. His rather bleak admission that much was lost, eradicated and destroyed by the establishment of British law in India must be set beside his otherwise self-congratulatory celebration of the progress of society from status to contract which had prompted Marx to ridicule his optimism. Maine came away with a great sense of the destructiveness of English law in India, that the introduction of right and contract had destroyed customary law and that this in turn fragmented traditional village communities.[86] Maine certainly did not invariably equate English law with progress: 'It must strike every observant man, that by our introduction of legal ideas and our administration of justice through regular courts, we give a solidity and rigidity to Native usage which it does not naturally possess.'[87] For Maine, the introduction of British law to India could never be unequivocally described as 'a moral conquest', intoxicating as the experience of writing law for the subcontinent must have been.

A powerful whig sensibility modulated the liberal individualism which was encapsulated in Maine's dictum that societies progress from status to contract. While he continued to regard the individual as the springboard for a vital and progressive society, he tended to describe even modern human society as organic rather than atomistic. While Maine asserted that stability and social cohesion were virtues of societies guided by status, he sought to minimize the atomism and the fragmentation of contractual societies. He repeatedly referred to the obligations entailed by contract as 'the "bond" or "chain" with which the law joins together persons'.[88] He described a balance of interests as essential to the stable, progressive society. This balance had in the past been secured by the skilful statesmanship of aristocratic elites. While as a writer for the *Saturday Review* in the 1850s, Maine had been highly critical of aristocratic political patronage, towards the end of his life he increasingly believed that aristocratic elites (both natural and intellectual) were essential for all improvements in civilization.[89] He came to regard unfettered individualism as inimical to progress. Like many other contemporary liberals, he also feared the new democratic spirit of the age, less because he regretted its flattening and homogenising force, but more because he believed that democracies were potentially explosive and prone to disintegration. The ideology of individual rights, which lay behind freedom of contract, was a potentially dangerous force. Again, he used India to illustrate this danger. Maine was scathing of the Bengali middle classes who threw aside custom and instead used the new rights which had been enshrined in Anglo-Indian law to challenge aspects of colonial rule, because he maintained they exercised individual rights without the requisite moral judgement. His emphasis on character and honour was strikingly redolent of a Burkean whiggism. He tended to regard individual rights as dangerous unless combined with high moral character. Introducing rights into the Indian legal lexicon had threatened the stability of the Raj because the Indian people had not yet acquired the manners to assert individual rights with wisdom.[90] He had little confidence that popular government in Britain could transcend the immediacy of individual desires and balance these desires against others in the state, though he looked to the American constitution with the hope that a balance of interests could be achieved through a system of checks and balances, and the dangers of popular government could be minimized.[91]

Maine was not an opponent of capitalism; he believed that civilization and private property, individual rights, freedom of contract and many other markers of capitalist society, have historically gone hand in hand.[92] In the choleric polemic he wrote against popular government in the last years of his life, he extolled the 'the springs of action called into activity by the strenuous and never-ending struggle for existence, the beneficent private war which makes one man strive to climb on the shoulders of another and remain there through the law of the survival of the fittest.'[93] For Maine, 'sacredness of contract and the stability of private property, the first the implement, and the last the reward, of success in the universal competition'.[94] However, Maine's experience as a colonial administrator and as a student of historical and comparative law led him to believe that the capitalist market economy was not the only form of social organization, and certainly not the oldest. As we have seen, others were less reluctant to draw more radical conclusions from the study of ancient and primitive societies. By the end of the nineteenth century, India inspired sharp and outspoken critiques of capitalism, like that developed by Annie Besant. Maine once reflected that the serious scholar of India finds not that 'he reverses his accustomed political maxims, but revises them, and admits that they may be qualified under the influence of circumstance and time'.[95] He left India far more sceptical of a utilitarian universalism, much more sceptical of the movement towards popular government in western societies, and more cognizant of the fragility of modern contract-based societies and the power of custom to secure social stability. His wide-reaching impact on late-nineteenth-century British and American writers lay not so much in his own distinctive blending of whig and liberal principles, as much as the bold and expansive power of his comparative study of law and society. Maine's fusion of anthropology and comparative law suggested to some of his contemporaries that there was no ineluctable justification for systems of private property or society organized around capitalist markets.

For others, Maine's account of the village community brought to the foreground organic relationships rooted in community. These ideas were to contribute to the intellectual milieu of the 1880s and 1890s when they mingled with such other strands as British idealism, social evolutionary theory, and cooperative socialism to form the basis for radical critiques that stretched beyond the more cautious convictions of the colonial administrator and legal scholar.

Notes

1. William Graham Sumner, *What Social Classes Owe to Each Other* (1883) (New Haven: Yale University Press, 1925), p. 26. See also his other early publications: *Collected Essays in Political and Social Science* (New York, 1885), *History of American Currency* (New York: Holt, 1878), *Problems in Political Economy* (New York: Holt, 1885), *Alexander Hamilton* (New York: Dodd, Mead, 1890).
2. Maine, 'Breaches of Contract' (17 Dec 1862), in M. E. Grant Duff, ed., *Sir Henry Maine* (London: John Murray, 1892), p. 90. On Maine, see R. C. J. Cocks, *Sir Henry Maine: A Study in Victorian Jurisprudence* (Cambridge: Cambridge University Press, 1988); A. Diamond, ed., *The Victorian Achievement of Henry Maine* (Cambridge: Cambridge University Press, 1991); G. Feaver, *From Status to Contract, A Biography of Sir Henry Maine* (London: Longmans, 1969). See also J. W. Burrow, *Evolution and Society* (Cambridge: Cambridge University Press, 1966); S. Collini, *Public Moralists: Political Thought and Intellectual Life in Britain* (Oxford: Clarendon, 1991); J. W. Burrow, S. Collini and D. Winch, *That Noble Science of Politics: A Study in Nineteenth Century Intellectual History* (Cambridge: Cambridge University Press, 1983); and E. Stokes, *The English Utilitarians and India* (Delhi: Oxford University Press, 1989).
3. Maine, 'Breaches of Contract', p. 91; Oriental and Indian Office Collections (OIOC) MSS Eur c 179/114/1 ff 12–18: Maine to Sir Charles Wood, 13 Feb. 1863.
4. This approach is in keeping with scholarship on the symbiotic relationship between the parts of the empire, and the recognition that the Empire had a vital impact on Britain. See, for example, A. Burton, 'Thinking Beyond the Boundaries: Empire, Feminism, and the Domains of History', *Social History* 26, 1, (2001), 60–71; C. A. Bayly, 'Ireland, India and the Empire c. 1780–1914', *Transactions of the Royal Historical Society* 10 (2000), 377–97; C. A. Bayly, 'Returning the British to South Asian History: The Limits of Colonial Hegemony', *South Asia* 17 (4) (1994), 1–25.
5. H. S. Maine, *Ancient Law* (1861) (Oxford: Oxford University Press, 1931), p. 141.
6. Ibid, p. 259.
7. Ibid.
8. Maine, *Village Communities in the East and West* (1871) (London: John Murray, 1881), pp. 110–11. The extensive scholarship on the encounter between colonial law and indigenous customary law forms a valuable context for this chapter: see, especially, B. S. Cohn, *Colonialism and its Forms of Knowledge: The British in India* (Princeton: Princeton University Press, 1996); J. D. M. Derrett, *Religion, Law and the State in India* (New York: The Free Press, 1968); M. Galanter, *Law and Society in Modern India* (Delhi: Oxford University Press, 1989); R. Dhavan, 'Introduction' in Galanter, *Law and Society in Modern India*, pp. xiii–c; and Lloyd I. Rudolph and S. Rudolph, *The Modernity of Tradition* (Chicago: University of Chicago Press, 1967).

9. OIOC V/9/9. 1865.
10. Maine, *Village Communities*, pp. 41, 68, 190–7.
11. S. Bose, *Peasant Labour and Colonial Capital: Rural Bengal since 1770* (Cambridge: Cambridge University Press, 1987), p. 141.
12. P. Robb, 'Law and Agrarian Society in India: The Case of Bihar and the Nineteenth-Century Tenancy Debate', *Modern Asian Studies* XXI(2) (1988), 330–54.
13. Bose, *Peasant Labour*, p. 74.
14. Ibid, p. 48. See Stanley Chapman, *Merchant Enterprise in Britain from the Industrial Revolution to World War I* (Cambridge: Cambridge University Press, 1992), pp. 11–119 for a sympathetic perspective on the agency houses involved in indigo cultivation. See also D. Kumar, *Cambridge Economic History of India Volume II 1757–1930* (Cambridge, Cambridge University Press, 1983).
15. OIOC MSS Eur c 179/114/1 ff 8–11: Maine to Sir Charles Wood, 4 Dec. 1862.
16. Sir Cecil Beadon introduced in 1861 a bill to punish by imprisonment fraudulent breaches of agricultural contracts. At the order of the Secretary of State, this bill was withdrawn; Wood also urged the withdrawal of a similar but more general bill the following year: G. Rankin, *Background to Indian Law* (Cambridge: Cambridge University Press, 1946), pp. 78–80.
17. Master and Servant Legislation: 1747 20 Geo.2,c.19s.2; 1765, 6 Geo.3,c.25s.4; 1823, 4 Geo.4,c.34s.3. See David Morgan, *Harvesters and Harvesting, 1840–1890* (London: Croom Helm, 1982), pp. 125–6. Sections 490–2 of the Indian Penal Code (1861) covered some breaches of civil contract.
18. OIOC MSS Eur c 179/114/1 ff 12–18: Maine to Wood, 13 Feb. 1863.
19. OIOC MSS Eur c 179/114/1 ff 79–84: Maine to Sir Charles Wood, 5 Nov. 1863.
20. OIOC MSS Eur c 179/114/2/ff 46–53: Maine to Sir Charles Wood, 19 March 1864.
21. *Third Report of the Commissioners Appointed to Prepare a Substantive Law for India* (London, 1867), p. 9.
22. See T. Metcalf, *Ideologies of the Raj* (Cambridge: Cambridge University Press, 1996).
23. Maine to Lawrence, 2 April 1864, IOL MSS Eur c 90/34/f 18.
24. J. F. Stephen, 'Legislation under the Earl of Mayo', in Sir William Hunter, ed., *The Life of Mayo* (London: Smith, Elder and Co., 1875), pp. 168–9. See R. Dhavan, 'Introduction', in M. Galanter, *Law and Society in Modern India* (Delhi: Oxford University Press, 1989), p. lxxvi; F. Snyder and D. Hay, eds., *Labour Law and Crime* (London, Tavistock, 1978), pp. 12–13.
25. J. Majeed, 'James Mill's "The History of British India" and Utilitarianism as a Rhetoric of Reform', *Modern Asian Studies* XXIV(2) (1990), 209–24; S. Chandra, 'Whose Laws: Notes on a Legitimising Myth of the Colonial Indian State', *Studies in History* VIII(2) (1992), 187–211.
26. Maine, 'Specific Performance', in Duff, ed., *Sir Henry Maine*, p. 164.
27. 'Contract Bill', *Allen's Indian Mail*, 23 Sept. 1868.
28. OIOC Mss Eur c 179 ff 31–32: Wood to Maine, 14 Feb. 1864.
29. Maine, 'Specific Performance', in Duff, ed., *Sir Henry Maine*, pp. 170–8.
30. OIOC Mss Eur F 90/51/ff115–118: Sir Henry Lawrence to Sir Cecil Beaden, 24 Aug. 1865.
31. OIOC Mss Eur C 179: Sir E. Perry to Maine, 23 Feb. 1864.
32. OIOC Mss Eur c 179/114/1 ff 12-18: Maine to Sir Charles Wood, 13 Feb 1863.
33. OIOC MS Eur F78: Maine to Wood, 2 April 1864.
34. OIOC Mss Eur C 179: Sir E. Perry to Maine, 23 Feb. 1864.

35. Act XV of 1865: An Act to define and amend the law relating to marriage and divorce among the Parsees followed from a Privy Council ruling that the Supreme Court of Bombay had no jurisdiction to entertain suits by a Parsee for restitution of conjugal rights and for maintenance. See also Act XXI of 1865, an act to define and amend the law relating to intestate succession among the Parsees.

36. See Blair B. Kling, *The Blue Mutiny: the Indigo Disturbances in Bengal, 1859–1862* (Philadelphia, 1966); R. Guha, 'Neel Darpan: The Image of a Peasant Revolt in a Liberal Mirror', *Journal of Peasant Studies* 1974 2(1): 1–46.

37. Bose, *Peasant Labour*, pp. 148–51.

38. This is not to suggest, as Immanuel Wallerstein has, that capitalism was introduced to the periphery by the western capitalist core; this hypothesis has been persuasively challenged by historians like David Washbrook, David Ludden and others who have argued that pre-colonial India exhibited features of a market society, and that the influence between the core and the periphery was interdependent: I. Wallerstein, *Historical Capitalism with Capitalist Civilization* (London: Verso, 1983); Sugata Bose, ed., *South Asia and World Capitalism* (Delhi: Oxford Univeristy Press, 1990); D. Washbrook, 'South Asia, the World System and Capitalism', *Journal of Asian Studies* IL(3) (1990), 479–508.

39. Washbrook, p. 495. See W. S. Jevons, *The State in Relation to Labour* (London: Macmillan, 1882); P. S. Atiyah, *The Rise and Fall of Freedom of Contract* (Oxford: Clarendon Press, 1979), p. 613.

40. Bose, *South Asia*, p. 68; Robb, 'Peasants' Choices? Indian Agriculture and the Limits of Commercialisation in Nineteenth-century Bihar', *Economic History Review* XL(1) 1992, 97–119.

41. See P. S. Atiyah, *The Rise and Fall of Freedom of Contract;* M. Horowitz, *The Transformation of American Law, 1780–1860* (Cambridge, MA: Harvard University Press, 1977), pp. 160–210; L. Friedman, *Contract Law in America* (Madison: 1965).

42. Atiyah, ch. 14.

43. See J. W. Burrow, *Whigs and Liberals: Continuity and Change in English Political Thought* (Oxford: Clarendon, 1988).

44. Macaulay, Minute No. 30, 13 November, 1835 in C. D. Dharker, *Lord Macaulay's Legislative* Minutes (Oxford: Oxford University Press, 1946), pp. 276–7.

45. D. J. Ibbetson, *A Historical Introduction to the Law of Obligations* (Oxford: Oxford University Press, 1999), pp. 233–84. Ibbetson argues that Indian lawyers, notably Henry Colebrooke, had a greater sense of how duress and fraud could constrain the voluntary nature of contractual agreements: p. 234.

46. See W. S. Jevons, *The State in Relation to Labour* , ch. 2; Aityah, pp. 613–618

47. J. S. Mill, *Principles of Political Economy*, V, ch. 1, sec. 2 cited in Atiyah, p. 331. Atiyah cites this as a rare example of discussion in classical political economists about the enforcement of contract.

48. W. Thornton, *On Labour* (London: Macmillan, now Palgrave Macmillan, 1869), p. 102.

49. Chandra, *Enslaved Daughters: Colonialism, Law and Women's Rights* (Delhi, Oxford University Press, 1998), pp. 6–7.

50. K. Orren, *Belated Feudalism: Labour, the Law, and Liberal Development in the United States* (Cambridge: Cambridge University Press, 1991), p. 105.

51. Kartik Kalyan Raman, 'Utilitarianism and the Criminal Law in Colonial India', *Modern Asian Studies* 28 (1994), 773.

52. See S. Risenfeld, 'The Influence of German Legal Thought in American Law: The Heritage of Savigny and His Disciples', *American Journal of Comparative Law* 37

(1989) 1–15; M. Hoeflich, 'Savigny and his Anglo-American Disciples', *American Journal of Comparative Law* 37 (1989), 17–37.

53. See J. W. Burrow, *Evolution and Society: A Study in Victorian Social Theory* (Cambridge: Cambridge University Press, 1966), and S. Collini, D. Winch and J. Burrow, *That Noble Science of Society* (Cambridge: Cambridge University Press, 1983), ch. 7; J. Whitman, *The Legacy of Roman Law in the German Romantic Era* (Princeton: Princeton University Press, 1990).

54. OIOC 142: Maine, Memorandum on Codification in India, July 1879, p. 1219.

55. See Kartik Kalyan Raman, 'Utilitarianism and the Criminal Law in Colonial India', *Modern Asian Studies* XXVIII(4) (1994), 739–91; and Uday S. Mehta, *Liberalism and Empire: A Study in Nineteenth-Century British Liberal Thought* (Chicago: University of Chicago Press, 1999) on the conflict between universalism and particularity in British liberal thought.

56. Maine, 'The Influence of India', p. 230.

57. Ibid, p. 233.

58. Maine, *Village Communities*, p. 197.

59. Maine, 'Minute: Selection and Training of Candidates for the Indian Civil Service, 12 Nov 1875', in G. Duff, ed., *Sir Henry Maine: A Brief Memoir of his Life With Some of his Indian Speeches and Minutes* (London: John Murray, 1892), pp. 406–7.

60. Maine, 'The Rede Lecture: The Influence of India on European Thought' in *Village Communities*, p. 224.

61. See J. W. Burrow, *Evolution and Society* (Cambridge: Cambridge University Press, 1966); R. Meek, *Social Science and the Ignoble Savage* (Cambridge: Cambridge University Press, 1976); G.W. Stocking, *Victorian Anthropology* (New York: Free Press, 1987).

62. G. Claeys, *Machinery, Money and the Millenium: From Moral Economy to Socialism, 1815–1860* (Cambridge: Polity Press, 1987), pp. 189–90.

63. L. Krader, *The Ethnological Notebooks of Karl Marx* (Assen: Van Gorcum, 1972), pp. 292, 309. see Alan Macfarlane, 'Some Contributions of Maine to history and anthropology', in A. Diamond, ed., *The Victorian Achievement of Henry Maine*, pp. 112–15 on the patriarchy/matriachy debate between Maine, Morgan and McLennan.

64. See T. R. Trautmann, *Henry Lewis Morgan and the Invention of Kinship* (Berkeley, University of California Press, 1987), p. 254 and D. Kelley, 'The Science of Anthropology: An Essay on the Very Old Marx', *Journal of the History of Ideas* 45(2) (1984), 258; on Morgan see C. Resek, *Lewis Henry Morgan, American Scholar* (Chicago, University of Chicago Press, 1960) .

65. J. Harris, 'General Introduction', in F. Tonnies, *Community and Civil Society*, edited by J. Harris (Cambridge: Cambridge University Press, 2001), p. xxiii. See H. S. Maine, *The Early History of the Property of Married Women* (Manchester, Ireland & Co., 1873) for the argument that modern contract has brought greater liberality towards women's property rights and that this liberality was a marker of social evolutionary progress.

66. Cambridge University Library. Mss Add. 7349/14 ff64–65. Stephen to Lytton, 23 August 1877.

67. C. Dewey, *Anglo Indian Attitudes* (London: Hambledon, 1993), p. 16.

68. H. Spencer, *Social Statics*_(London: John Chapman, 1851); and *Principles of Sociology* (London, Williams and Norgate, 1877). See also D. Wiltshire, *The Social and Political Thought of Herbert Spencer* (Oxford: Oxford University Press, 1978).

69. H. L. Morgan, *Ancient Society* (London: Macmillan, now Palgrave Macmillan, 1877), p. 552.

70. J. S. Mill, 'Maine on Village Communities', in R. Robson, M. Moir and Z. Moir, eds, *Writings on India: Collected Works of John Stuart Mill* (Toronto: University of Toronto Press, 1990), XXX: p. 215. see Lynn Zastoupil, *John Stuart Mill and India* (Stanford University Press, 1994), pp. 188–90; Bruce Kinzer, 'J.S. Mill and Irish Land', *Historical Journal* 27 (1984), 111–27.

71. Mill, 'Village Communities', 225.

72. Ibid, 221. See Mill to Maine, 1 Jan. 1869 in F. Minecke and D. Lindley, eds, *The Later Letters of John Stuart Mill. The Collected Works of John Stuart Mill* XVII (Toronto: University of Toronto Press, 1972), pp. 1536–9.

73. C. Dewey, 'Images of the Village Community: A Study in Anglo-Indian Ideology', *Modern Asian Studies* 6(3) (1972), 318.

74. A. W. Bob Coates, *On the History of Economic Thought: British and American Economic Essays I* (London, Routledge, 1992), p. 221. See G. Koot, *The English Historical Economists 1870–1926* (Cambridge: Cambridge University Press, 1988).

75. Cunningham cited in J. Maloney, *The Professionalization of Economics: Alfred Marshall and the Dominance of Orthodoxy* (London: Transaction Publishers, 1991), p. 101.

76. see E. H. H. Green, *The Crisis of Conservatism* (London: Routledge, 1995), pp. 162–83.

77. D. Ross, *The Origins of American Social Science* (Cambridge: Cambridge University Press, 1991). See also T. L. Haskell, *The Emergence of a Professional Social Science* (Urbana: University of Illinois Press, 1977), R. Seidelman and E. Harphan, *Disenchanted Realists: Political Science and American Crisis* (Albany: Albany State University Press, 1985).

78. Adams urged friends and colleagues to read Maine and taught Maine to his students at Harvard; see for example Adams to Henry Cabot Lodge, 2 Jan. 1873 in E. Samuels, ed., *Henry Adams: Selected Letters* (Cambridge, MA: Harvard University Press, 1992), pp. 126–7. See also E. Samuels, *Henry Adams* (Cambridge, MA: Harvard University Press, 1989), pp. 106–7; see Adams to Maine, 22 February, 1875 in Harold Dean Cater, ed., *Henry Adams and His Friends: A Collection of Unpublished Letters* (Boston: Houghton Mifflin, 1947), pp. 6–64.

79. See J. Fiske, *The American Revolution* (London: Macmillan, 1891)

80. See Sumner, 'What Social Classes Owe to Each Other', 1883.

81. See Matthew Hannah, *Governmentality and the Mastery of Territory in Nineteenth Century America* (Cambridge: Cambridge University Press, 2000) for a recent analysis of Francis Walker as the epitome of the gentlemanly social scientist; B. Newton, *The Economics of Francis Amasa Walker* (New York, A. M. Kelley, 1968). See F. Walker, 'The Present Standing of Political Economy', *Discussions* (New York: Holt, 1889) I, pp. 301–18; F. Walker, *The Wages Question* (New York: Holt, 1876).

82. Lester Ward, *Dynamic Sociology or Applied Social Science* (1883) (New York: Appleton and Co., 1898), 2nd edn., I, p. 53. see I, p. 580; II, pp. 398, 578.

83. See, for example, Peter T. Manicas, *A History and Philosophy of the Social Sciences* (Oxford, Blackwell, 1988), p. 209.

84. See Mary Morton, 'Competing Notions of "Competition" in Late Nineteenth Century Economics', *History of Political Economy* 25(4) (1993), 563–604 for an examination of how American exceptionalism was carried into contemporary

accounts of trusts and combinations by regarding them as a new and exceptional form of competition.

85. Cited in Duff, *Sir Henry Maine*, p. 75.
86. Maine, *Village Communities*, p. 112.
87. OIOC V/9/10: H.S. Maine, 'Native Marriage' (1868), 497–8.
88. Maine, *Ancient Law*, p. 269.
89. Maine, 'The Abolition of the East Indian Company', *Saturday Review* V (1858), 56.
90. Maine, *Village Communities*, p. 73.
91. Maine, *Popular Government* (1995, London: John Murray, 1886), essay four.
92. Maine, 'The Influence of India', 230.
93. Maine, *Popular Government*, p. 50.
94. Ibid, essay one.
95. Maine, 'Influence of India', 206.

4
British Socialism and American Romanticism[1]

Mark Bevir

In 1906 William Stead sent a questionnaire to prominent members of the British Labour Party asking what books had influenced them.[2] The most frequently mentioned authors were Carlyle and Ruskin but Emerson and Thoreau were not far behind. Much has been written about the influence of British romanticism on the British socialist movement, and perhaps the obvious impact of Carlyle and Ruskin has obscured that of Emerson, Thoreau and Whitman.[3] However, we can trace lines of influence from the tradition of American romanticism to British socialism through Thomas Davidson, Edward Carpenter and John Trevor, for these three consciously borrowed from the Americans rather than merely expressing a diffuse romanticism. In each case, the influence of the Americans was acknowledged, and also symbolized by the physical travels of the individual concerned. Moreover, some ideas were common in the tradition of American romanticism but not its British counterpart, and we can follow these ideas through Davidson, Carpenter and Trevor into the British socialist movement.

The influence of American romanticism on British socialism helps to explain the particular character of British socialism and thence the Labour Party. In Britain, the dominant socialist theory was that found within the Independent Labour Party (ILP), the organization that did most to convince the trade unions to form the Labour Party. The socialism of the ILP differed from most forms of Continental Marxism above all else in its reliance on an ethical tone deriving from a vision of socialism as a new religion requiring a new personal life.[4] From where did this ethic come? One source was the non-conformist heritage, particularly for workers in areas such as the West Riding of Yorkshire. Another was American romanticism, particularly for middle-class activists in the south of England.

Distinguishing romanticisms

American romanticism differed from British romanticism in its close relationship to both unitarianism and frontier individualism. The debt to unitarianism inspired an immanentist spirituality, which later reappeared in the idea of socialism as a new religion. The debt to frontier individualism inspired an ideal of self-sufficiency, which later reappeared in the idea of socialism as involving a new personal life. Of course romanticism is a vast and ill-defined movement, so our distinctions between its American and British forms must be concerned with delicate shades not strong contrasts.

What is the ideal? Emerson was the dominant figure of American romanticism. His home in Concord acted as a regular meeting place for the Transcendental Club, the name of which referred to Kant's use of the term transcendental so as to denote the way we can know things *a priori*. The American romantics followed their European counterparts in rejecting the narrow rationalism of the eighteenth century, especially Lockean empiricism. Emerson was influenced by German philosophers such as Schelling, and when he travexlled to Europe in 1832 and 1833, he became friendly with both Carlyle and Coleridge. American and British romantics thus shared a philosophical outlook indebted to German idealism.

However, the American romantics drew heavily on unitarianism in a way the British did not. Emerson studied theology at Harvard, and he remained a unitarian minister until 1832, and many other American romantics also were unitarians, including William Channing and George Ripley. The appeal of their unitarianism to Victorian Britons is evident from the popularity in London of preachers such as Moncore Conway, another member of the Transcendental Club. Unitarians stood for a rational and liberal approach to Christianity: they opposed what they considered to be the irrational concept of the Trinity, arguing instead for the single personality of God, and they rejected what they considered to be the immoral dogmas of eternal punishment, inherited guilt and vicarious atonement. Thus, unitarian theology readily opened the way to a belief in a single spiritual deity existing within nature, rather than a transcendent God standing outside of nature. Although this immanentism remained rare among orthodox unitarians until the close of the nineteenth century, the unitarian inheritance of the American romantics gave them a more immanentist outlook than was common among their British counterparts.

The immanentism of the American romantics appears in their view of God as present throughout the world, realizing his divine purpose through natural processes. Emerson was a spiritual monist who believed an Over-Soul unified a spiritual reality, a divine mind pervaded the whole of the material universe.[5] He argued that all things contain the divine spirit, so everything is united in a single whole; and because the divine dwells within everything, each thing contains the laws and meaning of the universe within itself. Some British romantics came near to deifying nature, as when Ruskin said, 'God paints the clouds and shapes the moss-fibres that men may be happy in seeing Him at His work.'[6] Ruskin argued that landscape painting can capture the truth and beauty of nature thereby witnessing to the glory of God. But while Ruskin suggested little more than that nature can offer spiritual solace, Emerson insisted on a spiritual reality in nature. While British romantics typically thought nature could inspire the imaginative faculty in man, or at most point towards the divine, American romantics typically believed God and nature actually were coextensive.

The immanentism of the American romantics encouraged them to argue that we come to know God through direct intuition of an absolute being, not through a miraculous revelation embodied in the Bible or the Incarnation. Emerson thought that individuals come into contact with the Over-Soul either by entering a mystical state in which they perceive the divine within themselves, or by discovering the divine in the truth, beauty and wholeness of nature.[7] The Emersonian sublime is a mystical, holistic freedom in which individuals recognize their true spiritual selves, and by thus finding the Over-Soul within themselves come to see the divine in everything else. True, many British romantics stressed the role of the imagination and nature as sources of harmony in a fragmented world, but they typically saw harmony in terms of either the individual or an organic society, without reference to the overt religiosity of Emerson.

How should we realize the ideal? The American romantics believed that personal intuitions have moral authority precisely because individuals contain the divine in themselves. Emerson argued that people should trust themselves, reject external rules, express their inner natures, and become self-reliant.[8] Henry Thoreau, another member of the Transcendental Club, proclaimed the individual conscience, not law, the supreme moral arbiter; political obligation depends on the moral judgement of the individual, and the best government is a government that does not govern.[9] Similarly, British romantics rejected the formal rules and public codes that had dominated the outlook of the Augustans in favour of a belief in the individual questioning and testing of values and experiences, and their rejection of Augustan limits sometimes spilled over into an opposition to all restrictive codes as evidenced by the appeal of Godwin's anarchism to Wordsworth and Shelley.

Yet the American romantics drew heavily on frontier individualism in a way the British did not. British romantics typically looked to the example of the middle ages, although they rarely agreed on the details of an ideal community, with, for instance, Coleridge calling for a clerisy and national church to balance the forces of progress with those of stability, and Ruskin trying to revive a moral economy based on craftsmanship and guilds.[10] In contrast, the American romantics eulogized an idealized picture of American democracy in a way that gave rise to two important themes. First, the American romantics saw their ideal as something that was being realized through the action of the divine purpose in history. Emerson, Thoreau and Whitman drew inspiration from Jeffersonian and Jacksonian democratic theory, which in turn restated the eighteenth-century belief in the perfectibility of mankind, a belief that fitted well with their own immanentism. Just as the democrats described the American polity as part of God's design, so the romantics could take the American ideal to be the summit of the immanent working out of the divine will. Just as the Jacksonian, George Bancroft wrote his famous history of America to show how America expressed the will of God, so William Channing spoke of the dawn of a new age in which people would surmount their political difficulties to realize their inner spirit.[11] Second, the American romantics inherited the ideal of a democratic republic composed of self-sufficient farmers. They believed in the virtue of a rough-and-ready life spent working the land. True, some British romantics called for the simplification of life and the rejection of unnatural wants created by industrial society, as when Ruskin used the example of Gothic architecture to illustrate how mechanism had replaced skill in the workplace.[12] But while Ruskin wanted a return to the skilled craftsmanship he thought produced artistic goods, Thoreau wanted people to minimize their possessions, and while Ruskin wanted workers to be able to exercise their creative impulses free from the regime of the machine, Thoreau wanted people to become effectively self-sufficient. Thus, whereas Ruskin established new guilds and revitalized the hand-made linen industry in Langdale, Thoreau lived alone in a hut at Walden Pond where he tried to 'simplify, simplify' so as to obtain spiritual wealth by living close to nature, reducing his material wants, and satisfying any residual needs by his own manual labour.[13]

We will find that some British socialists took from the American romantics both an immanentist theology expressing genuine religious conviction, not just a romantic pantheism that invested nature with imaginative appeal, and a rough-and-ready ideal which looked unfavourably on all possessions, not just commercial products, and which praised self-sufficiency and working the land, rather than the craftsmanship of skilled artisans. However, the imprecise nature of romanticism means our distinctions between its American and British forms have referred to matters of emphasis as much as doctrine. Thus, when we consider the particular examples of Davidson, Carpenter and Trevor, we also will be filling out these distinctions by showing how American romanticism influenced the beliefs and lives of specific individuals. What follows is the unfolding of a definite line of historical influence, where the evidence for this influence is both textual – certain ideas are common to American romantics and some British socialists but not British romantics – and biographical – the lives and autobiographical writings of some British socialists reveal their debt to the American romantics.

Davidson and the New Fellowship

It was on a first visit to Concord that I was told the story . . . of how when [Father Taylor] was asked whether he thought Emerson would have to go to hell, he replied that if he did the tide of emigration would likely turn that way.[14]

Thomas Davidson was born in Scotland and educated at Aberdeen before becoming a wandering scholar, moving from place to place, learning and teaching with equal enthusiasm, in a life akin to that of Giordano Bruno, the Renaissance pantheist he admired.[15] Davidson arrived in America around 1866. In Boston, he participated in a philosophical club, the members of which included the educationist and philosopher William Harris, a friend of Emerson who did much to introduce German philosophy into America when he founded the St Louis School of idealism. Davidson himself lectured alongside Emerson at summer schools and taught classics under Harris in the public schools of Missouri. In the early 1880s, Davidson moved on to Italy where he studied the life and thought of Antonio Rosmini-Serbati.[16] When he had joined the philosophical club in Boston he had talked incessantly of Aristotle, but by now he had adopted many of the beliefs he had discovered among the American romantics. Just as Rosmini had fused Aquinas and Hegel, so he hoped to combine Aristotelianism and American romanticism. His Emersonian immanentism suggested that forms might constitute the eternal essence of reality but he wanted to retain Aristotle's view that forms can not exist apart from matter – individual things, not forms, are the immediate objects of reality.

According to Davidson, the purpose of philosophy is 'to unify the world' by uncovering the 'unity of the human spirit', that is, God.[17] He argued that Kant demonstrates how Humean scepticism requires us to grant mind a determining role in the construction of the world. Again, Zeno's paradox of Achilles and the tortoise reveals our current understanding of motion to be mistaken: it demonstrates that change and time require us to postulate an unchanging subject of change existing outside of time. This unchanging subject is a universal mind that performs the creative role Kant showed to be necessary. Furthermore, this universal mind exists in each individual mind: God is an ideality present within all reality.

Davidson was an immanentist and an idealist who denounced materialists such as Comte and Spencer as obscurationists, but he also retained the Aristotelian belief that spirit or forms can exist only in matter or individuals. He criticized American romantics for considering Being only in its universal aspect and so neglecting individuals: like Schelling and Hegel, they 'functioned with the forms of thought, disregarding the content, without which the forms have no meaning (as Kant saw); and of course they arrived at a sort of Vedantic or neo-Platonic mysticism.'[18] Davidson replaced Hegel's single, thinking subject with a multitude of sentient individuals. Each individual is a bundle of feelings grouped together, and distinguished from one another, by reference to desires. Feeling, not consciousness or

matter, is the fundamental constituent of the world. God is not the form-
less universal of Hegelianism because spirit cannot exist apart from monads
of feeling.

Although individuals have separate identities, they are intimately related
because each individual's desires seek satisfaction through actions whose
effects are experienced by other individuals. As Davidson explained, 'I am a
feeling or sensibility, modified in innumerable ways by influences which I
do not originate,' and 'these modifications, when grouped, are what I call
the world, or *my* world, for I know no other.'[19] The world of each individual consists of their experience of the actions of other desiring monads.
When individuals comprehend and classify their sensations, they thereby
construct their world, since their world is the content of their consciousness. For Davidson, therefore, education gives individuals the conceptual
tools with which to arrange their feelings and build their worlds. Education
can create a new moral order by ensuring that people build harmonious
worlds. Society can be transformed by the propagation of new beliefs: 'we
have but to get a new economic faith, laid down in a new economic bible,
to transform our cities and our life into something as different from what
they are at present as human life is from brute life.'[20]

Davidson's proposals for moral reform through education again illustrate
his debt to American romanticism. While in America, he taught at summer
schools organized by Bronson Alcott, the instigator of various experiments
in education and communalism. Alcott founded the Temple School in
Boston as an attempt to use beautiful surroundings, play and imagination
to sustain a schooling that would develop all of a pupil's intellectual, physical, moral and aesthetic faculties. He also founded a co-operative community called Fruitlands, the members of which were to till the soil, eat
vegetarian food, and build social unity on religious love and progressive
education. (Although Fruitlands collapsed after a year the romantics' community at Brook Farm lasted three years before then becoming a Fourierist
phalanx).[21] The example set by Alcott inspired both Davidson's summer
schools at Farmington and Glenmore, where the teachers included Harris,
and his attempt to bring culture into the lives of the working people of
New York through his Breadwinners College. Like Alcott, Davidson
believed that education should promote a broad culture, including physical
exercise, morality and aesthetics. Like Alcott, he wanted education to
proceed by means of learning through activity within pleasant and natural
surroundings.[22]

More importantly, Davidson wanted a suitable education to inspire a
new world that encompassed the values taught by the American romantics
and lived by the monks in the Rosminian monastery in Domodossola. He
hoped to capture the high spiritual life of the monks, while freeing their
religious spirit from the dogmatic structure of the Church of Rome by
infusing it with the tolerant, all-encompassing outlook of American roman-

ticism. Hence, he regularly praised American republicanism as a noble religion of more promise than any other. He wanted people to adopt a simple communal life guided by a spiritual and ethical ideal free of all dogma. He spoke of 'a small devoted band of men and women of fearless character, clear philosophic insight, and mighty spiritual love, who, living a divine life in their relations to each other, shall labour, with all the strength that is in them to lift their fellows into the same divine life.'[23] Yet Davidson was no socialist. He criticized socialism for being incompatible with his desire to keep sight of the individual, and for being a materialist ideology denying the paramountcy of moral reformation. He also argued that socialism cannot come into being unless people adopt a new ethic as to the meaning and use of wealth and life, but that once they do this, the solution will come naturally by itself.[24]

Percival Chubb visited Davidson at Domodossola, and when the peripatetic Davidson moved to London in 1882, Chubb led the small group that gathered about him to discuss religion, ethics and social reform. At the second formal meeting of this group, Davidson suggested they take the name Fellowship of the New Life, and declare their purpose to reconstruct Society 'in accordance with the highest moral possibilities'.[25] The rules of the Fellowship reflect Davidson's utopian views.[26] Members initially were to perfect their individual characters in accord with an ethic of love, simplicity and kindness, before then forming a community to encapsulate these principles, and finally using the example of this community to regenerate humanity as a whole.

Within the Fellowship, Maurice Adams, Chubb and Hamilton Pullen were disciples of Davidson, while Havelock Ellis, a young sex-therapist, joined Mrs Hinton and her sister, Caroline Haddon, in preaching James Hinton's evolutionary mysticism.[27] Yet other members of the Fellowship, notably H. H. Champion and Edward Pease, placed social reform before moral regeneration. The differences between these attitudes surfaced at the third and fourth meetings of the Fellowship, after which the social reformers departed to found the Fabian Society. Those who remained adopted a spiritual basis:

The Fellowship of the New Life
Object. – The cultivation of a perfect character in each and all.
Principle. – The subordination of material things to spiritual.
Fellowship. – The sole and essential condition of fellowship shall be a
single-minded, sincere, and strenuous devotion to the object and principle.[28]

After this spiritual proclamation, there followed articles on simplicity of living, the importance of manual labour, and the desirableness of forming a community of fellows. Later, when Davidson returned to America, the members of the Fellowship adopted an explicitly socialist programme.[29]

Although Davidson combined American romanticism with the teachings of Rosmini, and although he opposed socialism, his followers in the Fellowship saw him as someone who brought them the teachings of Emerson and Thoreau, teachings that they believed pointed to socialism. In this way, Davidson acted as a conduit through which American romanticism reached a number of British socialists. Many of those involved with the Fellowship saw it as an expression of the ideals of American romanticism. Chubb, for instance, said 'England drew upon America for the new ethical inspiration,' and, in particular, upon Emerson whose home in Concord was 'the citadel of the new truth'.[30] Likewise, Pease described Davidson as a 'descendent of the utopians of Brook Farm', a view echoed by Ernest Rhys when he recalled how the Fellowship 'aimed, like Hawthorne's Brook Farm, at setting up a colony of workers and craftsmen'.[31] A decade after Davidson's stay in London, the official journal of the Fellowship published an editorial insisting that the Fellowship had been 'influenced by Thoreau and Emerson rather than Marx'.[32]

Many of the members of the Fellowship came to accept a form of socialism indebted to American romanticism. Chubb defended both an immanentist philosophy expressing a genuine religious conviction, and an ethic that identified this religious conviction with the republican ideal. The significance of Chubb's debt to American romanticism appears in a critical review he wrote of William Morris' utopian novel *News from Nowhere*, a socialist vision inspired by a more British romanticism. Chubb described the central defect of Morris' socialism as 'the absence in it of anything like a belief in a divine purpose running through nature and history, or in the divine essence of man'.[33] Morris was no immanentist. Rather, Chubb continued, Morris espoused a paganism that portrays nature as beneficent but lacks a truly religious impulse. This defect led Chubb to identify further weaknesses in Morris' political strategy and socialist ideal, weaknesses that again parallel differences between American and British romanticism. With regard to political strategy, Chubb argued that Morris failed to allow for the fact that socialism will arise through the divine purpose working in history. Morris' optimistic view of nature led him to a faith in the noble savage, or human nature as it is: he thought that to overturn society would be to free the good innate within a humanity corrupted by society, and so he believed that socialism could arise from a cataclysmic social revolution destroying bourgeois society. Chubb, in contrast, argued that once we recognize history represents the working out of a divine purpose, we must acknowledge that socialism will arise as the culmination of man's evolution, so we must seek to remodel society by improving, not abolishing, our political and social institutions. With regard to the socialist ideal, Chubb argued that Morris neglected the religious aspect of ethics. Morris envisaged a society of sensuous delights at the expense of the religious virtues found in Christianity: he did not appreciate the virtues of love and sympathy which encourage self-denial, and he ignored the role of the corresponding desire to serve others as a motive to action. Instead Chubb wanted a socialism infused with religion, a social expression of Emerson's concept of the sublime, a community of people consciously aware of being bound together by a shared relation to the divine. Such a community was fellowship. Because the true self is at one with the divine, true freedom consists of realizing one's good through the good of the community. Elsewhere Chubb described his religion of socialism as an extension of American republicanism. He wanted 'a religious union parallel with and harmonious with that which unites men under the aegis of the republican state or party – a religion of Democracy'.[34]

The crux of the socialism of the Fellowship was a faith in a religion of Democracy. The members viewed socialism as a moral ideal of brotherhood. They believed social change was dependent on an ethical transformation. They defined socialism as a vital moral life, not an institutional arrangement, asking 'cannot moral life itself glow with a passion which makes all other passions pale,' and answering 'we believe it can, and by fellowship and sympathy to raise it to a white heat, which shall make it a prevailing power in the world, is the ethical aim of the Fellowship of the New Life'.[35] They insisted that the 'radical reform of our social arrangements, which is now being made, will be powerful and salutary just so far as it is based upon a clear and intelligent moral purpose.'[36]

The members of the Fellowship tried to realize socialism – their religion of Democracy – by means of an ethical transformation in their personal lives. They shared the concern of the American romantics with education, communal living and the simplification of life. Their journal echoed Alcott, saying, schools 'ought to be communities, miniature commonwealths or states', and they themselves founded an experimental school at Abbotsholme on the edge of the Derbyshire moors, run by Dr Reddie and Bob Muirhead, though disagreements over the day to day running of the school led most of the members of the Fellowship to withdraw, leaving Reddie in sole charge.[37] More importantly, the Fellowship was committed to providing an example of communal living. Initially members merely tried to live near to each other, but later, after much discussion on the relative merits of Latin America and London as possible sites, they rented Fellowship House, a shared residence at 29 Doughty Street in the Bloomsbury district of London. Residents included Havelock Ellis, Edith Lees, Ramsay MacDonald, Sydney Olivier, an anarchist called Agnes Henry and Mrs Pagovsky and her daughter from Russia. The residents had separate bed sitting-rooms, and ate their meals together in the basement. Unoccupied rooms were let out to members of the Fellowship or friends who needed a temporary base in London. Things did not go well. Edith Lees, the dominant figure within the House, wrote to Macdonald complaining, 'Miss Henry is *awful*! – I hate the place without you.'[38] The Fellowship constantly reiterated the need for individuals to restructure their personal lives according to the precepts of simplicity and comradeship. When the Fellowship was dissolved in 1898, the farewell issue of its journal told readers: 'it is not to its meetings that the Fellowship must look for the spread of its teaching, but to the lives of those who have received the Fellowship ideal.'[39]

Carpenter and provincial socialism

> Thoreau [showed] . . . it is still possible and profitable to live . . . in accordance with nature, with absolute serenity and self-possession; to follow out one's own ideal, in spite of every obstacle, with unfaltering devotion; and so to simplify one's life, and clarify one's senses, as to master many of the inner secrets.[40]

Edward Carpenter, born in 1844, was educated at Cambridge, where he later became a clerical fellow. He held Broad Church beliefs, and was ordained despite telling the examining Bishop that he rejected the doctrine of the atonement.[41] At Cambridge, he decided he was gay in a sort of revelation upon reading the second-generation American romantic, Walt Whitman. In 1873, he toured Italy with his unorthodox cousin Jane Daubney.[42] The ancient statues seemed to him to express Whitman's vision of male comradeship. Broad Church Anglicanism appeared shallow and dogmatic. Upon his return, he renounced his Holy Orders, resigned his fellowship, and became a university extension lecturer. In 1876, he wrote to Whitman saying 'you have made the earth sacred for me.'[43] The following year he travelled to America where he spent a night in Concord with Emerson before going on to stay in Camden with Whitman.[44] He returned to America in 1884, visiting Walden Pond, where he swam and placed a stone on top of Thoreau's cairn.

When Carpenter first visited America, he looked through Emerson's translation of the Upanishads and discussed oriental literature with Whitman. This shared interest in Indian religion indicates Carpenter's affinity to the American romantics. True, British romantics such as Southey found poetic material in the legends of India, and in Hindu festivals such as the Rath Yaga at Puri, but American romantics such as Emerson also found religious inspiration in Hindu texts, and even equated Hinduism with their own immanentist belief in a single God existing throughout this world.[45] Of course, not all Indian philosophy is mystical and immanentist, but, like the American romantics, Carpenter picked out the idea that everything contains the divine. He described how with the Gnani with whom he studied in Ceylon 'one came into contact with the root-thought of all existence – the intense consciousness (not conviction merely) of the oneness of all life – the general idea which in one form or another has spread from nation to nation, and become the soul and impulse of religion after religion.'[46]

Carpenter shared the religious immanentism of the American romantics. Indeed, he argued that the logical nature of all knowledge proves there is a fundamental unity underlying everything. He divides the act of knowledge into three constituents: knower, knowledge and known. Neither object nor subject can be known either independently of the other or outside an act of knowledge. Objects can be known only by a conscious subject because something 'not relative to any ego or subject, but having an independent non-mental existence of its own, cannot be known'.[47] The subject can be conscious of itself only during an act of knowledge since 'when there is no act of knowledge there is no consciousness of the Ego.'[48] Moreover, he continues because dead matter is impossible – though he actually has shown only that matter can not be known in the absence of a knower – the objects we take to be matter actually must be other egos, and because egos can not exist outside of an act of knowledge – though he actually has shown only that egos can not know themselves outside of an act of knowledge – everything must be united in a fundamental act of knowledge. Thus, Carpenter concludes, the world consists of a universal subject coming to know itself: 'the World, the whole creation, is self-revealment.'[49] History is the evolution of an immanent God; it is the self-revealment of a universal subject. Carpenter shared the American romantics' vision of God at work in this world ensuring history will end with the fulfilment of the divine purpose, understood as a society based on the Emersonian sublime, the self-conscious unity of all.

According to Carpenter this final realization of the unity of all will be socialism. Like Chubb, Carpenter equated socialism, not with a particular institutional or legal structure, but with a spiritual recognition that we are all one. He himself turned to socialism as a result of such a spiritual experience:

> I became for the time overwhelmingly conscious of the disclosure within of a region transcending in some sense the ordinary boundaries of personality . . . I almost immediately saw, or rather felt, that this region of Self existing in me existed equally . . . in others. In regard to it the mere diversities of temperament which ordinarily distinguish and divide people dropped away and became indifferent, and a field was opened in which all were truly equal.[50]

Socialism is love or comradeship, fellowship or Democracy. In a socialist society, individuals will recognize they are mere outgrowths of a universal self, so they will be suffused with love and sympathy for their fellows. The triumph of love will establish a universal brotherhood in which there will be no place for the struggle for personal domination that underlies both political authority and private property. People will live in non-governmental communities based on cooperative systems of production.[51]

The socialist ideal promoted by Carpenter incorporated Whitman's belief that the soul needs religion, the mind needs Democracy, the heart needs love, and the body needs nature. Here Whitman defined his ideal in terms of 'the dear love of comrades', not a particular institutional arrangement, arguing that true Democracy is of the spirit, and consists of 'manly love'.[52] His poems combined natural simplicity, male comradeship and democracy into a mystical vision of the vitality of human life. Similarly, Carpenter argued that the growth of comradely love will result in a true brotherhood of all, a real Democracy. This advocacy of male love informs his views on what we now might call gay liberation. He identified the meaning and purpose of love with fusion not procreation; love requires comradeship and is divorced from sex. Moreover, he suggested that the love of gays crosses barriers of class, so gays are harbingers of Democracy. In general, though, people will embrace the principle of brotherhood only if they become aware of the divine in themselves, and they will do this only if they quieten their lower minds and remove the clutter of material existence by simplifying their lives, by returning to nature and undertaking manual labour. To build socialism, people have to transform their personal lives so as to connect with their inner selves. In particular, they have to simplify their lives, since extraneous wants drown out the voice of the true self, leaving us attending to the momentary self. Here Carpenter again followed the American romantics in advocating not a return to the greater beauty of hand-made goods, but rather the elimination of as many possessions as possible, and a commitment to make things oneself even if they then turn out to be rough and ready. By simplifying their lives, people can clear away the debris of convention thereby creating the space needed for personal expression. People should return to nature and manual labour, feeling 'downwards and downwards through this wretched maze of shams for the solid ground – to come close to the earth itself and those that live in direct contact with it.'[53] They should work in the open air, live in simple shelters, and eat a diet of fruit and nuts. They should adopt a measure of self-sufficiency and emphasize personal relationships. Carpenter called for the simplification of life, manual labour and gay liberation: 'lovers of all handicrafts and of labour in the open air, confessed passionate lovers of your own sex, Arise!'[54]

Our very health depends on our developing a proper awareness of the unity of all since disease follows the breakdown of oneness and the consequent disruption of the harmonious balance of the whole. As Carpenter explained, 'the establishment of an insubordinate centre – a boil, a tumour, the introduction and spread of a germ with innumerable progeny throughout the system, the enlargement out of all reason of an existing organ – means disease.'[55] Thus, neglect of the fundamental unity of all things explains the prevalence of disease in contemporary society as evidenced by the need for so many doctors, slow rates of recovery, any number of lunatic asylums, and a widespread feeling of uneasiness. The absence of simple living contributes to physical illness – processed food weakens the teeth and sedentary lifestyles produce flaccid muscles – while the doctrine of individualism contributes to mental illness – it is because people seek their own advantage without considering others that society has had to set up an arbitrary moral code which stimulates an unnatural sense of sin.

Carpenter provided the Social Democratic Federation with the money to begin publishing *Justice*, briefly joined the Socialist League, spoke at Fabian meetings, and sent Kropotkin notes to help with his research, but of all the socialist groups he was most at home in the Fellowship, which he joined in 1885. Later he recalled how 'those early meetings of the New Fellowship were full of hopeful enthusiasms – life simplified, a humane diet and rational dress, manual labour, democratic ideals, communal institutions.'[56] Yet Carpenter's penchant for comradeship in small groups led him to put more effort into his local Sheffield Socialist Society than into any national organization. Indeed, his work to establish a socialist movement in Sheffield illustrates the process by which some members of the Fellowship took their ideal out of London into the provinces. They inspired groups of local socialists to adopt a new way of life and to build new, moral communities among themselves. The Sheffield Socialists, for instance, concentrated their energies on charitable activities, such as tea-time outings for slum-children, and enjoyable social gatherings, such as those in their Commonwealth Cafe where Carpenter played the harmonium while others sang the songs collected in his *Chants of Labour*.[57] These provincial socialists combined popular culture with a moral belief in the transforming power of a rude simplicity.

The spread of the fellowship ideal throughout England owed much to the inspirational example provided by individuals such as Carpenter. Many provincial socialists looked upon his life as a model for the future: he had adopted the socialist ideal, and socialism was the adoption of the ideal. Carpenter hoped his university extension classes would bring him into contact with manual workers, but his audience actually consisted almost exclusively of artisans and middle-class women. Only in 1879 did he meet Albert Fearnehough, a scythe maker, and his wife, and move in with them in the village of Bradway, just outside Sheffield. Soon afterwards, he gave up extension lecturing, built a roofless hut by the river, and spent his days writing the first part of *Towards Democracy*, a poem in the style of Whitman. Later still he brought some land in rural Derbyshire and built a house where he lived first with the Adams family and then with his lover, George Merrill. He tried to become self-sufficient by growing vegetables and selling remaining produce from a stall in the local market.[58] He also tried to live close to nature by taking regular sun-baths and writing in an open-roofed shed built beside a stream running across the bottom of his garden. His simple lifestyle inspired numerous other socialists, including Harold

Cox who returned to the land at Craig Farm in Tilford. When Cox went to India, he sent Carpenter the pair of sandals that provided the model for those Carpenter began to make believing they liberated the feet.

The Sheffield Socialists fell apart after the Walsall anarchist case of 1892, but by then Carpenter had shifted his interest towards a number of humanitarian causes. In 1889, he had begun a campaign against smoke pollution, pointing out the environmental costs of industry, and showing how easily the smoke nuisance could be alleviated if only industrialists used suitable equipment.[59] An emphasis on humanitarian causes was an important feature of the socialism of the Fellowship. This broad benevolence appears, for instance, in the Humanitarian League, an organization founded in 1891 by Henry Salt, a member of the Fellowship and an old friend of Carpenter's, on the principle that 'it is iniquitous to inflict suffering on any sentient being.'[60] Salt himself was influenced by the American romantics. He wrote a biography of Thoreau, edited several volumes of Thoreau's writings, and began his plea for vegetarianism by citing Thoreau.[61] Carpenter became active in the Humanitarian League because, like Salt, he was a vegetarian who opposed cruelty to humans and animals alike, arguing, for example, that vivisection was immoral since all creatures contained the divine, and since, even from a utilitarian standpoint, hurting animals would not reduce human suffering but might well give rise to new diseases.[62]

Trevor and the Labour churches

> When Emerson died a friend said to me, 'It was a pity he should have gone. No doubt his work was done; he had no more to say to us. But it was good to think of him there, living on, serene and wise. It had been well if two or three of us could have died instead of him. It was a pity he should die.'[63]

John Trevor wrote that Emerson and Whitman 'became part of me'.[64] He described Whitman as 'nearer to God than any man on earth', and just before his marriage, he began to keep a copy of Emerson's writings 'to read occasionally as a Bible'.[65] Trevor was raised in East Anglia as a Calvinist, but in 1876 he both sailed to Australia and renounced the Bible as a religious guide. Soon after, he decided to become a unitarian minister by studying at Meadville in America. Earlier he had read Emerson. Now he 'discovered' him:

> What Emerson did for me was, not to give me a formula, but to stimulate my faith – I do not mean faith of any theological sort, but rather that commanding confidence in the soundness of life which is the first step towards true self-confidence, true courage, and true Religion. I can only have any true self-confidence when I realise my oneness with a Universe that I can confide in.[66]

In 1879, Trevor returned to England and took a house in the countryside where he experienced the Emersonian sublime through nature. As he explained, a 'new sense of oneness with flowers and trees and stars brought me to God in quite a different fashion.'[67] He spent a year studying at Manchester College, London before becoming an assistant to the Rev. Philip Wicksteed, and then accepting a post as minister of the Upper Brook Street Free Church in Manchester. In 1891, he attended a unitarian conference at which Ben Tillett called on the churches to respond to the demands of the workers before the workers left the churches. Soon afterwards, he met a lapsed member of his own congregation who said he had stopped attending chapel because he had felt unable to breathe freely. Trevor responded to these events by founding the Labour Church movement to provide workingmen with a suitable religious home. In the ensuing years, he published a number of newspapers to promote the Labour Church, often referring to the American romantics, and once exclaiming, 'I am wasting valuable time, writing myself when I might be quoting Walt Whitman.'[68]

The practice of establishing alternative churches to preach the new ethic proved very popular with members of the Fellowship such as Trevor. William Jupp, a founding member, preceded Trevor, when, in 1890, he formed a free religious movement in Croydon.[69] Jupp too had been raised as a Calvinist before becoming a Congregationalist minister, and then, influenced in part by Emerson, establishing his free religious movement on the principles of the Fellowship. For him, '*Leaves of Grass* [by Whitman], and *Towards Democracy* took their place with Thoreau's *Walden*, and Emerson's *Essays and Lectures*, and *Conduct of Life* as Scriptures "given by inspiration of God".'[70] J. Bruce Wallace was raised as a Presbyterian before becoming a Congregationalist minister and then, in 1892, founding a Brotherhood Church in Hackney, London. Somewhat later, in 1894, J. C. Kenworthy, who had just been elected to the Executive Committee of the Fellowship, established a Brotherhood Church in Croydon.[71] Throughout the 1890s, various members of the Fellowship formed religious groups to promote their socialist ideal of a moral community based on the divine unity of all.

Trevor rejected all dogma in favour of an immanentism, according to which 'one might have risen from the soil to the stars, returned from the stars to the home, expanded from the home to Humanity, and found God everywhere.'[72] His immanentism mirrored the religious conviction of the American romantics. Even his language was that of Emerson: he said a life with God could take 'many forms', so he pleaded only for 'the inward temple, where the lamp ever burns, and where the soul enters into communion with the great Over-Soul'.[73] Trevor contrasted his concept of God or the divine energy with the theological concept of God or tradition. He defined theology as the application of a religious doctrine to life, rather than a life in which God appears spontaneously; an abstract system taken from traditional sources, rather than a concrete discovery of God at work within oneself.[74] His immanentism implied that individuals contain the divine so individuals who follow their instincts will just find God working through them. In contrast, the Calvinism of his childhood suggested that God was beyond us so we should reject our instincts and follow the teachings of a theological tradition. Trevor rejected creeds, formal doctrines and rigid hierarchies. He sought a loosely defined religiosity expressed in life and deeds.

According to Trevor, the basis of the unity of all is a divine love, a vital force that puts people in a spiritual relationship with nature, and a relationship of mutual brotherhood with their fellows. More particularly, the divine life can be found in the labour movement as it battles to realize the truth of universal brotherhood. Indeed, 'the Labour Church was founded for the distinct purpose of declaring that God is at work, here and now, in the heart of the Labour Movement.'[75] The labour movement does not represent wage-earners alone; it stands for a labour consciousness which points to a growing sense of brotherhood among the downtrodden masses of the world, which in turn points to the gradual development of a 'human consciousness, world consciousness, God consciousness'.[76]

Like Chubb and Carpenter, Trevor held an evolutionary theory of history with the divine progressively revealing itself in a process that would climax in the self-conscious recognition of both the unity of all and the fact that all things partake of the divine. Socialism represents the harmonious society that will arise from the growth of this ideal of the divine unity of all. Like the American romantics, Trevor looked forward to the realization of the divine will here on earth, so he unsurprisingly complained of Ruskin exhibiting an unhealthy medievalism which 'tends back to the old life rather than forward to the new'.[77] Where he differed from many of the other members of the Fellowship was in his specific identification of the labour movement as the most advanced expression of the evolutionary process. The labour movement embodies an ideal of brotherhood extending beyond the workers themselves to embrace the whole of humanity. Once this ethic is explicitly linked to immanentism, the workers simply will adhere to the teachings of the Fellowship. Thus, the Labour Church aims merely 'to set free the tremendous power of religious enthusiasm and joy which is now pent up in the great labour movement'.[78]

Trevor accepted the rough and ready ethic of the American romantics, arguing the adoption of an ethic of fellowship would arise from greater self-reliance and greater simplicity in our personal lives. The triumph of socialism depends on people following a new life based on a new religion: only if we allow our lives to flow out from the presence of God can we establish a society truly devoted to the common good that is human well-being. Here too Trevor distanced himself from British romanticism, complaining of

Ruskin's failure to grasp the import of the new ethic of Liberty and Democracy.[79] Individuals should stand by the divine light within themselves rather than bowing to an external authority. True socialists reject the dead weight of theological tradition; they listen to their instincts and act in accordance with the divine energy within them. The true socialist 'is not afraid to follow the conclusions of his own reason and the feelings of his own heart, and to base his personal life and his social life upon both of them'.[80] Socialists are self-reliant. Here too, the labour movement is in the vanguard of history. Those who possess labour consciousness follow their own instincts; they work to cure the ills of the slums and thereby find God in their work, instead of wasting their time studying old texts where God can no longer be found. When people follow their impulses in this way, they are led inexorably towards nature and the simplification of life. Unfortunately, however, most people lack confidence in their spontaneous impulses, so they are unable to live life naturally and simply. It is the socialists who lead the way in showing us how we can come into contact with the divine by adopting a rough and ready life of comradeship and manual labour. Trevor described how 'the pleasure and wholesomeness' of growing his own fruit and vegetables had led him to God, and how his contact with 'the workings of Nature made Religion, for the first time, real and essential.'[81]

The first Labour Church service was held at Charlton Town Hall, Manchester on 4 October 1891.[82] The service opened with a reading of a poem by James Russell Lowell, after which a unitarian minister read the lesson; the congregation sang Carpenter's hymn 'England Arise', and Trevor then read a sermon on the entwining of religious sentiment within the labour movement.[83] At the next meeting, Robert Blatchford spoke to a crowd too large to fit into the building.[84] The movement spread rapidly throughout Lancashire and the West Riding of Yorkshire, with a few Labour Churches also appearing in other parts of the country. The movements' statement of principles echoed Trevor's beliefs:

The Labour Church is based upon the following Principles:

1. That the Labour Movement is a religious Movement.
2. That the Religion of the Labour Movement is not a Class Religion, but unites members of all classes in working for the Abolition of Commercial Slavery.
3. That the Religion of the Labour Movement is not Sectarian or Dogmatic, but Free Religion, leaving each man free to develop his own relations with the Power that brought him into being.
4. That the emancipation of Labour can be realized so far as men learn both the Economic and Moral Laws of God, and heartily endeavour to obey them.

5. That the development of Personal Character and the improvement of Social Conditions are both essential to man's emancipation from moral and social bondage.[85]

The Labour Church movement was designed to express and to promote Trevor's belief that the spiritual ethic of the Fellowship now inspired the labour movement.

In May 1892, Trevor and Blatchford founded the Manchester Independent Labour Party, and, at much the same time, Joseph Burgess began a campaign to unite such local organizations into a national body. On 13 January 1893, a conference at the Bradford Labour Institute founded the national ILP, with Trevor present as a delegate from Manchester, and with an associated Labour Church gathering.[86] The Labour Church movement maintained a close relationship with the ILP for the rest of the decade. In 1894 the executive committee of the ILP even passed a resolution saying, 'branches of the ILP, wherever practicable, should run a Sunday meeting on Labour Church lines.'[87] This relationship created difficulties as well as opportunities for the Labour Church. Trevor hoped his movement would fulfil humanity's need for God, but the relationship with the ILP raised the question of how the movement should relate to Party members who rejected the very idea of a God. This question caused much anguish especially as leading individuals such as Fred Brocklehurst, the first general secretary of the Labour Church Union, considered belief in God to be irrelevant to the movement. Sometimes compromises could be reached: when the question of prayer arose the matter was left to the discretion of individual chairmen.[88] But sometimes they could not: at the annual conference of 1894, Trevor and his supporters managed to retain the word God in the movement's statement of principles only after a close vote, and even then an official journal of the movement still noted that 'Labour Church folk do not bother much about God.'[89]

Labour Churches often became primarily political organizations, their religious role weakened by their rejection of formal professions of faith and their ambivalence about the very idea of God. At first the movement's paper carried the message 'God is King', but this soon changed to 'let Labour be the basis of civil society.' As political organizations, the Labour Churches provide further examples of the approach to cultural politics found within the Sheffield Socialists. They typically adopted a political style caught by Wicksteed's description of the Labour Church as 'an open recognition of the fact that the ultimate conditions of strength lie in our personal relations to each other, to nature, and to God, which no social machinery can in itself harmonise'.[90] Labour Church meetings represented a sociable form of politics more than a devout form of worship. They revolved around readings from writers such as Emerson and Ruskin, together with songs composed by people such as Carpenter and Salt –

although these songs were published as a hymn book, hardly any of them referred to God.[91]

Socialism and the ILP

Davidson, Carpenter and Trevor had considerable influence on British socialism in general and the ILP in particular. Although Ramsay MacDonald was a leading member of the Fellowship who lived in the communal residence in Bloomsbury, the Fellowship's main influence was through individuals such as Carpenter and Trevor. The Sheffield Socialists inspired many other local groups, including the one in Nottingham with which D. H. Lawrence was associated, and these groups often later became branches of the ILP.[92] Carpenter gave the Bristol Socialist Society some money with which to begin a library – MacDonald was the librarian. Katharine Conway, a member of the Bristol group who became prominent in the ILP., recalled, 'I came under Carpenter's influence as a morbid High Churchwoman with vague humanitarian impulses and the lead he gave me was literally from darkness and bondage out into life and liberty.'[93] More generally, Carpenter influenced a number of progressive groups who saw themselves as followers of Whitman, including the one that flourished in Bolton.[94] The close ties between the Labour Churches and the ILP have already been mentioned: a list of preachers at Labour Church meetings reads like a who's who of the early ILP: Blatchford, Conway, Hardie, Margaret MacMillan and Tillett were regular favourites.

The easy alliance between those socialists inspired by American romanticism and the other members of the ILP rested on a shared ethical socialism based on immanentism. In these doctrines the influence of American romanticism mingled with that of British romanticism and strands of nonconformity to inspire the peculiar ethical quality of much of British socialism. Many prominent members of the ILP, including Bruce Glasier and Kier Hardie, owed a debt to Carlyle and Ruskin and to congregationalism. The British romantics believed nature reflected the best in humanity, and the idea that nature was good inspired many early socialists with a faith that the Kingdom of God could be built in this world. Congregationalists led non-conformists in responding to historical criticism of the bible by moving towards a faith based on the example of Christ the man, and the idea of the humble carpenter's son who eschewed pomp and wealth then inspired many early socialists.

Nonetheless there were differences between those socialists indebted primarily to American romanticism and the other ethical socialists of the ILP. Glasier and Hardie did not share the religious outlook of Chubb, Carpenter and Trevor. Most ethical socialists did not view nature in the mystical terms of Emerson: some did not have any genuine religious convictions – Glasier had been an active member of the National Secular Society – and others, including

Hardie, described themselves as Christians. Most ethical socialists gave their socialism a religious dimension through references to Christ who almost never appeared in the writings of socialists inspired primarily by American romanticism: some such as Hardie actually believed in Christ as the Son of God, while others such as Glasier looked to the moral example of the human Jesus. The religious aspect of their socialism revolved around Christian symbolism, not the Emersonian sublime: Hardie told the Congregational Union, 'the Labour movement had come to resuscitate the Christianity of Christ', while Glasier attacked those usurers who cry 'communist' and thus 'crucify again the Christ.'[95] In contrast, Davidson, Chubb, Carpenter, and Trevor, did not talk of Jesus, or a God Incarnate, but solely of an immanent God found throughout nature. Trevor rejected the option of returning from Christianity to the religion of Jesus as yet another misguided attempt to 'restore the old' rather than 'build the new'.[96] These contrasting religious doctrines sustained different ideas of brotherhood. Hardie and Glasier held a primarily moral concept of brotherhood. They regarded all people as of equal worth, so they conceived of an ideal society in which equality would be established, and they regarded nature as benign, so they believed they could establish this ideal society in this world. They wanted to build a community of moral equals akin to that described in the Sermon of the Mount. Thus, Hardie said, socialism was 'entitled to the support of all who pray for the coming of Christ's kingdom upon earth'.[97] In contrast, Chubb, Carpenter and Trevor did not talk of building Christ's kingdom here on earth, but solely of giving expression to the divine already present within oneself. Their concept of brotherhood was primarily mystical; they claimed all things were fundamentally at one, and they conceived of an ideal society in which people realized their inner selves.

The tradition of American romanticism provided one important source of the peculiarly ethical socialism of the ILP. At the heart of this socialism was an immanentist belief in a God present throughout the world. Immanentism inspired a faith in brotherhood, in a moral transformation, in the need to recast our personal lives, and in a cultural form of politics. First, immanentism suggested that because individuals contain the divine, they can trust their instincts: there is no need to search for an intellectual basis for feelings, so action comes before theory. As Trevor said, when 'Life appears upon the scene, Tradition is compelled to weakly follow'.[98] Second, an immanentist outlook suggested that because we all contain the divine, we are all part of a single whole, so we should adopt an ethic of universal brotherhood. As a member of the Fellowship explained, each individual exists 'in organic relations with his fellows and only through these relations does he realise himself'.[99] Third, immanentist doctrines led the Fellowship, the Sheffield Socialists, and the Labour Church movement to adopt a primarily ethical socialism. A member of the Fellowship said that 'for the great work of Social Reconstruction we want above all a new morality.[100] Fourth, Davidson, Carpenter and Trevor all agreed the desired change in social morality has to begin with the transformation of our personal lives. Socialism has to begin with an inner conversion turning one into a new kind of person: to be a socialist is to give expression to the divine in one's personal life, for God is not a transcendent principle, but a real and living power operating throughout the universe. Finally, this stress on individual regeneration meant these socialists were preoccupied with a personal and cultural politics. The Fellowship insisted members should bear witness to a moral ideal and try to establish an example of communal living; Carpenter strove for sexual liberation and wrote songs for socialist meetings; and the Labour Church tried to bring 'the means of living' into the labour movement.[101] All these different facets of a socialism which drew on American romanticism appear in Trevor's claim that:

> We shall never do away with bondage, and this Religion of Bondage, until we have a Religion of Freedom to put in its place – not any mere theory thereof, but actually incarnating itself in our own flesh and blood. For the great work we have to do, Economics alone will not suffice, neither will Ethics added to Economics. We must expand and grow into the larger life, wherein we enter freely into living and loving fellowship with Man, with Nature, and with God.[102]

Notes

1. An earlier version of this chapter appeared in *English Historical Review* cx (1995), 878–901.
2. William Stead, 'The Labour Party and the Books that Helped Make It', *Review of Reviews*, xxxiii (1906), 568–82.
3. On British Romanticism and British socialism see Jonathan Mendilow, *The Romantic Tradition in British Politics* (London: Croom Helm, 1986); and Stanley Pierson, *Marxism and the Origins of British Socialism* (Ithaca, NY: Cornell University Press, 1973).
4. On ethical socialism see Mark Bevir, 'Welfarism, Socialism and Religion: On T. H. Green and Others', *Review of Politics* lv (1993), 639–61; Pierson, *Marxism*; and Stephen Yeo, 'A New Life: The Religion of Socialism in Britain, 1883–1896', *History Workshop* iv (1977), 5–56.
5. R. W. Emerson, 'Nature', in *The Complete Works of Ralph Waldo Emerson* (London: Routledge, 1903), Vol. I: *Nature, Addresses, and Lectures*, pp. 1–77; and 'The Over-Soul', in Vol II: *Essays, First Series*, pp. 265–97.
6. John Ruskin, *Works*, ed. E. Cook and A. Wedderburn (London: George Allen, 1903–12), Vol. V: *Modern Painters* (iii), p. 384.
7. Emerson, 'An Address', in *Works*, i. 117–51.
8. Emerson, 'Self-Reliance', in *Works*, ii. 43–90.
9. Henry Thoreau, *Essay on Civil Disobedience* (London, 1903).
10. Samuel Coleride, *On the Constitution of Church and State* (London: Chance, 1830); John Ruskin, 'Unto this Last', in *Works*, Vol. XVII: *Unto This Last, Munera Pulveris, Time and Tide, and Other Writings on Political Economy, 1860–73*, pp. 15–114.

11. George Bancroft, *A History of the United States from the Discovery of the American Continent to the Present Time* (London: Routledge, 1834–74); William Channing, *An Address Delivered before The Mercantile Library Company of Philadelphia* (Philadelphia: J. Crissy, 1841).

12. John Ruskin, 'The Nature of Gothic', in *Works*, Vol. X: *The Stones of Venice – II: The Sea Stories*, pp. 180–269.

13. John Ruskin, 'General Statement Explaining the Nature and Purposes of St George's Guild', in *Works*, Vol. XXX: *The Guild and Museum of St. George*, pp. 45–59; Henry Thoreau, *Walden* (Edinburgh: Douglas, 1884).

14. Percival Chubb, *On the Religious Frontier* (New York: Macmillan, 1931), p. 37.

15. See Thomas Davidson, 'Autobiographical Sketch', ed. A. Lataner, *Journal of the History of Ideas*, xviii (1957), 531–6; and William Knight (ed.), *Memorials of Thomas Davidson* (London: Fisher Unwin, 1907).

16. J. Blau, 'Rosmini, Domodossola and Thomas Davidson', *Journal of the History of Ideas*, xviii (1957), 522–8.

17. Thomas Davidson, *The Education of the Wage-Earners*, ed. C. Bakewell (London: 1904), p. 37.

18. Knight (ed.), *Memorials*, p. 149. Davidson's recollections show that he accepted much of American romanticism, as found in the Boston radicals, while rejecting much of their philosophy, as found in the St Louis Hegelians. He said, 'I came to America and fell first among Boston Radicals with whom I very cordially sympathized, and then among St Louis Hegelians with whom I never in any degree sympathized.' Davidson, 'Autobiographical Sketch', 532.

19. Thomas Davidson, 'Education as World Building', *Western Educational Review*, ix (1900), 327.

20. Thomas Davidson, *The Moral Aspects of the Economic Question* (London: W. Reeves, 1888), p. 25.

21. See E. P. Peabody, *Record of Mr Alcott's School, Exemplifying the Principles and Methods of Infant Instruction* (Boston: Roberts Brothers, 1888); Clara Sears (ed.), *Bronson Alcott's Fruitlands* (New York: Houghton Mifflin, 1915); and Henry Sams (ed.), *Autobiography of Brook Farm* (Englewood Cliffs, NJ: Prentice-Hall, 1958).

22. Thomas Davidson, *Aristotle and Ancient Educational Ideals* (London: Heinemann, 1892); Thomas Davidson, *Education of the Greek People* (London: Edward Arnold, 1895); and Thomas Davidson, *Rousseau and Education According to Nature* (New York: Heinemann, 1898).

23. Davidson, *Wage Earners*, p. 48.

24. Davidson, *Moral Aspects*.

25. Edward Pease, *The History of the Fabian Society* (London: A. C. Fifield, 1916), p. 31.

26. Knight (ed.), *Memorials*, pp. 21–5.

27. Havelock Ellis, *My Life* (London: Heinemann, 1940). On Hinton and his views see Ellice Hopkins, *Life and Letters of James Hinton* (London: Kegan Paul, 1882); James Hinton, *Life in Nature*, intro. H. Ellis (London: Allen and Unwin, 1932); and James Hinton, *Philosophy and Religion*, ed. C. Haddon (London: Kegan Paul, 1881).

28. Pease, *History*, p. 32. On the history of the Fellowship also see William Armytage, *Heavens Below* (London: Routledge and Kegan Paul, 1961), pp. 327–41.

29. Whether Davidson's individualism or the Fellowship's socialism best caught the spirit of American romanticism is a moot point. Although the socialists typically

denied there was any contradiction between individualism and socialism, it is interesting that the only criticism they made of the American romantics concerned Thoreau's individualism. Chubb complained: 'No concession to society" was the cry of the new Protestants; and so austere were some, that ... they decided to leave society altogether': 'Introduction', to *Select Writings of Ralph Waldo Emerson* (London: Walter Scott, 1888), p. xv. Henry Salt complained that Thoreau's 'intensely individualistic nature' prevented him from comprehending the enormity of the social problem: *The Life of Henry David Thoreau* (London: Bentley, 1890), p. 292. Even less critical members of the Fellowship, such as William Jupp, allowed that 'to many his [Thoreau's] individualism will seem too pronounced, and his social sympathies too weak': *The Religion of Human Nature and of Human Experience* (London: Philip Green, 1906), p. 91.

30. Chubb, *Religious Frontier*, pp. vii–viii; Chubb, 'Introduction', p. xix.
31. Pease, *History*, p. 26; Ernest Rhys, *Everyman Remembers* (London: Dent, 1931), p. 2.
32. *Seed-time*, April 1892.
33. *Seed-time*, October 1891. Note also Jupp's contrast between the British romantics with their 'earthiness' and the American romantics with their beliefs in 'homeliness in relation to things of the body with a view to Heavenliness in relation to things of the mind': *Wayfarings: A Record of Adventure and Liberation in the Life of the Spirit* (London: Headley Bros, 1918), p. 133.
34. Chubb, *Religious Frontier*, p. 29.
35. Maurice Adams, *The Ethics of Social Reform* (London: W. Reeves, 1887), p. 26.
36. *The New Fellowship* (Thornton Heath: New Fellowship, 1890), p. 5.
37. *Seed-time*, April 1890. On the founding of the school see *Seed-time*, July 1889. For later developments see Bernard Ward, *Reddie of Abbotsholme* (London: Allen & Unwin, 1934).
38. Cited from The MacDonald Papers, Public Record Office, London, in David Marquand, *Ramsay MacDonald* (London: Cape, 1977), p. 27. On Havelock Ellis see Ellis, *My Life*. Edith Lees, who later married Havelock Ellis, found inspiration in both Carpenter and Hinton: E. Havelock Ellis, *Three Modern Seers* (London: Stanley Paul, 1910). Sydney Olivier was one of the more moralistic of the Fabians: Sydney Olivier, *Letters and Selected Writings*, ed. M. Olivier (London: Allen and Unwin, 1948).
39. *Seed-time*, February 1898.
40. Salt, *Life of Thoreau*, p. 3.
41. Edward Carpenter, *My Days and Dreams* (London: Allen and Unwin, 1916); Stanley Pierson, 'Edward Carpenter: Prophet of a Socialist Millennium', *Victorian Studies* xiii (1970), 301–18; Sheila Rowbotham and Jeffrey Weeks, *Socialism and the New Life: The Personal Politics of Edward Carpenter and Havelock Ellis* (London: Pluto, 1977); and Chushichi Tsuzuki, *Edward Carpenter* (Cambridge: Cambridge University Press, 1980).
42. Carpenter depicted Daubney as Francesca in his *Sketches from Life in Town and Country* (London: George Allen, 1908).
43. Horace Traubel, *With Walt Whitman in Camden*, Vol. III: *Conversations 1 November 1888 to 20 January 1889* (New York: Appleton, 1914), p. 414.
44. Edward Carpenter, *Days with Walt Whitman* (London: George Allen, 1906), pp. 3–52.
45. See, for instance, Emerson, 'Brahma', in *Works*, Vol. IX: *Poems*, p. 195; and Whitman, 'Passage to India' in *The Complete Poems* (Harmondsworth: Penguin, 1975), pp. 428–37.

46. Carpenter, *My Days*, p. 143. For his account of his time in India see his *From Adam's Peak to Elephanta* (London: Swan Sonnenschein, 1892).
47. Edward Carpenter, *The Art of Creation* (London: George Allen, 1904), pp. 38–9.
48. Ibid, p. 42.
49. Ibid, p. 44.
50. Edward Carpenter, *Towards Democracy* (London: Gay Men's Press, 1985), p. 410.
51. Edward Carpenter, 'Transitions to Freedom', in *Forecasts of the Coming Century*, ed. Carpenter (Manchester: Labour Press, 1897), pp. 174–92.
52. Walt Whitman, 'I Hear It was Charged against Me', and 'For You O Democracy', in *Complete Poems*, pp. 161, 150.
53. Carpenter, *Towards Democracy*, p. 32.
54. Ibid., p. 33.
55. Edward Carpenter, *Civilisation: Its Curse and Cure* (London: Swan Sonnenschein, 1902), p. 14.
56. Carpenter, *My Days*, p. 223. He read to the Fellowship a paper on the 'Simplification of Life' which was later published in his *England's Ideal* (London: Swan Sonnenschein, 1902), pp. 95–120.
57. Carpenter (ed.), *Chants of Labour* (London: Swan Sonnenschein, 1888).
58. For his account of the experiment see his *England's Ideal*, pp. 95–120.
59. Edward Carpenter, 'The Smoke Plague and its Remedy', *Macmillan's Magazine*, July 1890.
60. *Seed-time*, July 1891. For his reminiscences see Henry Salt, *Seventy Years among Savages* (London: Allen and Unwin, 1921).
61. Salt, *Life of Thoreau*; Henry Thoreau, *Poems of Nature*, ed. H. Salt and F. Sanborn (London: Lane, 1895); Henry Thoreau, *Selections From Thoreau*, ed. and intro. H. Salt (London: Macmillan now Palgrave–Macmillan, 1890); and Henry Salt, *A Plea for Vegetarianism* (Manchester: Vegetarian Society, 1885).
62. Edward Carpenter and Edward Maitland, *Vivisection* (London: Humanitarian League, 1893).
63. William Jupp, 'Walt Whitman: The Man and His Message', *Seed-time*, July 1892.
64. John Trevor, *My Quest for God* (London: Labour Prophet, 1897), p. 135.
65. *Labour Prophet*, July 1896; Trevor, *My Quest*, p. 158.
66. Ibid, p. 135.
67. Ibid, p. 187.
68. *Labour Prophet*, April 1892.
69. His autobiography is Jupp, *Wayfarings*. On the formation of the Croydon movement see *Seed-time*, January 1891. Jupp also wrote a highly appreciative review of Carpenter's, *Towards Democracy* in *Seed-time*, April 1893.
70. Jupp, *Wayfarings*, p. 68.
71. *Seed-time*, April 1895.
72. John Trevor, *Labour Prophet Tracts* (London: Labour Prophet, 1896), Tract 3: 'Our First Principle', p. 34.
73. *Labour Prophet*, October 1894.
74. Trevor, *Tracts*, Tract 1: 'Theology and the Slums'.
75. *Labour Prophet*, September 1894.
76. Trevor, *My Quest*, pp. 235–6.
77. Ibid., p. 51. It was, Trevor added, Emerson who had taught him that, contrary to Ruskin's view, 'Life was reliable' (p. 175).
78. *Workman's Times*, 23 October 1891.
79. Trevor, *My Quest*, p. 51.

80. Trevor, *Tracts*, Tract 1, p. 5.
81. Ibid., Tract 3, pp. 33–4.
82. See Kenneth Inglis, 'The Labour Church Movement', *International Review of Social History* iii (1950), 445–60; and Stanley Pierson, 'John Trevor and the Labour Church Movement in England, 1891–1900', *Church History* xxix (1960), 463–78.
83. *Workman's Times*, 9 October 1891.
84. Ibid., 16 October 1891.
85. *Labour Prophet*, January 1892.
86. Ibid., February 1893.
87. Ibid., September 1894.
88. Ibid., June 1895.
89. Ibid., September 1894; *Labour Church Record*, April 1899.
90. Philip Wicksteed, *What Does the Labour Church Stand For?* (London: Labour Prophet, n. d.), p. 11.
91. John Trevor, ed., *The Labour Church Hymn Book* (London: Labour Prophet, 1895).
92. Émile Delavenay, *D. H. Lawrence and Edward Carpenter: A Study in Edwardian Transition* (London: Heinemann, 1971).
93. Gilbert Beith (ed.), *Edward Carpenter: In Appreciation* (London: Allen and Unwin, 1931), p. 183. On socialism in Bristol see Samson Bryher, *An Account of the Labour Movement in Bristol* (Bristol: Bristol Socialist Society, 1931).
94. Paul Salverson, *Loving Comrades* (Bolton: n.p., 1984).
95. J. B. Glasier, *On the Road to Liberty* (London: National Labour Press, 1920), p. 33.
96. Trevor, *My Quest*, p. 138.
97. *Labour Prophet*, November 1892; J. K. Hardie, *From Serfdom to Socialism* (London: n.p., 1907), p. 44.
98. Trevor, *Tracts*, Tract 1, p. 8.
99. *Seed-time*, April 1890.
100. *The Sower*, April 1889.
101. *Labour Prophet*, January 1892.
102. Trevor, *Tracts*, Tract 2: 'From Ethics to Religion', p. 32.

5
Britain, Europe and the Critique of Capitalism in American Reform, 1880–1920

Axel R. Schäfer

In the decades prior to World War I, an intricate network of personal friendships, organized exchanges, institutional ties and professional publications linked American progressives to European social reformers. The renewed focus on this transatlantic dimension of American reform in recent scholarship provides an important opportunity for reinterpreting progressivism. It challenges long-standing assumptions about the nature of American reform, and suggests that European social reform was constitutive of American progressivism and vice versa in ways that have previously been neglected.[1]

Much contemporary scholarship on turn-of-the century American reform tends to emphasize the repressive and reactionary aspects of progressivism. It charges progressives with defending traditional gender roles, racial distinctions, middle-class moral codes and class divides that were challenged by industrialization, new urban styles, working-class politics and immigrant culture. Likewise, many scholars maintain that the progressives paved the way for welfare capitalism, the 'associative state', and the corporate-oriented positive state.[2] While the study of the transatlantic dimension of progressivism validates some of these findings, it also reasserts the genuinely radical intellectual impulses of American reform and maintains that progressivism did not simply assert bourgeois norms and buttress industrial capitalism.

Looking at progressivism through the lens of intellectual and cultural transfer studies reveals a binary image. On the one hand, the narrative traditions the reformers used to link Europe, and especially Britain, to America opened up pathways for the translation of European social thought along radical lines and sharpened the emerging critique of laissez-faire capitalism. Recontextualized outside their restrictive cultural and institutional settings, such as British class politics and German 'reform from above', these ideas helped progressives break the stranglehold of liberal economics, find an intellectual grounding for their moral outrage against industrial society, legitimate domestic social reform, and assert sociocultural and political influence at home.

On the other hand, the political and cultural traditions and practices of American capitalism filtered, winnowed and coopted the social ideas gleaned from Europe, thereby limiting the radical potential of European social thought. The reformers' own class-bound fears of radical change, their grounding in established morality and cultural conservatism, and their backpedalling in the light of political attacks further softened the radical edges. In addition, the way progressives understood European reform tended to reaffirm the very traditions and practices they had set out to overcome.[3]

Britain and Europe in American progressivism

A transatlantic orientation shaped both the climate of opinion and the mental horizon of American progressivism. Even the most casual observer of American society in the late nineteenth century was often struck by the detailed reporting in newspapers and magazines about political and social developments in Britain in particular, and Europe in general. As William T. Stead remarked in 1902, 'the Chicago citizen on Sunday morning would find as a rule three special correspondents' letters from London, one from Paris, and one from Berlin … giving a very detailed, brightly written, sketch of the history of the week. We have nothing approaching to that from the other side in any of our English papers'.[4]

American popular magazines, such as *Outlook*, *Arena*, *Scribner's* and *Review of Reviews* were filled with articles such as 'The Municipal Spirit in England', 'How Germany Cares for Her Working People', and 'Public Ownership in France'. Professional journals and mouthpieces of social reform, such as the *Survey*, the *National Municipal Review*, and *City Plan*, alerted their readers to British municipal reform, German social insurance or French syndicalism. European models were scrutinized by Americans who embraced causes ranging from public playgrounds to public housing; from protective laws for women workers to unemployment insurance; and from prison reform to municipally owned utilities. At a time when the lines between genteel reform, social work and professional social science were not clearly drawn, self-taught economists and sociologists published widely read books on European reform. The backgrounds, causes, and strategies of American reformers differed tremendously, and they acted upon a variety of impulses, including middle-class guilt, evangelical fervour, civic responsibility, status anxiety, economic self-interest and a desire for political power. Nonetheless, they were largely united in their belief that European prescriptions offered remedies for the maladies of American society.

Several factors account for the era's openness to European precedent. For a start, a crisis of industrial confidence prompted a new interest in transatlantic affairs. As a writer in a leading magazine noted in 1905, in the past Americans had 'lacked a reason for having a keen practical interest in

European social and industrial conditions', but with the rise of industrial society and competition for markets 'the questions affecting the relative efficiency of the other great industrial countries in competition with us' became of practical importance to every American.[5]

In addition, American forms of government were perceived as creaking and losing legitimacy. There was a profound sense that following well-trodden political paths in order to achieve reform was a futile endeavour. The spoils system, the corrupt Civil War pensions, and party machine politics were anathema to the urban, cosmopolitan and newly assertive middle class that formed the backbone of progressivism. The reformers also found little worth commending in the record of home-grown economic interventionism, such as railroad subsidies and licensing laws. Distrustful of government corruption, and sidelined politically, they sought inspiration from abroad, rather than from indigenous traditions. Their emphasis on the transnational aspect of reform was thus part of an attempt to find a substitute for American policy trajectories.[6]

Another factor in opening American thought to European influences was the fact that post-Civil War government, though still largely reliant on spoils and party machines, increasingly needed skilled administrators and expert civil servants, particularly in federal and state bureaucracies. The expansion of regulatory agencies, administrative tasks and investigative functions as a result of industrialization, urban growth, and rising immigration and provided new job opportunities for the educated middle classes. Since European universities provided training not available in the US, European degrees were coveted credentials that eased access into new administrative positions.[7]

Finally, transatlantic travel became cheaper and access to European universities was more widely available. As a result, more and more middle-class Americans ventured abroad for study and travel, previously a privilege of the rich. The interplay of industrial convergence, lack of faith in domestic political paths, new professional opportunities and the growing accessibility of Europe provided an opportunity for European-trained progressives to assert themselves politically and culturally.

The strong linguistic, historical and institutional ties between Britain and the United States made British critiques of capitalism and reform proposals the first transatlantic conduits for late-nineteenth-century European social legislation. Nonetheless, in the progressive imagination the distinctions between the countries of Western and Central Europe were subordinated to the quest for usable models of reform across Europe. As the ubiquitous reformer Henry Demarest Lloyd exclaimed, Americans should 'have the wit to make a salad of all the good ideas of Europe and Australasia'.[8] Despite this pan-European outlook, however, progressive social thought reflected the biases against Southern and Eastern European culture long established in Western European thought. This was reinforced by the reformers' apprehensions about the new mass immigration to the US from places such as southern Italy, Slovakia and Russia. Progressives frequently invoked negative stereotypes about Southern and Eastern Europe when warning about the dangers of unchecked industrial capitalism. As an article in a popular magazine declared in 1902, the states in the Union that 'send their little tots to factories by lamplight, which consign them to long hours of poorly requited toil, which make no provision for the education of these children ... belong to the same class with effete Spain and semi-barbarous Roumania and are far behind the land of the Czar or industrially unprogressive Italy'.[9] Few references to urban reforms in southern European cities can be found in American progressive writings. Countries in that region were by definition seen as backward, despite the fact that some urban developments there antedated reforms in Britain and Germany. American progressives chose the Western European municipal experience as a model, because it tied in with their adulation of Anglo-Saxon and Teutonic democracy.

In their desire to link their own reformist fervour to European models, the progressives were keenly aware of the need to establish the relevance of European developments within the narratives of American society. Economically, the reformers advanced a theory of convergence and modernization as a way of establishing the comparability of European and American economic realities and depicting models of reform as mutually exchangeable. In the political arena, they skillfully modified the established narrative that saw America as liberated from the corrupting influences of feudalism with a script that reconstructed Europe as a force for revitalizing corrupted American republicanism. In the cultural realm, progressives linked the adaptation of European reform to high culture, tapping into the established reverence for European cultural expressions in the US.

Britain as the first nation to industrialize and as the leading economic competitor became the main focus of the progressives' construction of an *economic* narrative of transatlantic convergence. Henry D. Lloyd, social worker Vida Scudder and economist John R. Commons all saw British and American accounts of labour problems and poverty as interchangeable. Where conditions were comparable, solutions were equally applicable, they argued. Following closely David Lloyd George's budget battles, Cleveland's reform mayor Tom Johnson noted that Americans were 'interested in that struggle over there, not as outsiders but as insiders'.[10] Arguing that Britain and America were exposed to the same forces of industrialization, they stressed 'sameness' over 'exceptionalism'. Progressives believed that learning the lessons of European developments would enable the United States to continue on the path of social progress. Even a cursory look at the efficient municipal services, well-constructed working-class houses, effective social insurance systems and the high standard of public amenities in Britain, France and Germany, they maintained, revealed that the Old World was ahead of the US.[11]

The *political* reconceptualization of Europe in the American mind required a larger feat of the imagination. 'Europe does not learn at our feet the facile lessons of democracy, but has in some respects become our teacher,' progressive journalist Walter Weyl asserted in 1912.[12] A whole tradition that juxtaposed European despotism and feudalism with enlightened republican America had to be turned upside down. In muckraking stories of urban America with its seedy saloons, notorious amusements, overcrowded tenements, noxious fumes and urban unrest, reformers invoked a wide range of images that had long been associated with Europe. Economist Richard T. Ely and others depicted American government as closely resembling medieval fiefdoms. America's plutocratic exploiters, labour conflicts, and obscene displays of wealth in the face of abject poverty had made a mockery of the Jeffersonian vision of a republic of yeoman farmers. America had turned into a country that was lagging behind in democratic development.[13]

Since the American republic had been corrupted, the reformers maintained that revitalization could not come from within, but needed an impetus from abroad. Municipal ownership of utilities in Birmingham in particular became progressivism's most celebrated example of municipal civic-mindedness in Europe. Glasgow and London also put a spell on reformers as American popularizers such as Ely, journalist Albert Shaw, and social worker Robert A. Woods spread the gospel of British urban reform. As American Fabian W. D. P. Bliss's influential *Encyclopedia of Social Reform* noted, 'the European city has become, as compared with American cities, efficient and pure.'[14] When the London City Council with its progressive majority of Liberals, Fabians and labour radicals attempted to municipalize public utilities and transport, build municipal housing, and organize a public work force in the early 1890s, it became the most closely watched urban experiment in American progressivism.[15]

In the early twentieth century, city planning emerged as the progressive cause of choice. City planning advocates were no longer satisfied with the good government prescriptions of municipal reform. Replacing corrupt politicians with honest citizens, reorganizing the administrative structure of the city, or touting the financial benefits of municipal ownership, they argued, were no longer sufficient to address the complex issues of urban life. They demanded that the city be given the power to own land, build public housing, and pass zoning laws. As urban reformer Leo S. Rowe noted, 'a well-developed street railway system is of far greater importance to the social welfare and economic efficiency of the population than an adequate return to the city treasury.'[16]

Again, Britain was an important focus of attention, and images of Hampstead Garden suburb, Letchworth and Port Sunlight captured the progressive imagination. Garden cities, medieval street layouts, model housing plans, zoning laws and public funds for building societies became part of the progressive arsenal of urban reform in the US. European tours organized by reform groups such as the City Clubs, the National Conference for Good City Government and the National Municipal League, inevitably included visits to British cities and meetings with Fabian socialist Sidney Webb, urban planner Raymond Unwin, or labour firebrand John Burns.[17]

Advocates of city planning, such as Frederic C. Howe, looked at Europe, rather than the American West, as Frederick Jackson Turner had suggested, for blueprints for the revival of democratic life. Expanding on Herbert Baxter Adams's contention that democracy had originated in the Teutonic forests, Howe argued that 'in England and Germany I saw democracy coming into being in cities rather than in parliament.'[18] His *The City: The Hope of Democracy* was both book title and programme, challenging American anti-urbanism with visions of European-inspired urban political regeneration.[19] The city, long seen as a source of corruption, depravity and the nemesis of democracy in American thought, emerged as the beacon in the night.

Howe's perceptions of European municipal thought and reform informed the progressives' conception of the city as a civic centre and a social organism of interrelated and complementary parts. He regarded the city as more than an aggregation of separate individuals. In his view, the city was an intricate network of dependencies and relationships where the welfare of each individual was dependent on the harmonious integration of all members of society. He stressed the psychological and ethical advantages of municipal ownership, in addition to the financial and administrative gains, claiming that the 'communal ownership of many services has awakened a political reaction on the part of the community, that has undoubtedly created a better civic spirit.'[20] The city, its complexity, interdependence and intermingling of people, was to become the outward manifestation of the transformation from a democratic ideal based on independent yeoman farmers to a pragmatist concept of democracy based on diversity, interdependence and interaction. Land and tax reform, a broader sphere of public control and ethical transformation through aesthetic experience were all part of the rejuvenation of democracy. As Howe put it, '[i]t was not economy, efficiency and business methods that interested me so much as a city planned, built, and conducted as a community enterprise.'[21] In revivalist fashion reminiscent of his Methodist past, Howe's goal was not to impose regulations, but to awaken moral feelings as a result of aesthetic experiences and social interaction. Conscious order and planning were to be the result of intellectual and moral progress. In its emphasis on moral conversion, cultural reconstruction and the awakening of social ethics, progressive urban reform drew on the ethical socialism of T. H. Green, John Trevor and William Jupp.[22] Indeed, for American progressives such as Ely, W. D. P. Bliss, and E. R. A. Seligman the term 'socialism' referred to either Christian or ethical socialism, rather than Marxism.[23]

After 1906, The 'New Liberals' and David Lloyd George's flurry of German-inspired social legislation that established a public old-age pension system, compulsory health insurance, minimum wages and progressive taxation, became progressivism's leading cause célèbre.[24] Progressive insurance reformers emphasized the larger political meaning of insurance reform. To them, republican renewal through social insurance did not mean a redefinition of the functions of the state in order to restore economic individualism and liberal democracy. Instead, reformers such as Isaac M. Rubinow and Florence Kelley proposed a conception of social insurance that stressed the close link between participation in self-governing insurance funds and the development of social ethics. They regarded the state-sanctioned public participation that insurance funds offered as a means by which individuals could recognize that their freedom and happiness were intrinsically tied to their social being. Their organicist social philosophy based liberty on principles of mutuality, communal rights and obligations, local decision-making, and cooperative administration. The new republic was not to be defined by constitutional government and the protection of individual rights, but by industrial democracy and social justice.[25]

For Rubinow, social insurance was part and parcel of modern democracy, rather than of the autocratic state. It was class legislation in the best sense of the word, an effort 'to readjust the distribution of the national product more equitably', he argued. He regarded social insurance as an alternative to the injustice, degradation and insufficiency of welfare. The goal of insurance, he declared, was to eradicate poverty by attacking the origins of the problem. He was convinced that both Malthus, who thought poverty an inevitable law, and Marx, who believed in progressive impoverishment as a prerequisite for revolution, were mistaken. Inspired by Eduard Bernstein, Rubinow saw social insurance as a means of infusing modern society with more justice and rationality, because the scheme encompassed self-governed funds, equal representation of owners and workers, equal benefits to men and women, and entitlement to benefits. '[C]lass struggle does not necessarily mean class war,' he declared, 'conflicts, born out of despair, are more bloodthirsty, more destructive, and less productive of positive results than intelligent collective action for the common weal.'[26]

Other progressive causes drew inspiration from Britain, too. Toynbee Hall in London provided the blueprint for Hull House and other American settlements, after leading social workers, such as Jane Addams, Stanton Coit and Vida Scudder had made the trip across the Atlantic. American reformers also followed closely developments in the areas of labour unions, cooperatives, friendly societies and collective bargaining. Labour legislation was another main area of progressive attention. In particular, reformers noted with some satisfaction that even in the land of Smith, Ricardo and Mill, government intervention and regulation was widespread. Laissez faire appeared no longer viable, as workmen's compensation and the governmental purchase of the telegraph system indicated.

Proponents of city planning, social insurance and other reforms relied upon both reports of British social legislation and their well-developed transatlantic personal networks. Fabianism, in particular, had a strong transatlantic dimension. A striking number of Fabians criss-crossed the Atlantic, and a remarkable congruence of ideas ensued. In this fertile exchange of ideas, Sidney and Beatrice Webb corresponded and met with Albert Shaw, John Graham Brooks, Theodore Roosevelt, Carroll D. Wright, Jane Adams and Woodrow Wilson. William Clarke and Graham Wallas developed close ties with American reformers, particularly Henry Demarest Lloyd, Frances Willard, William English Walling and Charles Zueblin. Sidney Webb kept in close contact with Richard Ely. Their papers include extensive correspondence, trace the exchange of books, indicate repeated visits, and show that Webb helped Ely with his book *Socialism and Social Reform*. Social gospeller Walter Rauschenbusch stayed with the Webbs when he travelled to Europe to conduct research for his influential book *Christianity and the Social Crisis*. And although W. P. D. Bliss's attempts to establish an American Fabian society were short-lived, they popularized Fabian approaches.[27]

American progressives shared with the Fabians the embrace of gradual change grounded in the awareness that all knowledge was uncertain, and a dedication to democratic politics as a process of collective truth-testing. Fabians and progressives alike remained sceptical of large-scale central state intervention. Though they advocated nation-wide reforms, such as minimum standards and the nationalization of 'natural monopolies', they felt more comfortable with urban politics than with the authority of the centralized state.[28] Many progressives also subscribed to the Fabian strategy of permeation, which the Webbs and their circle used at different times to work inside the Conservative, the Liberal and the fledgling Labour parties. Both Fabians and progressives were torn between the desire for boring from within existing parties and for forming their own, alternative organizations.[29] However, American progressives, disillusioned with the Republican party and ever wary of the Democrats, were more reluctant to engage in party politics than British Fabians. They eschewed party politics, both because urban politics marginalized them and because they were disgusted with urban party machines. Most of them preferred civic organizations, though a significant number became involved in the Socialist and the Progressive parties.[30]

American reformers attached *cultural* legitimacy to their adaptation of European social reforms by linking them to American conceptions of European high culture. Again, British critics of industrialism provided the first inspiration. As avid readers of the late Victorian library, progressives approached social problems through aesthetics in the fashion of Carlyle, Ruskin, Morris and Matthew Arnold, denouncing capitalism as immoral, ugly and offensive. American progressives identified with the sentiments and sensibilities of British gentleman reformers and shared the class consciousness of British 'Tory radicals'. Building upon long-standing connections between British and American social movements, 'reform thinking of the Progressive Era was debtor to Britain, as Americans were attracted to a number of English thinkers who spoke the language of political economy in the accent of the moralist, or even the prophet.'[31] Writers such as Arnold Toynbee and Graham Wallas confirmed the progressives' belief that an educated elite needed to take on cultural and political leadership roles to redirect society. Economist Richard Ely even called for 'an American aristocracy', and Vida Scudder, the leading American scholar of British social thought, pointed out that reform 'ought to come from above and not from below'.[32] Progressives used the rhetoric of William Morris, John Ruskin and Charles Dickens to express their disdain for businessmen and to voice their patronizing view of the workers. As historian Arthur Mann points out, 'the first American book on the English social movements ... told more about the efforts of reformers to help workers than about the activities of workers to help themselves.'[33]

The cultural narrative of Europe was particularly prominent in progressive urban reform. Urban reform was never just about efficiency, but also about edification. As Albert Shaw maintained, 'residence in the centers of population can be made not only safe and wholesome physically for the masses of the people, but also conducive to mental and moral progress.'[34] In typical progressive fashion, Richard Ely noted in the late 1880s the painful contrast between the clean, aesthetically appealing features of European city streets and the squalor of American cities.[35] Unlike many of their European counterparts, however, American reformers embraced the social possibilities of industrial society, rather than idealizing the lost communal ties of pre-industrial culture. They did not follow the medieval utopianism of Ruskin and Morris.[36] Instead, their writings combined depictions of medieval cathedrals with the wonders of modern slaughterhouses, interweaving ancient and modern in urban reform, and stressing the cultural effects of new social institutions. By depicting Europe's cities as combining medieval past with modern social planning, they also reinforced both the sense of sameness and the sense that Europe offered solutions applicable to an American environment. Albert Shaw, for example, insisted that despite their medieval core and their hallowed customs, British and German cities were as new as American municipalities. For Shaw, urban planning replaced narrow medieval streets with wide open thoroughfares, allowing air and light to penetrate the dark and dank quarters that spawned gloom and vice, both literally and metaphorically.[37]

City planners in particular maintained that modern civilization might have supplied the technical means for progress and improvement, but culture alone could provide meaning and common purpose. Thus, Howe constructed an ideal in which engineers, architects, artists and experts saw themselves as contributors to a cooperative effort to create a work of art. Art, architecture and aesthetics were to give outward expression to the intuitive awareness that individual self-realization could be found only in the shared vision of the harmonious development of the social organism.[38]

The transformation of social thought

The three themes of economic convergence, republican revival and cultural redemption formed the ground upon which progressives legitimated their recourse to Britain, and Europe in general, for their models of reform. Intellectually, the progressives' concern with transatlantic reform derived primarily from their desire to find validation for a critique of laissez-faire economics, for democratic renewal through the expansion of the public sphere, and for social redemption through cultural self-realization. Progressives used their appeals to Britain and Europe more generally to bring genuinely radical ideas into the American debate. European social ideas were thus translated into a new theory of social reform in American thought.

This new way of thinking grew out of a philosophical sea-change that swept across Western Europe and America and challenged the epistemological, ontological and ethical foundations of nineteenth-century liberalism, a sea-change associated with progressive reformers such as Ely and Simon N. Patten, pragmatist philosophers such as William James and John Dewey, and European social thinkers such as T. H. Green, L. T. Hobhouse, Sidney Webb and the advocates of the German historical school of economics. Progressive social thought thereby emerged as a genuinely radical alternative to older philosophical master narratives.[39] The beliefs loosely associated with this radical alternative included the idea of the market as a social construct, the notion that truth was a social product, and the denial of mind–body and subject–object dualisms.

The intellectual cross-currents of the fin-de-siècle provided the reformers with an intellectual grounding for their moral outrage. [40] Relishing the 'mental emancipation from the tyranny of pessimism' of orthodox liberal economics, progressives often described their experiences by evoking images of epiphany, conversion and liberation. As economist Henry Carter Adams put it, European social thought suggested 'the possibility of industrial and social development by the process of artificial rather than natural selection'.[41] As the reformers infused these social ideas into the American economic, political and cultural debates via their conceptualization of Europe, so their radical potential began to unfold.

This process coincided with the gradual broadening of the transatlantic gaze across the Channel. While British reformers had given Americans a language to express their moral outrage, they rarely provided the theoretical framework for analysing industrial society and constructing a new theory of social reform. Though progressives identified more readily with British reformers, such as Sidney Webb and John Ruskin, than with German academic economists, such as Adolph Wagner and Gustav Schmoller, in their quest for analytical tools they also turned to continental traditions.[42] Indeed, American reformers grew increasingly disappointed with the limitations of the British precedent. Frederic C. Howe was critical of the power of the land-based aristocracy in Britain and the failure of the Housing and Town Planning Act to provide land-purchasing rights. He thus came to favour German urban reform over the British precedent. Likewise, government centralization and exemptions for commercial insurers in British social insurance legislation explain the disillusionment of American insurance reformers with British precedent.

A brief glance at the three narratives of Europe that Americans used to legitimate their crusades highlights the emergence of the new theories of reform. As indicated earlier, the narrative of *economic* convergence had established the applicability of European social reform. The same narrative now became the basis for a philosophical critique of *laissez-faire*. In particular, many reformers began to subscribe to European theories of the market as historically constructed and as reflecting socially and culturally established power relations. The allegedly absolute and universal laws of the market were thus portrayed as ideological legitimations of a historically developed economic set-up. Many progressives also adopted the view that ethics were formed through social interaction and participation. Suggesting a relativistic view of morality, this concept put all forms of social interaction, including market relations, to the test of their contribution to the development of social ethics. Social well-being was no longer to be left to market mechanisms, but needed to become a matter of the active political ordering of social and economic relations.[43]

These ideas captured the progressives' attention because they reestablished the connection between ethics and economics and stripped the market of its trappings as a natural, autonomous and self-regulating realm. Most progressives did not object to the concept of the market as such, but to the fact that the connection between the market and morality had been severed as a result of industrial capitalism. A mainstay of the progressive moral tale was that in the late-nineteenth century the close association between middle-class norms of self-help, industriousness and competitive achievement, and a Protestant code that demanded self-control, personal piety, and frugality had begun to diverge. William Dean Howells's novels typified this image of Gilded Age industrialism, which rewarded the ruthless exploiter and the unscrupulous businessman and severed the established link between individual entrepreneurship and moral development.[44] In the same vein, progressive sociologist Edward A. Ross maintained that modern sin lacked the tokens of guilt, the stigma and the images of wrongdoing, while at the same time being transformed from a personal threat to a danger to the fabric of society. Whereas the old-time villain wore a slouch hat, smelled of gin, and walked around with an evil scowl, he explained, the modern 'quack, the adulterator, and the purveyor of polluted water' wears 'immaculate linen, carries a silk hat and a lighted cigar, sins with a calm countenance and a serene soul'.[45]

Though reestablishing the connection between ethics and economics was important, the real nut to be cracked was *laissez-faire* packaged in naturalist thinking. Gilded Age capitalism rested on an ideological justification stronger than the concepts of the self-regulating market, entrepreneurial individualism and limited government. The naturalist revolution in thought, in particular the transliteration of Darwinism, provided a legitimation for *laissez-faire* above and beyond the natural rights philosophy of the eighteenth century. Darwinism reinscribed the teachings of English economics into the realm of nature.[46] Rephrased in terms of selection, mutation and survival of the fittest, the competitive market and the acquisitive individual were made part of the natural order of the physical world and were removed from their ties to the emancipatory narrative of the Enlightenment. By revealing the philosophical contradictions of the combination of *laissez-faire* economics and Darwinian thought, progressive social thinkers such as Patten, Thorstein Veblen, and John Dewey formulated a fundamental critique of the naturalist ideology underlying Gilded Age capitalism. In particular, the tension between the metahistorical foundationalist ideas of market economics and the relativist, anti-foundationalist implications of Darwinism became the basis upon which they systematically developed their theories. By linking truth to contingent experience, and society's progress to political reform, they helped progressives to establish agency, to embrace evolutionary thought and to reconnect morals to economics.[47]

These intellectual shifts came to fruition in the *political* realm. As indicated above, American progressives turned around the moral narrative that posited European despotism against enlightened republican America, and depicted Europe as the source for democratic revitalization. As progressive thought matured, a new progressive social theory emerged that constructed democracy no longer in terms of protecting individual rights, but in terms of social integration and social ethics. John Dewey in particular spelled out this progressive conception of democracy, which differed from the liberal insistence on protecting individual rights. Defining democracy as 'the effective embodiment of the moral ideal of a good which consists in the development of all the social capacities of every individual member', he argued that society needed to create structures of participation and communication that enabled each individual member to participate in the formulation of ethical goals and the scrutiny of political and economic decisions.[48]

Dewey regarded communication not simply as a functional instrument to coordinate social action, but as an event that enabled individuals to open themselves up to others and allowed for experiences that resulted in the attachment to norms and values.[49] Reform was not a matter of bureaucratic control and administrative efficiency. Rather, the primary goal of government intervention was to broaden the sphere of public control and to ensure equal opportunity of participation for all as a prerequisite for social progress, political tranquility and moral growth. Structured participation and communication, Dewey asserted, made people aware of their interdependence and gave them an opportunity to rationally connect with each other in order to solve specific problems of an interdependent industrial society.[50]

According to Dewey, 'new civic and political agencies' would open up new avenues for ethical self-realization. As W. E. B. Du Bois wrote, democracy was not a functional arrangement or a mechanical problem, but a system that gave meaning and significance to human strivings. Its real justification lay in its potential for promoting social ethics, not in its protection of individual rights.[51] In Dewey's view, social reform would thus safeguard against 'explosive change and intermittent blind action and reaction', allowing instead for the 'graduated and steady reconstruction' of society. At the same time, it would preserve the evolutionary dynamics of society, since the expanded public sphere of control 'will not subordinate individual variations, but will encourage individual experimentation in new ideas and new projects'.[52] Reform was thus a matter of reconnecting ethics to economics in conjunction with a theory of social evolution.

The Fabian and revisionist critiques of Marxism adopted from Britain further fuelled this democratic theory and gave voice to the reformers' desire to link both social progress to moral development and to heed the lessons of Darwinism. The Fabians frequently commented on the 'conscious growth of social feeling' brought about by working-class involvement in municipal and other self-governing bodies, arguing that an increase in economic interaction and interdependence would result in solidarity between classes. In addition, the *Fabian Essays* maintained that living conditions for workers were improving, rather than deteriorating, and the recurrent crises of capitalism were abating, rendering its collapse less likely. The growth of the middle class, as well as the improvements in the economic status of the working classes, pointed toward the emancipation of the workers through the internal dynamics of capitalist society.[53] In a similar vein, though with more radical implications, the revisionist Eduard Bernstein maintained on the basis of observing British developments that reform needed to precede revolution, because it would nurture the workers' moral strength, political expertise and intellectual abilities to prepare them for a broader view of socialist emancipation required for true social change. 'When the working classes ... have not attained, by means of education on self-governing bodies, a high degree of mental independence, the dictatorship of the proletariat means the dictatorship of club orators and writers,' he declared.[54]

The progressives' advocacy of municipal ownership of utilities, comprehensive city plans and self-governed insurance reflected these ideas. The campaigns were often phrased in terms of reconstructing American democracy as an ethical community, rather than in terms of protecting individual rights or promoting efficiency. The reformers' conception of social ethics differed from the older liberal concept of moral self-determination and its concomitant view of man as acquisitive and self-interested. It anchored values in social interaction and participation, locating the essence of individuality in inner feelings of belonging to a social whole. Reforms were designed to promote self-help and public participation, not to foster paternalism.[55]

The 1897 speech by urban reformer Leo S. Rowe at the meeting of the National Municipal League provided a cohesive expression of this approach. Pointing out that urban government was organized in analogy to state and national governments, Rowe complained that checks and balances and the division of powers did not adequately address problems of urban life. The conditions of urban existence revealed the 'close interdependence of the units and the sensitiveness of the whole body politic to the standards of individual action'. A new civic standard was needed that encompassed both individual responsibility and organized action. The city was not a corporation furnishing services, he insisted. Utilities, transportation devices or municipal buildings should be intelligently designed with their effect on social relations and civic activities of the community in mind. The ensuing new mode of life would, in turn, create a new view of life. The transition to a higher ethical standard, Rowe contended, relied heavily on public opinion and a 'new sensitiveness' which would condemn the 'overcrowded street car, the advertisement-covered fence, the chimney-like sky-scraper, the filthy alley-way'.[56] Rowe, who had been Simon Patten's student, expressed the belief that social consciousness and outside environment, subject and object, acted and reacted upon each other in the unfolding of the social organism.

This points toward the growing significance of the *cultural* narrative of progressivism. By asserting the political significance and evolving nature of aesthetic experience, American progressives parted with the formalism of nineteenth-century conceptions of art. Their faith in the connection between art and social ethics turned urban reform into an integral part of the progressives' departure from nineteenth-century liberalism. Urban reformers, such as Howe and Rowe, defined the city as a 'home' where a sense of belonging would emanate from aesthetic experience, social participation and ethical consciousness. For Frederic Howe the predominance of aesthetic considerations over bureaucratic control was more than a reflection of his middle-class cultural sensitivities. He saw new aesthetic experiences as part and parcel of fundamental social change. European city planning lent further support to these ideas. One of

Europe's foremost city planners, Camillo Sitte, regarded town planning as a distinct profession that went beyond technical engineering and administrative concerns. Sitte's focus on the character of the old parts of towns, his fetish for curved streets and finite perspective, and his definition of the city as *Heimat* (home) gained widespread attention through town planning exhibits that drew many American planners to Germany. In the same vein, Howe realized that broadening the sphere of public control required not only economic and administrative justification, but also a sense of belonging and participation in a common endeavour. 'Provision for happiness', he reflected, 'should be as obligatory on a city as provision for police protection.'[57]

Howe's approach to city planning reflected both established concepts of art and new ideas of social ethics introduced through the transatlantic community of discourse. In his eyes, the city plan expressed the power of the mind to recognize absolute harmony, beauty and virtue. This recognition, he believed, would creatively engage the mind in a process of self-reflection. The resulting intellectual inspiration and aesthetic satisfaction would allow for the development of a higher social and ethical consciousness. Thus, Howe and other urban reformers saw in the city plan a means of harmoniously ordering and connecting transportation, housing, utilities, industry, public space and social life in order to provide the best possible environment for the self-realization of each individual based on the awareness of the city as a shared civic endeavour.

Faith in the connection between art and morals was one of the defining characteristics of progressive urban reform.[58] 'City planning is the first conscious recognition of the unity of society,' Howe mused, 'it involves a socializing of art and beauty and the control of the unrestrained license of the individual.'[59] New social ethics would emerge from the development of new civic urban institutions, increased public participation and opportunities for aesthetic experiences in an urban environment. Urban well-being, the reformers argued, was dependent on the ability of urban man to think of each action in terms of its effects on the social organism. Ultimately, citizenship would no longer be defined in terms of protecting individual rights, but in terms of social integration and social ethics, and new aesthetic experiences were part and parcel of this process.

Reasserting the social order

The adaptation of British and continental European social thought helped progressives pry open the intellectual, political and social foundations of post-Civil War American society and allowed new visions, imaginations and ideas to inspire reform activism. However, the transatlantic orientation of progressivism also helped reinforce aspects of the existing social order in the United States. As James Kloppenberg put it, the radical impulses in progressive social reform 'filtered into the political process in a way that has enabled systems of welfare capitalism ... to perpetuate themselves'.[60] The reformers gradually relegated issues of ethics and democratic participation to the sidelines. In the end, the progressive call for a broad sphere of public control, social legislation based on ethical precepts, and participatory models of reform yielded to an emphasis on regulatory agencies, administrative problem-solving and government–business partnerships that became the main features of the liberal welfare state.

To a large extent the history of the limits of transatlantic reform can be told through the analysis of the impact of domestic American traditions and practices. Progressives failed to mobilize broad-based support for reform, encountered massive legal obstacles, and floundered under the impact of organized attacks by economic interest groups. The power of the courts often stymied the development of social legislation. Likewise, the decentralized political structure and competing levels of government hampered the development of social welfare policies. Moreover, social policies and state intervention in post-Civil War America did not create a lasting legacy of public bureaucratic and administrative capacities.[61] At the turn of the century the federal government had fewer employees than the steel industry. Hence, the private sector provided many of the conceptual models and organizational features upon which public programmes were eventually based: big business preceded big government in undergoing bureaucratic transformation in such fields as minimum wages, retirement plans, accident insurance and safety campaigns so that employer-initiated programmes were often central to the development of socially desirable welfare standards.[62] Many insurance reformers, including Isaac Rubinow, learned actuarial skills in the private insurance business. Although they designed compulsory social insurance in order to replace the waste and chaos of private plans, to substitute entitlement for charity and to replace private control with mutual administration, they were hampered by the administrative confines of late-nineteenth-century government. The frequent switch of insurance reformers from public service to private companies hindered rather than promoted reform.

The development of urban reform illustrates the marginalization of the radical impulses of progressivism. The most avid housing reformer of the period, Lawrence Veiller, was at the same time an outspoken and effective opponent of land and tax reform. A key figure behind the path-breaking 1916 zoning ordinance of New York City, Veiller had little to say about the transforming power of aesthetic experience or the formation of ethics through social interaction. He believed in creating social order and stability through regulation and the embourgeoisement of the working class.[63] Veiller's emphasis on regulation and his rejection of more radical land and tax reforms reflected his awareness that the courts had put effective limits on the progressive fervour. With uncanny frequency the courts struck down labour laws, minimum wage laws, health regulations and related pieces of legislation with reference to constitutional rights of liberty and contract. As a result, urban reformers and city planners increasingly modified their proposals to ensure that their laws would be upheld in the courts.[64] The Massachusetts legislature passed a law in 1904 that permitted condemnation of lots for public use and formation of large parcels of land from remnants, after a committee had studied European excess condemnation laws. Yet, in 1914 Pennsylvania was still the only state in which property-owners could be compelled to comply with municipal street plans without obtaining compensation. Municipal purchase of land remained outside of the authority of the cities.[65]

Progressive legal scholar Ernst Freund personified the cautious legal mind-set of progressivism that moved away from broader visions of social transformation and declared that 'governmental powers ought not to run very far ahead of that conservative sentiment which is represented by the courts.'[66] In his influential book *The Police Power*, Freund argued that a great deal could be achieved by making use of the existing legal framework, such as the municipal power to determine the location of public buildings, recreation grounds and the lay-out of streets. Though the courts frequently threw out restrictive legislation by asserting the constitutional right of liberty and contract, they often acknowledged that conditions that affected health or morality, such as unhealthy working conditions and fraud were areas of legitimate exercise of police power.[67]

The growing progressive awareness of these limitations and possibilities of reform led to the fundamental change in the approach of many urban reformers to city planning. In particular, concepts of increasing popular participation and redistributionist tax reform fell victim to this shift. Advocating the extension of the restrictive police power of government limited the scope of reform and pushed the more radical proposals to the fringes of the accepted discourse. With land reform sidelined and the concern with police power overshadowing the ethical impetus, housing reformers embraced narrower and more immediate goals, such as zoning, height restrictions and suburban housing codes.

Likewise, municipal ownership, encountered only limited success in the United States in the era before World War I. Although at the turn of the century 30 out of 38 major American cities owned their own water and sewer facilities, municipal control rarely reached beyond maintaining waterworks. Only nine cities operated electrical power plants, only three maintained municipal gasworks and, by the 1920s, only Detroit, San Francisco, Seattle and New York operated or owned transit lines.[68] Public utility commissions that regulated privately owned services became a more popular form of control in the United States than municipal ownership. Wisconsin and New York formed the vanguard in 1907 and within the next five years 14 additional states passed public utility laws.[69] These commissions had the power to approve rates, oversee capitalization and set minimum standards. The concept greatly appealed to progressives, because it seemed to insure public regulation and oversight, avoided the pitfalls of urban corruption and did not challenge the hallowed principle of private ownership. Newton D. Baker, Tom Johnson's successor as mayor of Cleveland and later Woodrow Wilson's secretary of war, summed up the consensus as it emerged in the mid-1910s. Municipal ownership, Baker declared, was not an ethical question. On the contrary, it was 'neither good nor bad', but 'a question of social organization, a question of economic policy, a question of large expediency'.[70] The utility companies soon recognized the advantages of these regulatory bodies. Not only were they able to staff the commissions with their own people, they also benefited from the depoliticizing of the franchise process. In addition, regulatory commissions effectively stymied the drive for municipal ownership.[71] As journalist Walter Lippmann grumbled in 1912 '[m]unicipal ownership under Socialists would pay for things that the people need; under reformers it would lighten the burden on property-owners'.[72]

The transatlantic nature of progressivism also acted so as to limit reform. Since the reformers' social vision and their sense of agency relied heavily on specific narratives of Europe, any changes to these narratives were likely to have an impact on the reform agenda. World War I in particular seriously undermined the narratives of Europe upon which the progressives relied. The high moral fervour of Wilsonian idealism turned the war into a crusade by the American knight in shining armour to rescue the European damsel in distress. Pro-war propagandists tapped into older American myths depicting American military involvement as a campaign against 'all that Europe historically represented in the American mind: coercive government, irrationality, barbarism, feudalism'.[73] As a result, progressives increasingly renounced the foreign influences on reform. The close ties of progressives to Europe, their cosmopolitan outlook and their attempts to forge an international movement for reform, were discredited in the wake of the war.

The political effects of the change in public opinion could not be overlooked, either, as the demise of the health insurance campaign revealed. War-time opponents of reform effectively exploited the declining public image of Europe to set up insurmountable cultural and political obstacles for insurance reformers. The immigrant roots of social insurance – the English fraternal orders, immigrant German sickness funds, Italian societies and Jewish lodges, eloquently defended by Isaac Rubinow – now proved a burden in promoting health insurance reform.[74] The reformers learned the lesson that 'the less identification with Europe, the better the prospects of social insurance'.[75] In 1920, the main lobbying group for public health insurance, the American Association for Labor Legislation (AALL) decided to cut the health care issue loose from 'the traditions of Rubinow and the German basis'.[76] This separation from the transatlantic context contained a clear political message. It sanctioned policies that reasserted business control and forestalled any reform in the direction of broader democratic participation of workers. The National Industrial Conference Board (NICB), for example, a business-sponsored research organization, derided 'the experience of foreign countries where sickness insurance has been tried'. It charged that these reforms had failed 'as a preventive agency' and had been marred by 'inefficiency and fraud'. The NICB urged preventive work, compulsory physical examinations and the amendment of existing workmen's compensation acts. Since the workmen's compensation systems were not based on the principle of effective worker control, basing changes in health insurance on the model of workmen's compensation effectively undercut the radical elements of the health insurance campaign.[77]

Moreover, war-time government intervention itself, despite gaining the support from many progressives, was based on a concept of state action that was at odds with the European-inspired ideal. Compulsory health insurance was a case in point. The government introduced health benefits for specific groups with exclusionary features and thus effectively thwarted the progressives' hope that insurance coverage would be extended to all workers. In addition, the war-time model of government insurance was based on state control, not on decentralized, self-governing funds. The war legitimized the use of the state as a restrictive police power and a regulatory agency, rather than as an instrument of social justice. War-time policies embraced government–business cooperation, moral regulation and centralized bureaucratic control. They thwarted the progressive agenda of a broader sphere of public control and social legislation based on ethical precepts.[78]

In turn, progressives in the post-war period shifted from advocating decentralized and self-governed mutual funds to urging preventive safety measures, compulsory physical examinations, Mothers' pensions and the amendment of existing workmen's compensation acts through state police powers. In 1919, for example, the majority of the Illinois Health Insurance Commission decided against compulsory health insurance and found 'no rational basis for a contribution by the employer'. Most wage-earners, the report asserted, could afford to buy insurance themselves. As an alternative, the commission recommended that the 'authority and powers of the state Department of Public Health be enlarged'.[79]

Above and beyond the impact of war, the way British and other European ideas and practices were translated imposed interpretive grids that limited the radical potential of progressive reform, as we can see with respect to each of the three narratives discussed above. As far as the *economic* narrative is concerned, the notion of convergence had been a useful tool for reformers to establish the relevance of European social thought. However, convergence also posited an ahistorical and essentialist concept that replicated the thought patterns familiar from *laissez-faire* liberalism. It implied that the differences that existed between the United States and the nations of Europe in regard to customs, traditions and institutions were less relevant than the shared experience of industrialization, urbanization and immigration. The notion that the forces of convergence were wiping away the cobwebs of history became the metahistorical axiom behind the progressives' critique of *laissez-faire* capitalism and their vision of social reconstruction. Hence, despite the historicist grounding of their critique of laissez-faire, late nineteenth-century social thought soon turned to the abstract concept of inevitable modernization, rather than historical analysis, to understand and examine the trajectories of social development. Reformers reinscribed universalistic assumptions that were more useful as defences of market-driven policies than as critiques of capitalism. They posited universal abstract laws of development, a self-regulating mechanism and a stage theory of civilizations that had been the hallmark of laissez-faire liberalism.[80]

In the *political* narrative, progressives had tied their visions of European-inspired republican revitalization to a growing consciousness of man's relational, interdependent and social nature. They questioned the liberal myth of the autonomous, self-interested individual, which had been linked to the assertion of the fundamental differences between Europe and the United States. Nonetheless, they were intellectually caught between a desire to overcome the philosophical, ethical and political limitations of nineteenth-century liberalism and the urge to uphold Victorian ideals of autonomy and propriety.[81] They talked about the ethical potential of public control, yet often regarded the corporation as the model for good city government. They desired non-commercial urban institutions, yet admired and courted 'enlightened businessmen'. A belief in thrift, frugality and self-discipline continued to bind the progressives to nineteenth-century Protestant America, despite their forages into the hazy realms of 'new ethics'.[82] Both Shaw and Ely described European town officials and expert administrators in terms reminiscent of nineteenth-century *laissez-faire* man. Their image of the expert as independent, prudent and self-controlled mirrored the liberal ideal of the householder and patriarch who fulfilled his social duties with a strong sense of responsibility emanating from his status as a self-sufficient citizen. In this manner they preserved a gendered view of 'male' independence despite the 'female' implication of their theory of mutual dependence and interconnectedness.[83]

Frederic Howe and others remained equally attached to the values of nineteenth-century Protestant America, where 'right living was living carefully, avoiding debts of any kind and husbanding for some distant future when sickness and old age would overtake one.'[84] They saw a central element of urban reform in convincing businessmen of the economic value of planning, broad powers of taxation and municipal ownership. Both Shaw and Howe wanted to lure businessmen to civic positions. The ensuing redefinition of status and wealth, Howe maintained, would allow businessmen to act in the interest of the well-being of the city, rather than according to their own self-interest. This would lead to 'an intelligent understanding and approval of municipal socialism by all classes'.[85] Thus, there was no need for radical actions to overcome capitalism and bourgeois liberalism. Instead, institutions needed to be organized in a way that would allow the potential of capitalism to be used for the welfare of the whole society.

For the latter-day mugwump Albert Shaw patriarchal corporatism was the model of city government. Politically, it was founded upon limited suffrage; organizationally, upon a broad sphere of public municipal control; administratively, upon experts serving the public interest; and culturally, upon middle-class pride in a conscious and purposeful civic endeavour. While the reformers thus embraced the concept of a socialized democracy, they turned a blind eye toward the authoritarian and class character of urban administration. In Europe the progressives met with city officials, planners and leading businessmen, but rarely talked to the man in the street or even to working-class representatives.

The medicalized rhetoric frequently adopted by progressives also placed urban reform squarely within the realm of professional experts, distinctly removed from democratic control. Howe's writings, for example, bristled with organicist terms such as 'lifeblood', 'arteries', and 'circulatory system' to describe integrated city planning. Transportation, gas, water and electric power were 'vital organs' of the city in his terminology.[86] The underlying tension between the goal of expert organization of urban life and the desire to expand the democratic potential of urban life by redefining the public sphere was never resolved in the Fabian or the progressive approach to reform.

Finally, the *cultural* narrative, which had enabled progressives to link reform and social ethics to a cultural awakening, ended up reinserting racialized images and themes into progressivism. The reformers were often more concerned with the cultural deviancy of immigrants than with their poverty; more focused on corrupt business practices than on the economic system that sanctioned them; and more obsessed with morals-testing than with redistributing income. They also frequently applied the rhetoric of sanitation gleaned from Europe to describe ways of dealing with immigrants and racial minorities. Progressives frequently juxtaposed American urban saloons, gambling dens and brothels with the clean and well-planned European public spaces that allowed for moral and decent recreational pursuits. They defined urban reform as a civilizing crusade and a campaign to save the fragile bourgeois family from the onslaught of immorality. Some, such as Jane Addams, identified the commercialization of urban recreation as the culprit that had led young people to confuse 'joy with lust, and gaity with debauchery'. Others, such as Albert Shaw elevated paternalistic regulation, traditional moral standards and benevolent class rule over concepts of the public sphere as a place for political self-realization through democratic participation.[87]

Black sociologist W. E. B. Du Bois's intellectual and personal journey during the Progressive Era revealed the significance of race in the transatlantic dimension of progressive social thought. Du Bois's student years in Berlin from 1892 to 1894 provided him with a theory of social ethics that had radical implications for his thinking on race and for his critique of the philosophical foundations of nineteenth-century liberalism. As a result, Du Bois rejected both Booker T. Washington's bootstrap ideology and the liberal civil-rights discourse as avenues for racial change. Instead, he favoured a historicist concept of social ethics that asserted the unfolding of the black civilizational gift through social interaction, liberal education, high culture and civic participation. Du Bois's emancipatory reading of the teachings of the German historical school of economics, however, cannot be separated from the larger dynamics of the recontextualization of European social thought in American progressivism. Leading progressives used the ideas of the historical school to advance the notion of black cultural deficiency. Du Bois's attempt to create black identity in the image of the progressive model of ethical awakening and social interaction thus clashed with white progressives' exclusion of blacks from the civilizational master narrative. In the final analysis, the discursive setting of progressivism did not allow for a profound intellectual challenge to racism. As Du Bois became increasingly aware of the ambivalence of progressive social ethics he renewed his commitment to extending civil and political rights, though historicist concepts remained prominent in Du Bois's thought.[88]

In conclusion, though a coherent progressive theory of reform never materialized, the transatlantic dimension of American reform was a crucial element in the progressives' quest to create an alternative to the liberal capitalist order. The analysis of American reform from a transatlantic perspective suggest both that progressivism was a genuinely radical attempt to overcome market capitalism and that the transatlantic dimension contributed to stabilizing the liberal social order.

In the late-nineteenth century, a number of factors came together that made American society receptive to European, and notably British, social thought and reform, among them the growing sense that the United States was lagging behind in 'social progress', the shared experience of the pitfalls of industrialization, the growing competition for world markets, the loss of faith in American institutions, the need for trained civil servants and the opportunities for transatlantic travel. Progressive reformers used these opportunities to position themselves as cultural mediators, constructing new images of Europe that posited the convergence of European and American societies, juxtaposed the corruption of America with the democratic potential of Europe and linked reform to visions of redemption through European high culture.

American progressives drew on British and European thought to pose radical challenges to the intellectual, political and socioeconomic foundations of Gilded-Age capitalism. They employed new economic, political and cultural narratives to develop a powerful critique of the epistemology, ontology and ethics of nineteenth-century liberalism. Most importantly, they spelled out a theory of social reform that viewed the market as a historical construct; regarded social interaction and political participation as the basis for value formation; and tied the progressive evolution of society to the promotion of social ethics. Upon this basis the reformers legitimated the expansion of a public sphere of control against the prerogatives of private interests. They saw the essence of democracy less in constitutional government and the protection of individual rights than in an expanded public sphere that provided new opportunities for social interaction and political participation.

Nonetheless, the institutional setting in the United States and the reformers' own intellectual inheritance circumscribed the radical potential of British- and European-inspired social reform. In the end, the broad vistas of progressivism gave way to the limited use of regulation and police power. Moreover, the same narratives that had framed the importation of radical ideas also contained elements that undermined their transformative potential. Despite the relativistic and historicist trajectory of transatlantic social thought, progressives reinscribed foundationalist concepts, sanctioned the racial divide, and embraced expert rule and administrative efficiency at the expense of democratic control.

Notes

1. The two seminal monographs on the transatlantic exchange of ideas in the Progressive Era are Daniel T. Rodgers, *Atlantic Crossings: Social Politics in a Progressive Age* (Cambridge, MA: Harvard University Press, 1998), and James T. Kloppenberg, *Uncertain Victory: Social Democracy and Progressivism in European and American Thought, 1870–1920* (New York: Oxford University Press, 1986).
2. For recent examples see Gwendolyn Mink, *The Wages of Motherhood: Inequality in the Welfare State, 1917–1942* (Ithaca: Cornell University Press, 1995); Alison M. Parker, *Purifying America: Women, Cultural Reform, and Pro-Censorship Activism, 1873–1933* (Urbana and Chicago: University of Illinois Press, 1997); David E. Bernstein, *Only One Place of Redress: African-Americans, Labor Regulations, and the Courts from Reconstruction to the New Deal* (Durham: Duke University Press, 2001); Elizabeth Lasch-Quinn, *Black Neighbors: Race and the Limits of Reform in the American Settlement House Movement, 1890–1945* (Chapel Hill: University of North Carolina Press, 1993).
3. This chapter expands on themes I develop in Axel R. Schäfer, *American Progressives and German Social Reform: Social Ethics, Moral Control, and the Regulatory State in a Transatlantic Context* (Stuttgart: Franz Steiner Verlag, 2000).
4. William T. Stead, *The Americanization of the World* (New York and London: H. Markley, 1902), p. 158, quoted in Gertrud Almy Slichter, 'European Backgrounds of American Reform, 1880–1915' (PhD diss., University of Illinois, 1960), p. 9.

5. Frank A. Vanderlip, 'Political Problems of Europe As They Interest Americans', *Scribner's Magazine*, 37 (January 1905), 1.
6. For a good discussion of the political meaning of the reformers' fight against patronage democracy see Theda Skocpol, *Protecting Soldiers and Mothers: The Political Origins of Social Policy in the United States* (Cambridge, MA: Harvard University Press, 1992), pp. 261ff. On the relationship between reformers and urban machines see ibid., pp. 96–101. On the interventionist role of nineteenth-century American government see Rodgers, *Atlantic Crossings*, p. 80; Sidney Fine, *Laissez Faire and the General-Welfare State: A Study of Conflict in American Thought, 1865–1901* (Ann Arbor: University of Michigan Press, 1956), pp. 19, 21.
7. On the development of administrative capacities see Ballard C. Campbell, *The Growth of American Government: Governance from the Cleveland Era to the Present* (Bloomington: Indiana University Press, 1995); and Stephen Skowronek, *Building a New American State: The Expansion of National Administrative Capacities, 1877–1920* (New York: Cambridge University Press, 1982).
8. Caroline A. Lloyd, *Henry Demarest Lloyd, 1847–1903: A Biography*, 2 vols. (New York and London: Putnam, 1912), II, 181, quoted in Arthur Mann, 'British Social Thought and American Reformers of the Progressive Era', *Mississippi Valley Historical Review*, 42 (March 1956), 675.
9. Henry W. Wilbur, 'Labor Laws in Europe', *Gunton's Magazine*, 22 (February 1902), 158–60, quoted in Slichter, 'European Backgrounds', p. 32.
10. Tom L. Johnson, *My Story*, ed. Elizabeth J. Hauser (New York: B. W. Huebsch, 1911), p. 302.
11. Daniel T. Rodgers has called this the emergence of a 'third frame' of Europe in American consciousness, which replaced the older imagery that juxtaposed European despotism and feudalism with enlightened republican America, and the aesthetic conception that regarded Europe as static and pre-modern, in contrast to the newness and rawness of America. See Rodgers, *Atlantic Crossings*, pp. 34–45.
12. Walter Weyl, *The New Democracy: An Essay on Certain Political and Economic Tendencies in the United States* (New York: Macmillan, 1912), p. 2, quoted in Benjamin R. Beede, 'Foreign Influences on American Progressivism', *Historian*, 45 (1983), 530.
13. See, for example, Richard T. Ely, *The Coming City* (New York: T. Y. Crowell, 1902).
14. W. D. P. Bliss, *The Encyclopedia of Social Reform* (New York: Funk and Wagnalls, 1897), p. 905.
15. For a good discussion of this aspect see Rodgers, *Atlantic Crossings*, pp. 126–30.
16. Leo S. Rowe, review of *Municipal Monopolies*, ed. Edward Bemis, in *Annals of the American Academy of Political and Social Science*, 14 (September 1899), 83.
17. Beede, 'Foreign Influences', p. 534; Rodgers, *Atlantic Crossings*, pp. 68, 163–5, 178–93.
18. Frederic C. Howe, *Confessions of a Reformer* (New York: Macmillan, 1925), pp. 8, 238.
19. Frederic C. Howe, *The City: The Hope of Democracy* (New York: Charles Scribner's Sons, 1905).
20. Frederic C. Howe, 'Municipal Ownership – The Testimony of Foreign Experience', *Annals of the American Academy of Political and Social Science*, 57 (January 1915), 205.
21. Howe, *Confessions*, p. 113.

22. See Mark Bevir, 'Welfarism, Socialism, and Religion: On T. H. Green and Others', *Review of Politics,* 55 (Fall 1993), 639–61; and Mark Bevir, 'The Labour Church Movement, 1891–1902', *Journal of British Studies,* 38 (April 1999), 217–245.

23. For a recent reassessment of urban reform as a movement toward substantive social change see Mary Corbin Sies and Christopher Silver, eds, *Social Planning: Planning the Twentieth-Century American City,* (Baltimore: Johns Hopkins University Press, 1996). See also Roy Lubove, 'The Twentieth-Century City: The Progressive as Municipal Reformer', *Mid-America,* 41 (October 1959), 207; Michael H. Frisch, 'Urban Theorists, Urban Reform, and American Political Culture in the Progressive Period', *Political Science Quarterly,* 87 (Summer 1982), 295–315; Patricia Mooney Melvin, *The Organic City: Urban Definition and Community Organization, 1880–1920* (Lexington: The University Press of Kentucky, 1987). For a good introduction to progressivism and urban reform see Arthur S. Link and Richard L. McCormick, *Progressivism* (Arlington Heights: Harlan Davidson, 1983), pp. 28–34, 78–9, 93.

24. Rodgers, *Atlantic Crossings,* p. 60; Mann, 'British Social Thought', pp. 675, 684–5.

25. See, for example, Isaac M. Rubinow, *Social Insurance: With Special Reference to American Conditions* (New York: Henry Holt, 1913); and Florence Kelley, *Modern Industry in Relation to the Family, Health, Education, Morality* (New York: Longmans, Green, 1914).

26. Rubinow, *Social Insurance,* pp. 491, 480–2, 500–1.

27. See Rodgers, *Atlantic Crossings,* pp. 63–66, 100; Kloppenberg, *Uncertain Victory,* p. 209; Mann, 'British Social Thought', p. 688; Richard T. Ely Papers Boxes 2/II and 3, (State Historical Society of Wisconsin, Madison).

28. Kloppenberg, *Uncertain Victory,* pp. 203, 205, 256, 257–8, 267.

29. These different strategies of permeation were embraced by Sidney Webb and George Bernard Shaw, respectively. See Mark Bevir, 'Fabianism, Permeation, and Independent Labour', *Historical Journal,* 39 (March 1996), 179–96.

30. For a good discussion of the marginalization of the urban professional middle classes see Marcus Graeser, 'Chicago 1880–1940: Urbanisierung ohne administrative Kompetenz?', *ZENAF Arbeits- und Forschungsberichte,* 1 (2001).

31. Mann, 'British Social Thought', p. 678.

32. Richard T. Ely, 'Plan for an American Aristocracy', unpublished mss., n.d., Folder 5 Box 8, Richard T. Ely Papers; Vida D. Scudder, 'A Protest', June 16, 1887, Vida D. Scudder Papers, quoted in Mann, 'British Social Thought', p. 683.

33. Mann, 'British Social Thought', pp. 682–3. Mann is referring to Robert A. Woods, *English Social Movements* (New York: Charles Scribner's Sons, 1894).

34. Albert Shaw, 'European Town Life', *Chautauquan,* 9 (June 1889), 520.

35. Richard T. Ely, 'Administration of the City of Berlin', *The Nation,* 34 (23 March, 1882), 245–6, and *The Nation, 34* (30 March 1882), 267–9. See also Benjamin Rader, *The Academic Mind and Reform: The Influence of Richard T. Ely in American Life* (Lexington: University of Kentucky Press, 1966), p. 1.

36. Mann, 'British Social Thought', p. 678.

37. Albert Shaw, 'Government of German Cities', *The Century,* 48 (June 1894), 297–8.

38. Frederic C. Howe, *Socialized Germany* (New York: Charles Scribner's Sons, 1916), p. 300.

39. Kloppenberg, *Uncertain Victory,* p. 3.

40. Rodgers, *Atlantic Crossings*, esp. ch. 3. On the intellectual sea-change see also Dorothy Ross, *Modernist Impulses in the Human Sciences* (Baltimore: Johns Hopkins University Press, 1994); Peter Conn, *The Divided Mind: Ideology and Imagination in America, 1898–1917* (New York: Cambridge University Press, 1983); H. Stuart Hughes, *Consciousness and Society: The Reorientation of European Social Thought, 1890–1930* (New York: Knopf, 1958); Morton White, *Social Thought in America: The Revolt against Formalism* (New York: Viking Press, 1949); Melvyn Stokes, 'Progressivism, Poststructuralism, and the Writing of American History', in David K. Adams and Cornelis A. van Minnen, eds, *Religious and Secular Reform in America: Ideas, Beliefs, and Social Change* (Edinburgh: Edinburgh University Press, 1999), pp. 205–29; Kloppenberg, *Uncertain Victory*.
41. Henry C. Adams, 'The Outlook of a Political Economist', typescript, 1900, p. 9, Address File, Box 25, Henry C. Adams Papers (Bentley Historical Library, University of Michigan, Ann Arbor).
42. Rodgers, *Atlantic Crossings*, pp. 140–1, 180; Schäfer, *American Progressives and German Reform*, esp. ch. 1.
43. For useful discussions of the ideas of the historical school of economics, see Thorstein Veblen, 'Gustav Schmoller's Economics', in *The Place of Science in Modern Civilization and Other Essays* (1901; New York: Viking Press, 1932), pp. 259, 264–5; Jurgen Herbst, *The German Historical School in American Scholarship: A Study in the Transfer of Culture* (Ithaca: Cornell University Press, 1965), pp. 132–9; Fine, *Laissez Faire*, pp. 198–200.
44. On the link between the market and morality in nineteenth-century thought see Christopher Lasch, *The True and Only Heaven: Progress and Its Critics* (New York: W. W. Norton, 1991), p. 487. The novels by William Dean Howells that address the divergence include *A Hazard of New Fortunes* (1890; New York: Bantam Books, 1960) and *The Rise of Silas Lapham* (1885; New York: Random House, 1951). See also *Atlantic Crossings*, pp. 77–80.
45. Edward A. Ross, *Sin and Society: An Analysis of Latter-Day Iniquity* (Boston: Houghton Mifflin, 1907), pp. 9–10, 13, 16.
46. Charles Gillespie, 'The Darwinian Heritage', in Norman F. Cantor and Michael S. Werthman, eds, *The Making of the Modern World: 1815–1914* (New York: Thomas Y. Crowell, 1967), p. 91.
47. See Simon N. Patten, *The New Basis of Civilization* (New York: Macmillan, 1907); Thorstein Veblen, 'The Preconceptions of Economic Science', in Wesley C. Mitchell, ed., *What Veblen Taught: Selected Writings of Thorstein Veblen* (New York: Viking, 1936), pp. 39–150; John Dewey and James Tufts, *Ethics* (New York: Henry Holt, 1908).
48. Dewey and Tufts, *Ethics*, p. 474.
49. Hans Joas, *Die Entstehung der Werte* (Frankfurt: Suhrkamp, 1997), p. 184.
50. Dewey and Tufts, *Ethics*, pp. 439, 481.
51. W. E. B. Du Bois, *Darkwater. Voices from Within the Veil* (1920; New York: AMS Press, 1969), pp. 144, 158–9.
52. Dewey and Tufts, *Ethics*, pp. 446, 485.
53. See Kloppenberg, *Uncertain Victory*, pp. 241–5.
54. Eduard Bernstein, 'Evolutionary Socialism – Ultimate Aim and Tendency', in Rosa Luxemburg, *Reform and Revolution* (1909; New York: Pathfinder Press, 1970), pp. 69, 72.
55. See Fine, *Laissez Faire*, pp. 211, 374; Kloppenberg, *Uncertain Victory*, p. 199; Dorothy Ross, 'Socialism and American Liberalism: Academic Sosial Thought in the 1880s', *Perspectives in American History*, (1977–78)', p. 11.

56. Leo S. Rowe, 'American Political Ideas and Institutions in Their Relations to the Problem of City Government', *Proceedings of the Louisville Conference for Good City Government and the Third Annual Meeting of the National Municipal League* (1897), 76, 80–1, 88.

57. Frederic C. Howe, 'The City as a Socializing Agency. The Physical Basis of the City: The City Plan', *American Journal of Sociology*, 17 (March 1912), 596. On Camillo Sitte see Brian Ladd, *Urban Planning and Civic Order in Germany, 1860–1914* (Cambridge, MA: Harvard University Press, 1990), pp. 120, 127–36; see also Carl Schorske, *Fin-de-Siècle Vienna: Politics and Culture* (New York: Knopf, 1981), pp. 24–5, 62–72.

58. On the link between art and morals in progressive thought see, for example, Jane Addams, 'Youth in the City', in Richard L. Rapson, ed., *The Cult of Youth in Middle-Class America* (Lexington: D. C. Heath, 1971), p. 45; see also Jane Addams, 'Problems of Municipal Administration', in *Congress of Arts and Sciences, Universal Exposition, St. Louis, 1904*, vol. 7, ed. Howard J. Rogers (Boston: Hougton Mifflin, 1906), pp. 434–50.

59. Frederic C. Howe, 'The Remaking of the American City', *Harper's Monthly*, 127 (July 1913), 186.

60. Kloppenberg, *Uncertain Victory*, p. 11.

61. For a good discussion of the institutional limitations on reform see David Brian Robertson, 'The Bias of American Federalism: The Limits of Welfare State Development in the Progressive Era', *Journal of Policy History*, 1 (1989), 272; see also Skocpol, *Protecting Soldiers and Mothers*.

62. Edward Berkowitz and Kim McQuaid, *Creating the Welfare State: The Political Economy of Twentieth-Century Reform* (Lawrence: University Press of Kansas, 1992), pp. x, 4–5, 35, 39.

63. Lawrence Veiller, 'Housing Reform through Legislation', *Annals of the American Academy of Political and Social Science*, 51 (January 1914), 68, 75–6; Lawrence Veiller, *Housing Reform: A Hand-Book for Practical Use in American Cities* (New York: Russell Sage Foundation, 1910), p. 6. See also Roy Lubove, *The Progressives and the Slums: Tenement House Reform in New York City, 1890–1917* (Pittsburgh: University of Pittsburgh Press, 1962), pp. 129ff.

64. Theda Skocpol uses this term in the context of insurance reform. Skocpol, *Protecting Soldiers and Mothers*, p. 260. For a good discussion of the impact of judicial opposition on progressivism see pp. 254–61.

65. Slichter, 'European Backgrounds', p. 179; Anthony Sutcliffe, *Towards the Planned City: Germany, Britain, the United States and France, 1780–1914* (Oxford: Basil Blackwell, 1981), p. 115.

66. Ernst Freund, remarks, *Proceedings of the Third Conference on City Planning* (1911), 246–8.

67. Ernst Freund, *The Police Power: Public Policy and Constitutional Rights* (Chicago: Callaghan & Co., 1904), pp. iii–iv; see also Seymour I. Toll, *Zoned American* (New York: Grossman Publishers, 1969), p. 138.

68. Rodgers, *Atlantic Crossings*, pp. 131, 152.

69. Slichter, 'European Backgrounds', p. 219.

70. Newton D. Baker, 'Municipal Ownership', *Annals of the American Academy of Political and Social Science*, 57 (January 1915), 191.

71. Rodgers, *Atlantic Crossings*, pp. 149–51.

72. Walter Lippmann, 'On Municipal Socialism, 1913: An Analysis of Problems and Strategies', in Bruce M. Stave, ed., *Socialism and the Cities* (Port Washington: Kennikat Press, 1975), p. 192.

73. David M. Kennedy, *Over Here: The First World War and American Society* (New York: Oxford University Press, 1980), p. 42.

74. Rubinow, *Social Insurance*, p. 283; see also J. Joseph Huthmacher, 'Urban Liberalism in the Age of Reform', *Mississippi Valley Historical Review*, 49 (September 1962), 231–41.

75. Roy Lubove, *The Struggle for Social Security, 1900–1935* (Cambridge, MA: Harvard University Press, 1968), p. 115, see also pp. 168–70; Isaac M. Rubinow, *The Quest for Security* (New York: Henry Holt, 1934), p. 213.

76. Alexander Lambert to John B. Andrews, May 3, 1920, AALL Papers, quoted in Ronald L. Numbers, *Almost Persuaded: American Physicians and Compulsory Health Insurance, 1912–1920* (Baltimore: Johns Hopkins University Press, 1978), p. 105.

77. National Industrial Conference Board, 'Sickness Insurance or Sickness Prevention', *Research Report*, 6 (March 1918), 22. On the popularity of workmen's compensation laws in business circles see Berkowitz and McQuaid, *Creating the Welfare State*, p. 43; Gaston Rimlinger, *Welfare Policy and Industrialization in Europe, America, and Russia* (New York: Wiley, 1971), p. 120; Lubove, *Struggle for Social Security*, p. 57.

78. Clarke Chambers, *Seedtime of Reform: American Social Service and Social Action, 1918–1933* (Minneapolis: University of Minnesota Press, 1963), p. 156; Hugh Heclo, 'Toward A New Welfare State?', in Peter Flora and Arnold J. Heidenheimer, eds, *The Development of Welfare States in Europe and America, 1850–1950* (New Brunswick: Transaction Books, 1981), p. 285.

79. *Report of the Health Insurance Commission of the State of Illinois* (Springfield: Illinois State Journal Co., 1919), pp. 165, 167.

80. As Mary O. Furner put it, progressive social scientists, '[i]n order to survive professionally', retreated to the security of technical expertise, elitist language and scientific claims to objectivity. They repressed partisanship and left ethical considerations by the wayside. Furner, *Advocacy and Objectivity: A Crisis in the Professionalization of American Social Science, 1865–1905* (Lexington: University Press of Kentucky, 1975), p. 7. On the long-term political implications of this shift see, for example, Alice O'Connor, *Poverty Knowledge: Social Science, Social Policy, and the Poor in Twentieth-Century U.S. History* (Princeton: Princeton University Press, 2001).

81. See Roscoe C. Hinkle and Gisela J. Hinkle, *The Development of Modern Sociology* (New York: Random House, 1954), p. 7; see also Geoffrey Blodgett and Daniel Walker Howe, *Victorian America* (Philadelphia: University of Pennsylvania Press, 1976).

82. Simon N. Patten, for example, maintains that through social reform and the elimination of fear, the 'fruits in security and welfare' would become apparent. He also declares, however, that the new *zoon politicon* would be 'a vigorous, self-reliant, aggressive, and often dominating man'. Simon N. Patten to Frank A. Manny, October 23, 1905, Box 1, Correspondence Folder, Frank A. Manny Papers (Bentley Historical Library, University of Michigan, Ann Arbor).

83. For a more detailed discussion of gender and progressivism see Linda Gordon, ed., *Women, the State, and Welfare* (Madison: University of Wisconsin Press, 1990).

84. Howe, *Confessions*, pp. 14, 180.

85. Howe, *Socialized Germany*, p. 265.

86. Howe, 'City as Socializing Agency', p. 594.
87. Addams, 'The Spirit of Youth', p. 41; Albert Shaw, *Municipal Government in Continental Europe* (New York: The Century Co, 1895), p. 301.
88. See Axel R. Schäfer, 'W. E. B. Du Bois, German Social Thought, and the Racial Divide in American Progressivism, 1892–1909', *Journal of American History*, 87 (2001), 925–49.

6
Getting *Your Money's Worth*: American Models for the Remaking of the Consumer Interest in Britain, 1930s–1960s[1]

Christopher Beauchamp

> We were attempting a feat never before performed in public, that of
> bowing simultaneously to Tom Paine and Adam Smith. (Paul Fletcher,
> 'When We Were Very Young')[2]

In 1958 the *Sunday Graphic* trembled with anticipation at the 'quiet but
major revolution ... happening in British shopping. The customers –
already a hundred thousand families of them [meaning the subscribers of
Which?] – are beginning to hit back.' The development of modern consumerism in Britain is indelibly associated with the 'consumer revolution'
in the late 1950s and 1960s, coinciding with the advent of the affluent
society.[3] Within a decade of its onset, the institutions of a consumer movement were in place: regular columns in newspapers, local consumers'
groups, and specialized research organizations. At the centre of the story
was the Consumers' Association (CA), founded in 1957. Energetic and
vocal, the Association was hoisted onto the shoulders of an enthusiastic
press and rapidly acquired subscribers for its product-testing and consumer
advice magazine, *Which?*. The impact of this one organization came to
stand for the novelty of the mobilized consumer; and the Association did
much to write the narrative of an emerging consumer consciousness.[4] The
orthodox founding-myth of the new consumer movement took Britain's
postwar affluence as its Genesis: with the expansion of home-ownership
and the diffusion of household consumer durable goods after 1953, consumers were confronted by a 'benevolent flood' of unfamiliar new products, competing brands and aggressive marketing. Sheer uncertainty,
accompanied by the possibility that vendors would exploit their ignorance,
drove shoppers into collective action and elevated consumer protection to
the political mainstream.[5]

Along with most luminaries of the new consumerism, the CA claimed no
continuity with earlier traditions of consumer politics from within Britain.
Looking for the ancestor of the Association, they identified 'the immediate,
obvious origin of the first consumer organisation – the publication of *Your*

Money's Worth by Chase and Schlink in 1927', moving on the face of the waters.[6] This book was the work of an American economist, Stuart Chase, and a mechanical engineer from the American Standards Association, Frederick J. Schlink.[7] It laid bare the vulnerability of the individual before the variety of mass-produced goods, unable to judge value accurately and thus at the mercy of corporations and advertisers: 'to talk of his bargaining power is to talk about a non-alcoholic America. There is no such thing.'[8] *Your Money's Worth* was a bestseller, reportedly the volume most often stolen from public libraries. From this base Schlink launched a subscriber-funded comparative-testing organization, Consumers' Research Incorporated, which reported on competing products' quality and value and sought particularly to prick the bubble of inflated advertising claims. In choosing this heritage, the consumer movement of *Which?* acknowledged the inspiration for its own testing and publishing form. But it also chose to attach its brand of activism to a particular tradition of thinking about the consumer interest – a tradition of consumer protection based on fair dealing for the shopper, value for money, and the information necessary to evaluate quality and match wants to products.

The assertion of consumers' rights in the marketplace and the importance of the consumer in political economy were not new. In Victorian and Edwardian Britain the thick mesh of radical and liberal attachments to free trade had kept consumers and the sanctity of the 'cheap loaf' central to political economy. The Co-operative Movement, with its mass customer-membership, a campaigning women's organization and a parliamentary party affiliated to Labour after 1917, stood for the organized working-class consumer. Thus, the self-styled revolution after World War II did not invent the consumer interest so much as redefine the needs of the consumer around a politics of 'consumer protection': it installed the rational, informed, individual shopper at the heart of a set of practices intended to represent, advise and protect her in the world of goods.

The tradition of consumer protection in the postwar decades, with its accent on choice, value for money and private exchange, its concern with informative advertising, labelling and manufacturing quality, provides a contrast with the tenor of earlier perspectives on consumer politics. In various traditions of radical political economy, the moral and economic characteristics of consumption were inseparable: whether in the free civil society invoked by free trade, or in the romantic socialism of William Morris and J. A. Hobson who saw a craft economy as the way to aesthetically and morally elevated consumption as well as humanized production. The 'cooperative commonwealth' offered a socially responsible collectivism and located consumer power within a critique of competitive capitalism.[9]

The eclipse of these earlier traditions by that of consumer protection involved a recasting of the situation of the consumer and the public benefits of empowering the consuming public in particular ways. This disjunction can be mapped onto a shift from the politics of scarcity and necessity to the preoccupations of abundance, in accordance with the CA's narrative of a 'benevolent flood'. Nonetheless, while the chronology of affluence suits some aspects of the consumer revolution, especially the success of *Which?* as a publishing phenomenon, the distinctive and programmatic tradition of consumer protection had itself begun to emerge before the war. The CA's narrative ignores the earlier roots of the tradition of consumer protection with its belief in the asymmetry of buyer and seller, the helplessness of the purchaser before the resources of organized production, and so the significance of consumer power as a problem of organization, representation and collective action. In its earlier guises, moreover, the tradition of consumer protection appears as a genuine reform tradition, embodying an impulse to balance or decentralize power in modern capitalism, and a challenge to the ideal of a free competitive market in which the consumer is sovereign.

'The dark side of the moon': Planners discover the consumer

In the mid-1930s the research group Political and Economic Planning (PEP) championed American models of consumer organization, and thus became the first group in Britain to conceive of consumer protection in the terms that would later delineate the field: quality standards, comparative testing and information. In several editions of its journal and in the meetings of its various committees, PEP reported, assessed and adapted American developments to reformulate consumer questions and open a bridgehead of research. Direct links run from PEP to the consumer revolution, not least through its wartime Director, the later founder of the CA, Michael Young. PEP itself, however, chose not to establish a product-testing service because of legal worries about 'slander of goods'. The reflections of the planners exhibit the emergence of the tradition of consumer protection as far back as the inter-war period, and thereby show how this tradition derived from broader thinking about an administered economy.

America's New Deal was a testing-ground for consumer politics even at the time of PEP. If the consumer in America was the 'most sought after, most flirted with debutante of 1934', her suitors were making quite different propositions informed by various traditions.[10] One was a tradition of activism of Schlink's Consumers' Research (CR), infused by the 'mobilization culture' of the decade. The formal organization of CR made it a centre of gravity for thinking about consumption in the early 1930s; hence the enduring appeal of *Your Money's Worth* as a point of origin. Yet CR's activism created tensions. At first a lot of progressives and radicals were drawn into its orbit, but later a split formed between those whose concern was with the scientific evaluation of consumer goods alone and those who favoured campaigning and were concerned with the conditions of the labour that made the products. The latter formed Consumers Union in 1936, which carried on product testing but gave itself more leeway in social campaigning and solidarity with labour. The Consumers Union, which soon surpassed CR to become the leading consumer organization, sustained the testing type: although, unlike CR, it was openly progressive in sympathy, it entrenched an advice-based consumerism, which, as the publisher of *Consumer Reports*, it continues to practise.[11]

A second tradition was redistributive. An alliance of working-class leaders, consumer activists, administrators and liberal economists forged a powerful appeal based on mass purchasing power. Given their chance by an 'underconsumption' analysis of Depression and the prospect of economic recovery through boosted domestic demand, they prosecuted a campaign for consumer mobilization from within the Roosevelt administration and the New Deal agencies.[12] In doing so, they relied on the elevation of the consumer within the New Deal's transformation of state power. Organs such as the National Recovery Administration (NRA) and Agricultural Adjustment Administration (AAA) had formal consumer representatives as a 'countervailing power'.[13] More generally, the elevation of the consumer identified the 'consumer interest' as the best expression of the 'public interest' and as the solemn charge of government, and hence as able to provide legitimacy to the expansion of federal authority. Although the consumer representatives struggled to influence the course of actual policy within the NRA or the AAA, they wasted no time in using their pulpit to assert the overriding, universal claim of the constituency for which they stood.[14] The American case revealed different visions of the consumer, jostling for influence in a context where their separate objectives were not always distinct or distinguished from each other. From across the Atlantic, it 'revealed the consumer problem' only in general terms, leaving its British interpreters to announce just what was at stake.

In Britain, as in America, the theme of an organized consumer interest resonated most where the wholesale re-orientation of the economy was at stake. In the 1930s planning constituted the axis around which thinking about economic change revolved, with industrial concentration and the perceived dysfunction of competition being the dilemmas that competing proposals sought to address through the vision of a stabilized, planned economy.[15] PEP was one group promoting a planned economy. It consisted of an assemblage of journalists, civil servants, economists, academics and others, describing themselves as 'those on whose service technical civilisation depends – the administrators, the managers, the engineers, scientists, teachers and technicians'.[16] They came together from March 1931 with the intention of drafting a capitalist plan of national reconstruction as the basis for a 'Planning Party' and ultimately a 'planned society'.[17] This project guided PEP's early years, though from the mid 1930s it settled on the role of an independent research institute providing a technocratic and empirical slant.[18]

PEP's main concerns, which it found echoed in American consumer politics, were change in economic and government structures, as expressed in Britain through the planning debate, and the administrative use of economic knowledge, especially the relatively untouched field of research into the consumer and consumer economy. Above all, PEP's sense of the political need for a new consumer order came from the obsolescence of free trade, abandoned in 1931 for external tariffs and state reorganization of domestic agriculture. The shifting plates of political economy in the inter-war period, particularly seismic rumblings around the nation's food provision, underlay the planners' thinking about the democratic implications of an administered economy. The tradition of free trade in Victorian and Edwardian times represented both an ideal of civil society in liberal and radical thought, and a guarantee for consumers against state domination, high prices and hunger. By ruling out producer tariffs, it promised a political economy immunized against the organized power of production. The consumer, in this order, was doubly sovereign: individually free from exploitation in the marketplace; and collectively, as the consuming public embodied the public interest. As Trentmann remarks, 'the political nation was defined as a nation of consumers, represented in Parliament.'[19] During and after World War I, however, economic liberalism came to be identified with corporate monopoly, and free trade was supplanted in popular politics by growing demands for state control, protection against trusts, and the support of health and nutritional standards.[20]

PEP defined its agenda for the consumer against the older tradition of free trade:

> We must give up supposing ... that we can help the consumer by repeating parrot-like the catchwords of an economic phase which for good or ill is rapidly passing away ... The consumer found in competitive free trade during the nineteenth century a nice labour-saving device which protected some of his main interests without much action on his part. Now that this device is ceasing to operate it must be improved upon or the consumer will suffer.[21]

The intellectual shift from the free-trade vision of an automatic balancing of interests to one of the positive representation of forces was crucial to PEP's position. As in the New Deal, it implied the state recognizing, and awkwardly sponsoring, a formal consumer interest.

In the inter-war period, Britain experienced consumerist issues – and there is a clear link here to the tradition of free trade – through the politics of food, where popular antipathy towards profiteering, trusts and combines mingled with widespread economic denunciations of the waste inherent in an unplanned distributive system. From 1918 to 1920 an advisory Consumers' Council, drawn largely from the cooperative, women's and labour movements and reporting to the Ministry of Food, framed demands for greater economic controls.[22] This pressure continued for the rest of the inter-war period. A series of government initiatives tried unconvincingly to give institutional form to the consumer interest. All kept the food issue firmly centred on the analysis of chains of production and retailing. From 1925 a Food Council raked through information on the productive and distributive food trades to look for 'excessive' margins; despite publicity, however, it remained a departmental advisory body on the margins of policy. The public scrutiny of whole chains of food provision reached its height in 1929–31. August 1929 saw a political storm over the price of milk in London, where the United Dairies combine held sway. In 1930 and 1931 the Labour government introduced unsuccessful Consumers' Council Bills, proposing another powerful investigative body with a hugely ambitious remit of investigation into raw materials, locally varying farm prices, industrial wage structures – in fact, the entire economy.[23] The incoming Conservative-dominated National Government in 1931 re-badged the Food Council as a formal, and clearly defensive, part of its agricultural marketing schemes, hoping to

> give the public a feeling of reassurance in that there is a body especially constituted to look after their interests as consumers ... it will give to producers and their marketing boards a measure of protection from the type of attack that today is frequently aimed at the distributive interests.[24]

The bureaucratic representation of a consumer interest thus became a practical reality, if not a success story. While sceptical about its achievements, PEP hailed the consumer appendage to agricultural marketing along with the New Deal consumer agencies as a sign of the new relationship between states and consumers in the reorganized economy.[25]

In holding this outlook, PEP lay within a broader tradition of economic reform politics. However, with American examples before it, the group now began to pull together an idea of consumer protection couched in terms of its distinctive preoccupations with industrial management from the 'consumer end' and the importance of information. The group's version of planning was particularly aware of the end user. Within PEP, the Industry Working Group adopted the principle that industrial problems could be advantageously approached from 'the consumer end'. This principle gained much of its weight within the working group from the advocacy of Israel Sieff, joint Managing Director and Vice Chairman of Marks and Spencer. Sieff preached the retailer's responsiveness to demand, along with vertical integration, and thus introduced the consumer as the ultimate arbiter of her own needs; and he could back his position with the phenomenal success of his firm's vertically integrated processes. [26]

The counterpart to responsive production and distribution was a discriminating public. PEP thus stressed the allocative efficiency or 'social value' of the properly educated consumer:

> The theoretical case for helping the consumer is unassailable: the more you increase the consumer's knowledge of alternatives and his powers of judgement, the more satisfaction he gets as a result of a given amount of income, and the greater is the number of wants which the productive system will be adapted to satisfying. In short, society will get better value for less effort.[27]

Testimony of the waste already rampant in distribution stung PEP. A radio manufacturer attending one meeting as an observer attested to the lack of price transparency, speaking of a 'margin of ignorance' – the margin by which supposedly competitive products could differ in actual value – of 25 per cent by the time a wireless reached its buyer.[28] And consumer culture showed itself to be disordered in other ways. 'Mass suggestion' ranked alongside ignorance of alternatives in impeding rational choice; a new more forceful advertising had put the purchaser, previously the active party choosing from the sellers' offerings, 'on the defensive ... his choices are more and more the consequences of chance and less and less those of his considered judgement.'[29] Excessive influence was wielded 'by the mentality and tastes of the salesman'.[30] The idea that advertising constituted yet more waste in the distributive system and created 'anarchic irresponsibility' among the buying public went back to the nineteenth century, and was being applied, for example, by the Fabians in the 1920s.[31] But unlike the Fabians, PEP pursued the potential of consumer choice, with Schlink's Consumers' Research providing it with the means of doing so. While the British planners' critique of advertising was much less fiery, they espoused the methods of the American consumer activists as the most promising means to access the social value of informed consumers, who would discipline the economy from the demand side.

It was no coincidence that information and research were at the centre of this project, nor that Britain's servitors of 'technical civilization' should discover an affinity for the American consumer movement. PEP's sense of 'discovering' the consumer anew sprang not from her absence from politics, but from the potential for formal research to define her needs and her place in the economy. According to the Secretary of its Research Group, F. R. Cowell, 'Hitherto the consumer, rather like the side of the moon unseen by human sight, has existed in political economy on presumptive rather than on empirical evidence.'[32] It now seemed that social and economic knowledge, 'in common with the design of goods, has so far been dominated by a producer's rather than a consumer's point of view'.[33] PEP sought to map out (and hence make amenable to planning) the situation of consumers in the world of information, choice and products, and as themselves objects of technical knowledge.

It is this positivist, scientific approach that ties PEP most closely to Consumers' Research in the United States. Lawrence Glickman has characterized Consumers' Research as the seedbed of 'technocratic individualist' consumer advocacy: expert, concerned with efficiency, based on product testing and 'truth in advertising', conceiving consumer power as the shopper's emancipation from the asymmetry of information, rather than as an organized front for attacking capitalist structures or pursuing social aims.[34] Notably, PEP's survey of the organization took place before disgruntled progressives reacted against the narrow ambitions of Schlink's model and decamped to form Consumers Union. Other kinds of expertise also resonated with the planners. On the staff of the New Deal's consumer boards, social scientists not only came together in common cause but intermingled their technical specialisms. Among the most important figures, the sociologist of *Middletown*, Robert Lynd, brought a critical view of consumer culture to the table, the labour statistician Paul Douglas his work on working-class purchasing power, and the economist Gardiner C. Means an analysis of corporate power and price-setting by the fiat of large-scale capitalism.[35] The New Deal's consumer boards also embraced a quality standards agenda entirely in keeping with the Chase and Schlink tradition of disdaining the package and looking scientifically inside the tin.

PEP stood shoulder to shoulder with this technical way of locating the consumer interest. Its Research Group did most to drive a specifically consumer agenda within the organization.[36] Particularly involved, and again linking PEP's version of the consumer with the politics of food, was the biologist and nutritionist Julian Huxley.[37] Contributors to *Planning* saw both quality standards and spending data as barren territory. In the apparent absence of substantial formal economic knowledge about either the individual consumer or the structure of demand the Research Group did its best to stimulate an effort, including lobbying the Ministry of Labour to gather more detailed household budgeting data.[38] Information professionals thus directed the new constructions: of consumers in sociology and the administrator's lexicon, and of their goods in science between the technician's callipers. Henceforth research was to be the flywheel of the consumer movement. The inter-war years had posed the consumer problem anew, in terms of power and protection, the visible hands of corporation and state. PEP's response was as yet one among many, but the question had been asked: 'How can one put knowledge at the disposal of the ordinary consumer?'[39]

1945–51: consumer protection and the shape of things to come

The tradition of consumer protection emphasis that defined the legitimate remit and the chosen instruments of both activists and government by the end of the 1950s ploughed a clear and careful furrow. It ran through a diffuse but stable group of policies relating to the marketplace, from advertising to quality labels to anti-competitive business activity. It defined itself by distinctions: not only did it mark off a set of identifiably 'consumer' issues; it also privileged the independence of the consumer's representatives. These developments are typically traced to the later 1950s, the affluent consumer consciousness partly released and partly invented by the assertiveness of *Which?* and in due course anointed by the government in the Molony Committee on Consumer Protection (1959–62).[40] Certainly the 'benevolent flood' of consumer goods provided much of the impetus, but other factors in the making of this kind of consumer interest had already fallen into place before the deluge. They drew on a number of developments that had far more to do with the 1940s than with the 1950s: the possibilities opened up by the wartime development of the state; an emerging strain of thought within the Labour Party prompted particularly by a critique of the nationalized industries; and party political confrontation amid debates over Britain's emergence from austerity.

These themes came together when the Labour government in its brief second term (February 1950 to October 1951) drew up a programme of consumer protection. Prompted by Michael Young, who had moved from the wartime directorship of PEP to become research director of the Labour Party in 1945, the agenda consisted of a consumers' advice service based on American product-testing organizations, legislation on restrictive trade practices, hire-purchase and false description, and measures on quality standards. While choked off by political events, the programme is an important hinge for the tradition of thinking about the consumer that this chapter considers. It delineated a field of consumer affairs around information and protection in the marketplace. And, in struggling to establish itself within Labour thinking, consumer protection challenged traditions that resisted the separation of producer and consumer interests.

War and austerity drew government attention to the conditions under which goods were supplied. Existing legislation on trading practices took on a new significance in the light of controls, especially as mis-selling or short measures compounded rationing. The Utility Goods Schemes were introduced to classify products for purchase tax exemption, but in setting design specifications the Utility mark became a *de facto* quality standard in clothing, footwear and furniture.[41] The nationalization of energy and transport industries committed the government – and the Labour Party specifically – to an additional set of relationships with the consuming household. Rapidly growing housewives' organizations in the later 1940s engaged with and participated in the government's management of scarcity.[42] All these channels of state obligation had been called into being, but how would they be represented?

Between 1945 and 1950 the Labour government framed the consumer interest collectively and saw its expression in effective public control of the economy. Rationing, subsidies and price controls were maintained as part of a policy of 'fair shares'.[43] Efficiency in production and distribution alone held the promise of lower prices. Thus in party pamphlets the first few promises under a consumer heading would concern supply: fruit and vegetable distribution, meat wholesaling, the sugar monopoly, and so on.[44] The cabinet set up a Distribution and Marketing Committee in 1950 to coordinate these efforts in a way that continued the inter-war tendency to interrogate the distributive system, looking for waste or exploitative middlemen.[45]

The design of the nationalized industries also subsumed the consumer interest within public control. On their conversion into public corporations, the coal, gas and electricity industries had all been issued with consumers' councils, but the government never used these councils as more than totems of a countervailing power. Ministers cleaved to the principle of autonomous managing boards, effectively a unicameral constitution for the industries. The boards were believed to be capable of dissolving competing claims to the public interest – for example, those of workers against consumers – in the win-win gains of improved efficiency.[46] A typical rejoinder to any doubts voiced was to ask 'How can an organisation which is running an industry for the public interest exploit anybody?'[47] The pre-nationalization model of price tribunals overseeing public utilities was unceremoniously swept away, to the spluttering horror of some observers.[48] Where in Labour's approach, asked the senior civil servant at the Board of Trade, was the 'feeling of moral obligation to safeguard the consumer'?[49] These sentiments appeared to be vindicated when price rises in the nationalized industries, especially during the winter fuel crisis of 1947, eroded the consumers' councils' standing as servants of the public. The councils were impotent on price decisions and usually revealed as the creatures of the managing boards, 'tak[ing] up cudgels on the Boards' behalf' in disputes with other nationalized industries.[50] They cringed from publicity, on the grounds that they 'must be careful not to encourage widespread complaints for which no remedy may exist'; accordingly, the press were generally excluded from meetings.[51] Thus, while the government had not seen the need for a credible consumer watchdog, others did. From around 1950 a clamour arose, much of it from Labour parliamentarians and commentators, damning the councils as creatures of the producer interest, and seeking more decentralized, democratically engaged, genuinely influential consumer representation.[52] Despite such condemnation, however, the councils slunk onwards unreformed, protected by departmental condescension.[53]

Michael Young had already begun to provide a counterpoint to Labour policy from within the party's research department. Reacting to the nationalization model, his 1948 pamphlet *Small Man, Big World* tried to initiate a discussion of the tension between the large scale of organization sought for efficiency and the direct community relations needed for participation.[54]

Young drew on PEP's work on citizenship and participation, conducted under his directorship during the war.[55] Also from PEP came the idea of an independent consumer advice service, which Young had 'managed to smuggle in' to the 1950 election manifesto.[56] Just as PEP's appropriation of the Consumers' Research model in the 1930s had differentiated them from the Fabians' dissolution of consumer control into planning and socialized ownership, so in the postwar period Young's consumer agenda stood somewhat apart from Labour's collectivist approach.

The political opportunity for consumer protection came after the February 1950 general election, as Conservative gains prompted anxiety in the Labour cabinet about the opposition party's consumer appeal. Harold Wilson, then President of the Board of Trade, did most to formulate the problem and the response. Presenting a paper to senior ministers on 'The State and Private Industry' he pressed home the importance of stabilizing the party's version of the mixed economy:

> it is pretty clear that at the last election a good number of those who voted against us (whether they voted for us or abstained in 1945), were voting as consumers, and were expressing their (albeit wrong-headed) view about the cost of living, and the performance of the nationalised industries. Apart from housing, the Conservative Party will presumably base their main appeal once more on questions affecting the consumer, and there is every danger that once again many electors will vote against us because they regard their gains as *producers* (full employment, high wages, better working conditions, higher shop or firm incomes etc.) as being not due to the Labour Government, but to act of God, or to their own merit, while the responsibility for their *consumer* troubles they are ready to lay at the Government's door. By being vigorous in protecting the consumer, both against public and private industry, we can help to redress this electoral balance.[57]

Suddenly and shockingly, Labour's heritage as 'a party of producers' now looked like a potential liability; it would have to reinvent itself without delay and 'come forward as the party of the consumer'.[58] Wilson's memorandum proposed a Consumers' Charter involving a range of protective legislation and Young's consumers' advice centre. These lines converged only at the horizon: apart from the consumer as the ultimate object of policy, they had little in common. Their promise from a political point of view was a connection with the evidently disgruntled shopping voter, a distinct and immediate appeal to the consuming sensibility. The consumer critique of the nationalized industries was a clear point of reference, with action against restrictive trade practices and monopoly set to be the prime weapon for deflecting criticism back onto private industry.[59] 'The State and Private Industry' was quite well received by Labour ministers. A meeting of junior ministers debated the details but concurred on the consumer emphasis. The Prime Minister felt it would help define 'the shape of things to come'.[60]

Throughout the period discussed in this chapter, from the preoccupations of PEP in the 1930s to the methods of the Consumers' Association in the 1950s, information was the preferred instrument of representatives of the tradition of consumer-protection. The 1950 episode was symptomatic. The consumer advisory service proposal was a belated attempt by Labour to reconfigure its approach to consumers, instigated under electoral pressure. But it fitted into a model of public relations close to Labour's heart, and rode the tide of economic information that swelled out of the wartime state. The exchange of information between the state, economy and people had mushroomed during World War II. Many of those services were consumption-related, such as the Ministry of Food's weekly 'Food Facts' bulletin. Public economic information was particularly important to the Attlee government, for some ministers – including Herbert Morrison, who chaired the propaganda committee – the cornerstone of government public relations.[61] The Treasury's Women's Organizations Committee on Economic Information held conferences, provided speakers for meetings of the various housewives' groups, and until 1952 published the monthly 'Talking Points' and 'Report to Women'. It was chaired by Eirlys Cullen, who was to become the first editor of *Which?*.[62] It was out of these earlier intersections of economic affairs, government information, public relations and publishing that several prominent consumer activists of later years emerged.

The Attlee years were more formative for consumer protection than the plan for a Consumers' Charter ever was for Labour. Consumer protection came as a promising political sideline out of the tangle of issues around austerity and consumption in the early postwar period, but was cut short by political events. Labour itself killed the consumer advice service proposal in early 1951. With the pressure of defence spending rising in January, the Chancellor wrote to the Prime Minister growling about the service's potential cost, and it was shelved.[63] The government fell that year before the other elements saw the light of day, though the legislation drafted on hire purchase and merchandise marks reached the statute books under the Conservatives shortly afterwards. The consumer protection agenda moved out of government departments and the cabinet room for the next few years, onto the Opposition back benches and, more importantly, into the pages of newspapers, where it took the form of exposés like 'They Fleece You With Phoney Labels!'.[64] Yet the 1940s had ingrained particular relationships of responsibility and engagement between consumers and the state, and it was this that grounded the rationale for strengthening consumer protection in quality standards and the regulation of trading practices. Austerity and scarcity pushed the woman with the shopping basket to the political front line. And in this context, a developing tradition of consumer protection sought to represent the buyer's interests in some way other than public control and planning. The experience of the nation-alized industries drove a wedge between consumer power and socialized ownership. Thus consumer protection was drawn away from the position, still strongly articulated by social movements such as the Women's Co-operative Guilds and Labour Women, that saw consumption as an axis for the collectivism of society.

The revolution and the sovereign consumer

Consumer protection had been identified with both a distinctive pro-gramme and a claim on the public interest in the years after World War II, but in the late 1950s it took a step further and became the basis for a 'con-sumer movement'. As a value-seeking individual, the British shopper gained a cohort of guardians: the Consumers' Association began publishing *Which?* in October 1957 and within five years reached a quarter of a million homes every month; the British Standards Institution (BSI) estab-lished its own *Shopper's Guide*; regular consumer columns appeared in the press.[65] From 1961 the CA seeded local consumers' groups, which federated nationally in 1963.[66] The 1962 Molony Report prompted government to establish an official Consumer Council to 'secure presentation of the con-sumer viewpoint at high national levels'.[67] This accretion of consumer resources gathered around a vision of the discriminating shopper most influentially articulated by the CA and most clearly represented in the Association's comparative testing and advice method.

Organization and method were never incidental to the consumer protec-tion tradition. The seminal importance of *Your Money's Worth* in both Britain and the USA was precisely the presumption that new forms rather than exist-ing institutions were needed to pursue the consumer interest. 'Institutional entrepreneurs' took charge of the consumer cause.[68] Organizational format became the key to defining and renegotiating the consumer interest, and this underpinned the British consumerists' act of cultural borrowing. American consumer politics was neither monolithic nor uncontentious, but Consumers Union stood out as a coherent and successful model. It tempered its critique of business by emphasizing the formal and scientific practices of consumer testing.[69] Framed as technological scrutiny rather than radical politics, testing and consumer information were more readily imitated and, as we have seen, incorporated into different political projects.

CA was only one – although it was the largest – of the product testing groups that proliferated across Europe in the 1950s and 1960s. Along with standard-setting and labelling bodies, the testing organizations were inte-grated into an ecology of 'consumer information systems' spreading throughout the rich world.[70] National variegation remained, however, as strategies for campaigning or advocacy, engagement with governments and party politics took different routes.[71] The CA's mode of operation reflected the tradition of consumer protection as it had evolved in Britain since the 1930s. The Association was attentive to two relationships: first between the buyer and her goods, to ensure that she chose and received the 'best buy' for her needs, and secondarily between the buyer and the seller, to make sure that the exchange took place on transparent and fair terms. Information and research could determine consumers' needs and guide their choices. As a result the CA's strong characteristics were its tight focus on shoppers' affairs, organizational coherence, redoubtable positivism and scientific method, and publishing success. Its weak valences were with party politics and social campaigning.

The Association's first office, a borrowed garage, suggests a certain style of social entrepreneurship, but its origins harked back more to the high-policy concerns of consumer protection. The British Association of Consumers first met in November 1956, after which a number of attendants produced an informal 'dummy' consumer bulletin, following the format of the American *Consumer Reports*. These were the first incarnations of the Consumers' Association and *Which?*. Michael Young chaired the Association, able now to author the consumer power envisioned in 1950. At the meeting Labour and Conservative researchers and MPs rubbed shoulders with engineers, journalists, civil servants, members of the British Productivity Council, the Directors of PEP, the National Institute of Economic and Social Research and the Government Social Survey, the Chief Scientific Officer of the Department of Industrial and Scientific Research and – accompanied by a reader's exclamation mark in the original list of those present – an advertiser.[72] The 1956 group assembled because they saw an informed, empowered and discriminating consuming public as a means as well as an end. Once again, spillovers from economic analysis and policy discussion gave the promoters of a consumer cause a rallying-point and a useful lever on public affairs. The problem at that time was the plight of the British export industry. Founders of the Association later remembered the export drive among its founding objectives; its role to give the British economy a form of 'in-built self-criticism'.[73] Indeed, many of the events and organizations bringing together discussion of the consumer from the 1940s to early 1960s acknowledged this priority, including the Council of Industrial Design and the British Standards Institution.[74] In 1956 a conference of the National Council of Women of Great Britain called for well-informed customers if manufacturing standards were to rise and the export drive succeed.[75]

The economic desirability of efficient markets secured through information and discriminating consumption was the hidden span that attached the aims of the British consumer movement to Chase and Schlink's original product-testing form. The explicit link between Consumers' Association and the consumer movement of 1930s America was the fortification of the buyer against confusion and the wiles of salesmen. Consumerism thus became a reform tradition posed between a brisk analysis of how a lack of information was failing both consumers and (indirectly) producers, and a surveillance of business methods that threatened at times to shade into a critique of the culture of consumption.

The consumerists' view of the affluent society and the balance of power between buyer and seller became an exploration of the meaning and the problems of choice. The uncontroversial starting-point was that the new appliances and materials remodelling the household guaranteed uncertainty for the shopper, who might get to grips with nylon only to encounter terylene, perlon, acrilan, courtelle, tricel and sumptuous 'plastahide'. Yet the intensity of affluent acquisition prompted the leading edge of the consumer movement to ask a deeper question: did consumers even make their own desires? A group of writers portrayed the shopper as irrational, gullible, the plaything of advertisers.[76] The canon of critical writings was presided over by American works: Vance Packard's denunciations of marketing *The Waste Makers* and *The Hidden Persuaders*, and J. K. Galbraith's *The Affluent Society*.[77] These exposed a new economic logic governing consumption: producers created wants to meet production, rather than vice-versa. Consumer sovereignty was inverted.

Against this prospect, the Consumers' Association held out the idea of the rational shopper. This figure encompassed not only the discriminating connoisseur of nutrition or quality integral to the efficiency concerns of earlier projects, but also an independent consumer impervious to the 'emotional' appeal of advertising. Eirlys Roberts cited sheer intellectual discomfort with the irrationality and emotion of most shopping as one motivation of the Association's founders.[78] The philosophy of *Which?* was arch-objectivity: the absolutes of 'best buy', and 'the more blobs the better'.[79] Consumerists began to distinguish between desirable 'informative' advertising and the 'persuasive' kind.[80] CA's contribution to the call for dedicated 'consumer education' wanted a 'kerb drill' of shopping to transmit the rationalist discipline.[81] While it did not carry out product tests, the government Consumer Council also privileged the calculus of consumer rationality, publicly tangling with retailers over the probability that promotional trading stamps would cloud the relationship between price and value.[82] However, although the rational shopper ideal had critical potential – offering to one of the CA's founders 'a peculiarly heady blend of social defiance, intellectual grace and moral satisfaction' – even such limited confrontation between consumer representatives and industry was uncharacteristic.[83] Despite the Galbraithian strain within the Association, consumer choice and information *per se* generated no clash with business. The Molony Committee leaned strongly towards producers and was more interested in casting aspersions on CA's limited internal democracy than in recognizing its contribution, but nevertheless developed a similar understanding of consumers' needs.[84]

Yet consumer protection did juxtapose producer and consumer interests. The collectivist tradition of the Co-operative and Labour movements had mobilized consumers around the politics of employment and wages as well as prices and standards, but the newer consumer movement was not characterized by this kind of integration. Unlike in Japan, where postwar consumer organizations allied with labour and agricultural interests and supported protectionist national policies as the means to growth, or France where trade unions and political parties conducted consumer advocacy, British groups privileged independence as a signifier of countervailing power.[85] Conceiving shoppers' needs in terms of information meant operating in a market for trust; CA Council members could have no commercial links and funding came entirely from *Which?* subscriptions, to guarantee unimpeachable impartiality in testing. When *Shopper's Guide* folded in 1962 the CA and others pointed to its lack of independence: as part of the BSI it had been jointly funded by government and industry.[86] This test of legitimacy was applied wholesale to the Co-operative movement. The Co-op was compromised by its production and retail activities and could not be considered a consumers' body: outside the movement itself it was a matter of principle that 'the relative purity of a consumer-group is a matter of importance, and on this score the co-operative movement must rate poorly.'[87] Likewise, the nationalized industries' consumer councils were regarded as thoroughly contaminated, even lumping industrial and domestic consumers together, and in bed with the industry boards.[88]

The standard of independence and functional distinction enabled a new class of 'professional consumers' to seize the agenda of representation. The dilemma of finding people to stand for the organized consumer had previously been resolved by picking from local authority members, cooperators and housewives with party-political connections. Selection by expertise had meant taking people from the industry in question. From the 1950s, specialists in consumer research and publication embodied the criteria of independence and expertise. They sought to insert a policy-oriented discipline between the burgeoning fields of professional marketing and social research. *The* consumer view would then be on hand as required, simply by referring to 'this year's Baedeker' of their needs and opinions.[89]

In becoming increasingly formalized and professional, Britain's consumer movement circumscribed its activities and its legitimate remit. CA initially approached its role in an extremely Spartan way. *Which?* represented its one strength, a business model as much as a social movement, successful solely through 'the sheer utility of reliable and objective advice on mundane problems of choice'.[90] Making a thoughtful judgement about their mandate from *Which?* readers, as well as their diverse personal views on the matter, the leaders of CA repeatedly foreswore any clear political or social role – they sought 'to strengthen the individual consumer, rather than all consumers in aggregate'.[91] As its deputy research director Jeremy

Mitchell acknowledged in 1964, 'the draw-back of this concentration on comparative testing is that the growth of the consumer movement, in Britain anyway, has been extremely lop-sided'; no politicized consumers' pressure group had emerged.[92] Only gradually did the Association begin to act as a lobbyist for consumers generally, pressing for legislation and giving the 'consumer view' in evidence to government inquiries.[93]

Beyond the revolution

Consumer protection, information and choice provided a relatively stable and successful framework for much legislation and regulation in the remainder of the twentieth century. Consumer sovereignty was an accessible and consensual way of representing the consumer interest, around which activists, business and state actors could converge. Regulators like the Office of Fair Trading, set up in 1973 with an explicit consumer information remit, or the watchdogs of privatized industry in the 1980s and 1990s could adopt this largely economic conception of the consumer interest with ease.[94] Companies applied themselves to customer information and satisfaction by developing their own market research efforts and consumer affairs departments, and opening channels of complaint and redress.[95]

The campaign to install consumers as a distinctive force in postwar Britain had stamped down the legitimate ground for the consumer interest, but the boundaries of that interest were continuously tested. The consumer movement began to face dilemmas arising from the very practices and intellectual framework that had nurtured the rational-shopper idea, and the consumerists' unified conception of the consumer interest as simply the problem of the individual in the economy began to break down. The collective action solution of information and of private self-help in purchasing turned out to be a partial one. Overwhelmingly middle-class composition was an acknowledged feature of the CA and local consumer groups; the consumer information project seemed to have an in-built middle-class bias that trapped the existing movement behind a 'class barrier'.[96] Consumer organizations were thus ill-equipped to respond to the challenge of the 'disadvantaged consumer', as research in the 1960s began to identify groups whose problems in the marketplace would not be solved by information. David Caplovitz's pioneering *The Poor Pay More*, published in 1963 with the support of Consumers' Union, revealed that the inhabitants of New York housing projects participated in a 'low-income marketing system' with limited local choice, exploitative merchants and permanent, precarious exposure to credit.[97] Growing attention to the disadvantaged consumer mainly focused on poverty, though it took in other groups such as the elderly.[98]

A consumerist analysis of social marginalization went beyond either the useful scope of product testing or the lobbying activity of the CA, and contributed to a tension between the aspiration of value-for-money and a wider conception of the consumer. The organizing motif for these debates was the distinction between consumer and citizen. CA, having been so successful in creating a paradigm of independent organization, has consistently seen the practical distinction of consumer interests from submergence in general citizenship as the price to pay for the Association's own coherence and survival.[99] Careful circumscription of the CA's operations involved a conscious attempt to 'fillet out the consumer from the person'.[100] This tendency was tested by an alternative conception that sought to do much the opposite: to mesh together the empowered consumer and the progressive cause. Its main spokesman was Michael Young who, while chairing the CA, realized that it could not accommodate a broader vision of consumer politics. In his independently published pamphlet *The Chipped White Cups of Dover* in 1960, Young related consumerism to citizenship in two senses: as a focus for social values rather than simply economic self-interest, and as deeply tied to the role of the state. He revisited the theme of *Small Man, Big World*: the attempt to make government and public services democratic in the broadest way.[101] From 1975 he was able to turn his consumer–citizenship principles into political practice as chairman of the new National Consumer Council. In its first few years the NCC staked out ground for a consumerist approach in housing and benefits policy, local government and public services, spreading its attentions from the grass roots of credit unions and local consumer advice to the heights of inflation and taxation policy. The citizen–consumer approach flared for a few years in the late 1970s and early 1980s, before the Conservative government pulled the NCC back towards markets and efficiency. By then, however, the NCC had established a web of contacts with single-issue groups that continues to tie consumerism to an arena of campaigning social politics.[102]

The engagement between this citizen–consumerism and environmentalists, disability rights organizations, health charities and pensioners' groups recalls the liberal-radical free trade and collectivist traditions of consumer politics: able to present consumption as a site of consequences and responsibilities, and of opportunities for protest and collective action. Consumer protection, by comparison, stands accused of an inability to go 'beyond the toaster', refusing to raise its gaze beyond the horizons of private market exchange and unable to apply its analysis of consumer benefit to the ethical and social implications of rich-world consumption.[103] This chapter has suggested that consumer protection in Britain was born and bred in policy rather than politics; oriented towards the identification of a stable and coherent 'consumer interest' rather than the attempt to link consumption to a critical set of public meanings. Tellingly, the looser coalitions of groups that have concurrently engaged in a politics of consumption since the 1960s have looked to a newer set of American writings than *Your Money's Worth*: Caplovitz's *The Poor Pay More*, Rachel Carson's *Silent Spring*, and the first thunderbolt of an anti-corporate citizen's movement, Ralph Nader's *Unsafe at any Speed*.[104]

Notes

1. For discriminating consumption of earlier drafts of this chapter I would like to thank Mark Bevir, Anisha Dasgupta, Martin Daunton, Emma Reisz and Frank Trentmann.
2. Paul Fletcher, 'When We Were Very Young', in *Which?* tenth anniversary issue, 5 October 1967.
3. 'Consumerism' is used throughout this chapter to refer to the promotion of a distinctive consumer interest, rather than in its alternative usage as the materialist preoccupation of a rich society.
4. Archive of the Consumers' Association (Henceforth CA), box 27, Press cuttings: J. Robertson 'Cars, Customers and Which?-hunts', *Sunday Telegraph*, 14 January 1962.
5. CA 27, Eirlys Roberts, 'Cool Customers', an article written for *New Society* but not published, 9 December 1963; see also for example Ronald Wraith, *The Consumer Cause: A Short Account of its Organisation, Power and Importance* (London: Royal Institute of Public Administration, 1976), p. 11; John Martin and George W. Smith, *The Consumer Interest* (London: Pall Mall Press, 1968), p. 5.
6. Eirlys Roberts, *Consumers* (London: Watts, 1966), p. 1; see also Martin and Smith, *Consumer Interest*, p. 242.
7. Stuart Chase and Frederick J. Schlink, *Your Money's Worth: A Study in the Wastes of the Consumer's Dollar* (New York: Macmillan, 1927). See also Charles McGovern, 'Consumption and Citizenship in the United States, 1900–1940', in Susan Strasser, Charles McGovern and Matthias Judt (eds), *Getting and Spending: European and American Consumer Societies in the Twentieth Century* (Cambridge and New York: Cambridge University Press, 1998), pp. 37–58 esp. 52–4; Lizabeth Cohen, 'The New Deal State', pp. 115–16 in ibid., esp. pp. 111–26.
8. Chase and Schlink, *Your Money's Worth*, pp. 34–5.
9. Matthew Hilton, 'Consumer Politics in Post-War Britain', in Martin Daunton and Matthew Hilton (eds), *The Politics of Consumption: Material Culture and Citizenship in Europe and America* (Oxford and New York: Berg, 2001), pp. 241–60, esp. 244–7; Noel Thompson, 'Hobson and the Fabians: Two Roads to Socialism in the 1920s', *History of Political Economy* 26 (1994), 203–20, esp. p. 209; Peter Gurney, *Co-operative Culture and the Politics of Consumption in England, 1870–1930* (Manchester: Manchester University Press, 1996); Mark Bevir, 'William Morris: The Modern Self, Art, and Politics', *History of European Ideas* 24 (1998), 175–94.
10. 'Jeannette Eaton, our "Counselor to the Consumer"', *Pictorial Review* 35 (February 1934), 2, quoted in Lawrence B. Glickman, 'The Strike in The Temple of Consumption: Consumer Activism And Twentieth-century American Political Culture', *Journal of American History* 88(1) (2001), 99–128, p. 100.
11. Glickman, 'Strike in the Temple'. On Consumers Union's adherence to testing rather than campaigning see Norman I. Silber, *Test and Protest: The Influence of Consumers Union* (New York: Holmes & Meier, 1983), pp. 23–38, 121–7; Hayagreeva Rao, 'Caveat Emptor: The Construction of Nonprofit Consumer Watchdog Organizations', *American Journal of Sociology* 103(4) (1998) 912–61, pp. 940–4.

12. Meg Jacobs, '"Democracy's Third Estate": New Deal Politics and the Construction of a "Consuming Public"', *International Labor and Working-Class History* 55 (1999), 27–51.
13. Persia Campbell, *Consumer Representation in the New Deal* (New York: Columbia University Press, 1940). On countervailing power see John Kenneth Galbraith, *American Capitalism: the Concept of Countervailing Power* (Boston: Houghton Mifflin, 1952).
14. Cohen, 'The New Deal State', pp. 114–19; Jacobs, 'Democracy's Third Estate', pp. 232–5.
15. Daniel Ritschel, *The Politics of Planning: the Debate on Economic Planning in Britain in the 1930s* (Oxford: Clarendon, 1997), pp. 47–9.
16. PEP, *Planning*, 23, 27 March 1934, p. 5. *Planning* was the monthly broadsheet of PEP.
17. Ritschel, *Politics of Planning*, p. 145.
18. Ibid., p. 230.
19. Frank Trentmann, 'Political Culture and Political Economy: Interest, Ideology and Free Trade', *Review of International Political Economy* 5(2) (1998), 217–51, p. 229. See also now Frank Trentmann, 'National Identity and Consumer Politics', in Patrick O' Brien and Donald Winch (eds), *The Political Economy of British Historical Experience, 1688–1914* (Oxford: Oxford University Press, 2002), pp. 187–214.
20. Frank Trentmann, 'Civil Society, Commerce and the "Citizen–Consumer"', in Frank Trentmann (ed.), *Paradoxes of Civil Society* (New York and Oxford: Berghahn, 2000), pp. 306–31, p. 321; Frank Trentmann, 'Bread, Milk and Democracy', in Daunton and Hilton (eds), *The Politics of Consumption*, pp. 129–64.
21. PEP, *Planning*, 36, 'What Consumers Need', 23 October 1934, p. 2.
22. Trentmann, 'Bread, Milk and Democracy', pp. 146–53.
23. British Parliamentary Papers (hereafter PP) 1929-30 I, Consumers' Council Bill.
24. Public Record Office, Kew (hereafter PRO), files of the Ministry of Agriculture (MAF): MAF 194/815, 'Extract from Parliamentary Papers, Ministry's notes on amendments to be moved in committee', attached as appendix 'Background to Consumers' Committees'.
25. British Library of Political and Economic Science, Political and Economic Planning archive (hereafter PEP archive) WG 6/2 Distribution Group memorandum on Consumers' Committees, 14 April 1934.
26. Oliver Roskill, 'PEP Through the 1930s: The Industries Group', in John Pinder (ed.), *Fifty Years of Political & Economic Planning: Looking Forward, 1931–1981* (London: Heinemann, 1981), pp. 54-80, p. 54. Roskill was himself a member of the working group.
27. PEP archive 12/164/30F 'Draft Broadsheet on Consumer Research', 13 November 1935.
28. Ibid., Minutes of Research Group meeting 19 November 1935.
29. Ibid., 'Draft Broadsheet on Consumer Research', 13 November 1935.
30. PEP archive 12/154, Minutes of Research Group meeting 22 May 1934.
31. Thompson, 'Hobson and the Fabians', p. 205.
32. PEP archive 12/154 memo by F. R. Cowell, 'Research for Consumers' 17 July 1934.
33. PEP, *Planning*, 17, 'The Output of Knowledge', 2 January 1934.
34. Glickman, 'Strike in the Temple', pp. 109, 115–16.
35. Jacobs, 'Democracy's Third Estate', pp. 29–34.
36. PEP archive 12/164/30F covering note to 'Draft Broadsheet on Consumer Research', 13 November 1935.

37. For Huxley's emphasis on how consumer needs should drive research in a context of national planning, see Julian S. Huxley, *Scientific Research and Social Needs* (London: Watts & Co., 1934) and *TVA: Adventure in Planning* (Cheam, Surrey: The Architectural Press, 1943). Huxley would later serve in an honorary capacity on the council of the Consumers' Association.

38. PEP archive WG 6/2, 'Points referred to the Distribution Group by the Research Group', 19 March 1934; PEP archive 12/154, Minutes of Research Group meeting 22 May 1934.

39. PEP archive 12/164/30F 'Draft Broadsheet on Consumer Research', 13 November 1935.

40. See Hilton, 'Consumer Politics in Post-War Britain', for detailed discussion of the Molony Committee.

41. PRO, files of the Board of Trade (BT): BT 258/352, Con. P.3 'Consumer Protection: the Improvement of Quality'.

42. James Hinton, 'Militant Housewives – The British Housewives League and the Attlee Government', *History Workshop Journal* 38 (1994), 128–56, p. 131.

43. The political results of this policy are somewhat contested. Although Labour's opponents kept discontent with shortages and queues to the fore, Labour Women and the Womens' Co-operative Guilds organized strongly behind 'fair shares'. Housewives were evenly divided over bread rationing in 1946. It is clear that there was a 'consumerist' constituency for controls, just as there was a 'consumerist' critique of them. While Conservative electoral victory in 1951 spelt the end of controls, which were subsequently dismantled, it is less clear that austerity was bankrupt, since Labour's share of the vote was higher in defeat than it had been in victory in 1945. For this debate see Ina Zweiniger-Bargielowska, *Austerity in Britain: Rationing, Controls, and Consumption 1939–55* (Oxford: Oxford University Press, 2000); Hinton, 'Militant Housewives'; Trentmann, 'Bread, Milk and Democracy', pp. 156–8.

44. Labour Party, *Labour Believes in Britain* (London: Labour Party, 1949), pp. 16–17; Labour Party, *Let Us Win Through Together* (London: Labour Party, 1950), p. 8.

45. BT 258/352, 'President's brief for first meeting of the Cabinet Committee on Distribution and Marketing', 21 April 1950.

46. See for example PRO, files of the Cabinet Office (CAB): CAB 124/950, Official Committee on the Socialisation of Industries, Second Report, 'Price Policy in the Socialised Industries', May 1946.

47. Foster, the Parliamentary Secretary to the Ministry of Fuel and Power, speaking on coal nationalization, *House of Commons Debates*, Standing Committee C, 5 March 1946, col. 310.

48. W. A. Lewis, 'The Price Policy of Public Corporations', *Political Quarterly*, **21**(2) (1950), 184–96.

49. CAB 124/950, letter from J. H. Woods to Sir Edward Bridges, 8 July 1946.

50. PRO, files of the Ministry of Fuel and Power (POWE): POWE 17/82, 'Assessment of the work of Gas Consultative Councils', 27 January 1953.

51. POWE 28/177, memorandum from Minister of Fuel and Power to Socialisation of Industries Committee, 1 May 1950.

52. A. M. de Neumann, *Consumers' Representation in the Public Sector* (London, 1950); 'The Consumer's Interest', *The Economist*, 5 August 1950; L. Freedman and G. Hemingway, *Nationalisation and the Consumer* (London: Fabian Society, 1950); J. A. G. Griffith, 'The Voice of the Consumer', *Political Quarterly* 21(2)

(1950), 171–83; J. W. Grove, 'The Consumer Councils for Gas and Electricity', *Public Administration* 28(3) (1950), 221–30; Ernest Davies, *Problems of Public Ownership* (London: Labour Party, 1952); F. Milligan, 'The Consumer's Interest', in William. A. Robson (ed.), *Problems of Nationalised Industry* (London: George Allen & Unwin, 1952), pp. 144–70; William. A. Robson, 'General Conclusions' in ibid.; Acton Society Trust, Studies in Nationalised Industry 12, *Relations With the Public* (London: Acton Society Trust, 1953); Mary Stewart, *Consumers' Councils* (London: Fabian Society, 1953).

53. For a fuller discussion see Christopher Beauchamp, 'Consumer Sovereignty and Consumer Protection in Britain, 1945–65' (unpublished MPhil dissertation, University of Cambridge, 2000), ch. 2.

54. Michael Young, *Small Man, Big World* (London, Labour Party, 1948); see also Milligan, 'The Consumer's Interest', pp. 166–7.

55. Abigail Beach, 'Forging a "Nation of Participants": Political and Economic Planning in Labour's Britain', in Abigail Beach and Richard Weight (eds), *The Right to Belong: Citizenship and National Identity in Britain, 1930–60* (London and New York: I. B. Tauris, 1998), pp. 89–115.

56. Quoted in Naomi Sargant, 'Consumer Power as a Pillar of Democracy' p. 190, in Geoff Dench, Tony Flower and Kate Gavron (eds), *Young at Eighty: the Prolific Public Life of Michael Young* (Manchester: Carcanet, 1995), pp. 187–98.

57. PRO, Files of the Prime Minister's office (PREM): PREM 8/1183, Wilson, 'Personal covering note to memorandum on "The State and Private Industry"'. Emphasis in original.

58. Ibid. The phrase was coined by Wilson's junior minister Christopher Mayhew. See also PREM 8/1183, minutes of meeting held to discuss 'The State and Private Industry', 17 May 1950.

59. PREM 8/1183, Wilson, 'Personal covering note'.

60. Keith Middlemas, *Power, Competition, and the State, volume1: Britain in Search of a Balance, 1940–61* (Basingstoke: Macmillan, now Palgrave Macmillan 1986), p. 183; PREM 8/1183, minutes of meeting held to discuss 'The State and Private Industry', 17 May 1950; PREM 8/1183, letter from Attlee to Wilson, 7 May 1950.

61. Abigail Beach, 'The Labour Party and the Idea of Citizenship, c. 1931–51' (unpublished PhD thesis, University of London, 1996), p. 257; William Crofts, *Coercion or Persuasion? Propaganda in Britain after 1945* (London: Routledge, 1989).

62. PRO, Files of the Treasury (T): T 245/9, minutes of the Women's Organisations Committee on Economic Information. Cullen had reverted to her maiden name, Roberts, by the time she helped to found the Consumers' Association, and will be referred to on following pages as Eirlys Roberts.

63. CAB 124/2749, Gaitskell to Prime Minister, 8 January 1951.

64. BT 258/355, unidentified press cutting attached to 'Fooling the Housewife', circular letter from Roger Diplock of the Retail Trading Standards Association to newspapers, 6 March 1950.

65. Consumer advice was provided by Elizabeth Gundrey in the *News Chronicle* and Marghanita Laski in the *Observer*, and arrived in the weeklies with the 'Consuming Interest' column in the *Spectator*, followed by 'Information' in the *Listener*, and 'Value Judgement' in the *New Statesman*. See A. Robertson, 'The Campaigners', *Twentieth Century* no. 4 1968/no. 1 1969, pp. 11–13.

66. The National Federation of Consumer Groups boasted a membership of 18,000 in 1967. See Hans B. Thorelli and Sarah V. Thorelli, *Consumer Information Handbook: Europe and North America* (London and New York: Praeger, 1974), p. 30.

67. PP *Final Report of the Committee on Consumer Protection*, Cmnd. 1781 (London: HMSO, 1962), p. 286.
68. Rao, 'Caveat Emptor',
69. This deflection was necessary: after the split from Consumers' Research, Consumers Union was hounded by F. J. Schlink and others as a subversive group with Communist links, leading to hearings before the House Un-American Activities Committee. Silber, *Test and Protest*, pp. 122–3.
70. The Association formalized links with its Dutch, Belgian and Australian equivalents, and with Consumers Union, in an International Office of Consumers' Unions (IOCU) in 1960, initially a clearing-house for testing but broadening both its membership and its range of discussion in the 1960s. Thorelli and Thorelli, *Consumer Information Handbook*, pp. 481–2.
71. See for example Gunnar Trumbull, 'Strategies of Consumer Group Mobilization: France and Germany in the 1970s', in Daunton and Hilton (eds), *Politics of Consumption*, pp. 261–82.
72. CA 27, 'European Consumer Organizations – A Digest of Their Work: Great Britain', undated.
73. CA 27, Untitled draft of an article by Roberts, 1 August 1966; Fletcher 'When We Were Very Young', *Which?*, tenth anniversary issue, 5 October 1967; CA 27, Michael Young's foreword to 'Consumer Information and Protection – Evidence Submitted to the Departmental Committee on Consumer Protection by Consumers' Association Ltd', March 1960.
74. Central Office of Information, *Consumer Protection and Guidance in the UK*, (London: HMSO, 1959), p. 13.
75. CA 27, Roberts, 'Cool Customers', pp. 4–10; CA 27, memorandum 'Proceedings of Conference on Consumer Protection 1956'.
76. Colin Harbury, *Efficiency and the Consumer* (London: Fabian Society, 1958); Robert Millar, *The Affluent Sheep: A Profile of the British Consumer* (London: Longmans, 1963); Robin Wight, *The Day the Pigs Refused to Be Driven to Market: Advertising and the Consumer Revolution* (London: Hart-Davis MacGibbon, 1972); Hilton, 'Consumer Politics in Post-War Britain', p. 256.
77. Vance Packard, *The Hidden Persuaders* (New York: D. McKay Co., 1957), *The Waste Makers* (New York: D. McKay Co., 1960); John Kenneth Galbraith, *The Affluent Society* (Boston: Houghton Mifflin, 1958).
78. Roberts, *Consumers*, p. 78.
79. Alan Aldridge, 'The Construction of Rational Consumption in *Which?* Magazine: The More Blobs the Better', *Sociology* 28(4) (1994), 899–912.
80. BT 258/885, Submission to Molony Committee by Advertising Inquiry Council, August 1960; CA 27, 'Notes on Consumers' Association', 1962; M. Tilleard and G. Clegg, 'Consumer Advisory Services', p. 57, in *Aslib Proceedings* 28(2) (1976), 56–68.
81. Research Institute for Consumer Affairs, *Consumer Education: Conceptions and Resources* (London: RICA, 1964).
82. Christina Fulop, *Consumers in the Market: a Study in Choice, Competition and Sovereignty* (London: Institute for Economic Affairs, 1967), p. 40.
83. Fletcher, 'When We Were Very Young'.
84. Hilton, 'Consumer Politics in Post-War Britain'.
85. Steven K. Vogel, 'When Interests are not Preferences: the Cautionary Tale of Japanese Consumers', *Comparative Politics* 31(2) (1999), 187–207; Trumbull, 'Strategies of Consumer-Group Mobilization'.

86. CA 27, Internal Memoranda: Notes On the Collapse of *Shopper's Guide*; Martin and Smith, *Consumer Interest*, p. 188.
87. Len Tivey, 'The Politics of the Consumer', p. 198, in Richard Kimber and Jeremy Richardson, *Pressure Groups in Britain: A Reader* (London: Dent, 1974), pp. 195–209.
88. Consumer Council, *Consumer Consultative Machinery in the Nationalised Industries* (London: HMSO, 1968).
89. BT 258/1505, Letter from Michael Young to R. H. King [Board of Trade], 29 August 1962.
90. Fletcher, 'When We Were Very Young'.
91. CA 27, 'Notes on Consumers' Association', 1962; Peter Goldman, 'Consumerism: Art or Science?', *Journal of the Royal Society of Arts* 127(5157)(1969), 632–40; Thorelli and Thorelli, *Consumer Information Handbook*, p. 31. On the divisions within CA see Matthew Hilton, 'The Fable of the Sheep; or, Private Virtues, Public Vices. The Consumer Revolution of the Twentieth Century', forthcoming in *Past and Present*. I am grateful to Dr Hilton for letting me see the manuscript before publication.
92. CA 21, Jeremy Mitchell, Introductory speech, in IOCU, *Consumers on the March: Proceedings of the Third Biennial Conference of the IOCU, Oslo 22–24 June 1964*.
93. Thorelli and Thorelli, *Consumer Information Handbook*, pp. 31–2.
94. Joel D. Wolfe, 'Power and Regulation in Britain', *Political Studies* 47(5) (1999), 890–905.
95. Jeremy Mitchell (ed.), *Marketing and the Consumer Movement* (London: McGraw-Hill, 1978).
96. CA 21, J. Mitchell, Introductory speech, in IOCU, *Consumers on the March*. In 1969 CA made a foray beyond the class barrier with a consumers' clinic in Kentish Town, an experiment followed up by a number of local councils: CA 27, Consumers' Association, *The Development of Consumer Advice Centres in the UK*, 1978.
97. David Caplovitz, *The Poor Pay More: Consumer Practices of Low-Income Families* (New York: Free Press of Glencoe, 1963).
98. Research Institute for Consumer Affairs, *Elderly Consumers: the Problem Assessed* (London: RICA, 1964). See also Alan R. Andreasen, *The Disadvantaged Consumer* (New York: Free Press, 1975).
99. See for example Jeremy Mitchell, 'Management and the Consumer Movement', *Journal of General Management* 3(4) (1976), 46–55, p. 52; CA 66, Rachel Waterhouse [then Chairman of CA], 'New Frontiers for Consumerism', speech to Royal Society of Arts, 22 February 1988.
100. Benet Middleton, 'Consumerism: A Pragmatic Ideology', *Consumer Policy Review* 8(6) (1998), 213–17.
101. Michael Young, *The Chipped White Cups of Dover: A Discussion of the Possibility of a New Progressive Party* (London: Unit 2, 1960), pp. 13, 18.
102. Hilton, 'Fable of the Sheep'.
103. For this debate between two prominent consumer-policy professionals see Colin Brown, 'Consumer Activism in Europe', *Consumer Policy Review* 8(6) (1998) 209–12 and Middleton, 'Consumerism: A Pragmatic Ideology'.
104. Caplovitz, *The Poor Pay More*; Rachel Carson, *Silent Spring* (Cambridge, MA: Houghton Mifflin, 1962); Ralph Nader, *Unsafe at Any Speed. The Designed-in Dangers of the American Automobile* (New York: Grossman, 1965).

7
Trust and Self-determination: Anglo-American Ethics of Empire and International Government

Kevin Grant

Great Britain and the United States built empires and international governments upon trust. Between the eighteenth and twentieth centuries, politicians, colonial officials and legal authorities on both sides of the Atlantic invoked trusteeship as the ethic of their imperial governance over dependent peoples, including native Americans, Asians, Pacific islanders and Africans. The idea of political trusteeship had originated in England during the Reformation, then come to fruition in the politics of radical Calvinism articulated by John Locke in the seventeenth century. By the late-eighteenth century, trusteeship had gained currency not only in Britain, but in the British colonies in North America, reflecting the strong political traditions which British subjects shared even as adversaries in the age of revolution. Subsequently, as Britain and the United States extended their separate empires, the governments of both countries developed the tradition of trusteeship in response to particular political and economic objectives, and changing relationships of power. Above all, trusteeship enabled British and US officials to reconcile their commitments to the expansion of modern capitalism and social justice by making a social virtue of capitalist development under their political authority. This chapter offers a preliminary outline of the genealogies of imperial trusteeship in Britain and the United States and particularly examines Anglo-American negotiations over the transition from empire to international government as a 'sacred trust' under the League of Nations and the United Nations.[1]

In the founding era of international government, new advocates of trust argued that social justice depended not only on capitalist development, but on support for human rights, and, by extension, political self-determination. While the proponents of the different concepts of trust disagreed over imperial policy, they shared three basic ideas, which together distinguished Anglo-American trusteeship from other traditions of imperial expansion.[2] First, trustees acknowledged that their colonial 'wards' retained their natural rights to ownership of land. Second, trustees declared their authority to be temporary, attributing this authority to their superior

151

position in the hierarchy of 'civilization', as conceived on a European social model. Finally, trustees committed themselves to the social improvement of their wards, especially through commerce and labour reforms suitable to modern capitalist development. When such development had elevated the wards to a comparable level of 'civilization', the trustees would cede their political authority, just as parents acknowledge the independence of their children who have become adults.

The tradition of trusteeship was reinvented in a wide range of imperial contexts. This chapter illuminates different ideas about the trustee's accountability, and about the relationship of the duty of trusteeship to the right of political self-determination. When Edmund Burke declared Britain's rule over India to be a 'sacred trust' in 1783, he believed that the British government answered ultimately to God for its imperial policies. In 1919, when President Woodrow Wilson included the idea of a 'sacred trust' in the Covenant of the League of Nations, he believed that imperial powers should ultimately be accountable to each other for their treatment of their colonial wards under the mandatory system. Furthermore, while the 'sacred trust' of the League of Nations did not preclude the future, political self-determination of most of Europe's colonial wards, it did relegate some 'barbaric' peoples to virtually perpetual wardship. On a different colonial front, the US government had already subjected native Americans to a trust that foreclosed their self-determination, requiring them to assimilate into US society and eventually accept US citizenship.

'Trust' is a multifaceted concept, with innumerable applications across scholarly disciplines.[3] This chapter is specifically concerned with political trusteeship as a safeguard of social justice in British and US colonial rule over peoples who were neither of European descent nor predominantly Christian. This emphasis highlights the importance of social prejudices and biases in determining political rights and recognition, and in defining the ethics of empire and international government.[4] The social prerequisites of justice under colonial rule can be seen from another angle in the protests of American colonists, who decried 'taxation without representation' as a violation of their rights and privileges as Englishmen.[5] By contrast, this chapter examines the application of trust to peoples who could not demand justice on the basis of a social identity shared with their rulers.

Trustees, wards and empire

The tradition of political trusteeship developed in England after the sixteenth century under the influences of Lutheran theology and radical Calvinism.[6] Political trusteeship was a product of the rejection of divine-right theories of monarchy, and it reflected a momentous turn in ecclesiological and political theory toward popular sovereignty and the right of resistance to unjust rule. The Lutheran origins of political trusteeship are found in the principle of justification by faith, *sola fide*, which established the equality of the faithful in the eyes of God, regardless of worldly ranks and orders. In privileging an individual's trust with God, Lutherans freed commoners of their dependence upon the spiritual mediation of priests and monarchs, laying the groundwork for a new conception of self that would reshape the political world.[7]

Luther believed that the existing social and political hierarchies were direct reflections of God's will and Providence, and he therefore opposed violent rebellion against rulers, however unjust they might be.[8] Subsequently, the persecutions of Protestants during the Counter-Reformation prompted radical Calvinists to reconceive Luther's idea that any individual could covenant directly with God as the basis of popular revolution.[9] Faith constituted one's trust with God, and the equality of the faithful entailed the Christian duty of the subject to enforce the sacred trust of a ruler to govern in a godly manner. This identification of trustee-ship with popular sovereignty became prevalent in England during the Civil Wars of the seventeenth century, and it was fully articulated by John Locke in his classic text on radical Calvinist politics, the *Two Treatises of Government*, in 1690.[10] Locke did not conceive trust as a legal contract, but as a Christian duty borne by rulers and by subjects, who gave legitimacy to government through their consent. But how did trusteeship apply to the governance of foreign peoples who did not consent to form an imperial society? One can derive an answer to this question from Locke's discussion of the land rights of British colonists and native Americans and from his views on the rights of children and the duties of parents.[11]

Locke acknowledged that native Americans had a natural right to own land, but he did not regard their societies as sovereign in a European sense, because they existed in an inferior state of nature from which European civilization had already developed.[12] Locke was committed to the idea of a universal hierarchy of civilization, measured by European social standards, but he asserted that even non-Christians had property rights, if not sover-eignty comparable to that of Europeans.[13] He believed that native Americans, like Europeans before them, could advance their societies up the civilized hierarchy through trade and through labour in commercial agriculture, which would promote universal social virtues such as discipline and honest industry. This connection between property rights, commerce and social improvement would remain an integral feature of the tradition of trusteeship, establishing the basis for a connection between modern cap-italism and social justice under colonial rule after the late eighteenth century.

Building upon his views on property relations, Locke asserted that people can give legitimacy to government, including an imperial government, not only through explicit consent, but also through 'tacit trust', which is dis-played by their continued residence in a given territory.[14] Moreover, the imperial ruler can perceive this tacit trust from the priviliged perspective of 'paternal power', which prefigures political power in Locke's analysis. Subsequent traditions of trusteeship would liken the relationship of the imperial ruler and subject to that of a father and child, rendering imperial violence an instrument of social justice, rather than political domination. Behind the simile, however, was the belief, evident in Locke, that the natural order of the Christian, European family could extend to mankind. According to Locke, parents hold authority over their children due to their natural affection and their superior capacity for reason, which enables them to comprehend the natural law of God and, in turn, to evaluate the development of the child according to standards of social behaviour that presumably manifest this law. 'Neither can there be any pretense why this parental power should keep the Child, when grown to a Man, in subjection to the Will of his Parents any farther.'[15] It is, nonetheless, for the paternal authority to determine when the child, like the imperial subject, has reached maturity. Social justice thus depends not only on the father's reasonable discipline, but upon the father's duty to guard the child against the perils of independence.

Locke identifies the grounds upon which imperial subjects can justly deny their tacit trust to their paternal governors. 'The Power of the Father', Locke explains, 'doth not reach at all to the Property of the Child, which is only in his own disposing.'[16] The property of the child, like the property of the imperial subject, is comprised fundamentally of his own person and his own labour.[17] The arbitrary coercion of the body, or the use of coercion to extract labour, constitutes a violation of tacit trust and justifies rebellion.[18] But to whom, then, can the imperial subject turn for justice in the face of the regime that oppresses him? Whereas Englishmen, as Christians, can appeal directly to God in the last resort, the imperial subject can appeal to God only through the mediation of Christian representatives in the legislature of the imperial government.[19] In Lockean terms, then, the social justice of imperial trusteeship depends on property rights, toleration of cultural difference, and social improvement through commerce. It further depends on tacit trust, recourse to God through Christian representatives in the imperial government, and, ultimately, the prospect of self-determination.

Almost one hundred years later, Edmund Burke asserted trusteeship in similar terms as the guiding ethic of the British Empire, an ethic that would reconcile social justice with an idealistic vision of the emerging capitalist order. In 1783, the same year in which Britain lost its war against the American revolutionaries, he endorsed an important bill concerning the administration of the East India Company. Burke declared in the House of Commons that all forms of political power and commercial privilege imposed upon men should be exercised as a 'trust' for their benefit.[20] Like Locke, Burke conceived Britain's trust as a Christian duty, but he further asserted that the British Empire was providential, and that Protestantism had imbued Britain with a unique capacity for just rule overseas.[21] He informed his fellow members of Parliament that they had a duty to watch over India, for, despite cultural differences, 'men separated by every barrier of Nature from you, by the Providence of God are blended in one common cause, and are now become suppliants at your bar.'[22] Burke did not believe that these suppliants were under any obligation to assimilate the culture of their distant British representatives. On the contrary, Burke argued, 'If we undertake to govern the inhabitants of such a country, we must govern them upon their own principles and maxims, and not upon ours. ... We have more versatility of character and manners, and it is we who must conform.'[23] While Burke believed that social justice depended upon a British government that tolerated cultural differences, he was not opposed to the reform of Indian society. Rather, he opposed the creation of a colonial administration that intervened in society to impose reforms. He believed alternatively that the reform of Indian society should occur through political economy, which he regarded as a divinely ordained engine for material and moral development.[24] Commerce and capitalist competition should be governed by the laws of God, which rendered subordination natural and respect for one's own subordination moral. Moreover, the Christian principle of trust constituted the duty of each person in a position of privilege to insure that his actions benefited those people under his power. In these terms, Burke established an ideological foundation upon which to reconcile capitalism and social justice in the Empire.

In contrast to Locke's denial of the sovereignty of native Americans, Burke believed that the people of India retained their natural sovereignty over their land, even under the authority of the East India Company. Burke's conception of trusteeship nonetheless suited imperial officials, because it articulated the social justice of political and economic subordination, while discouraging administrative intervention to impose social reforms. Imperial officials were, and would remain, generally averse to such reforms, because these reforms tended to produce dangerous social and economic instability. The principle of trust, furthermore, gave officials the authority to determine when the ward had achieved civilization and become entitled to his freedom. Consequently, as in Locke's political philosophy, the social justice of trusteeship was both temporary and indefinite in its duration.

The political principle of trusteeship, situated firmly in the Whig tradition, was challenged in Britain by the revival of the evangelical tradition after the 1780s.[25] In contrast to the Calvinist concept of an Elect destined for salvation, evangelicals emphasized that grace was available to all people who performed good works and lived in accordance with Biblical precepts. Granted, evangelicals and the advocates of trusteeship shared a strong faith in the religious superiority of Christianity, and a firm commitment to capitalist development. Moreover, the advocates of evangelicalism and trusteeship acknowledged a close connection between commerce and

Christianity. In contrast to Burke, however, most evangelicals advocated an interventionist programme bent upon systematic social reform as an integral part of Christian conversion. While evangelicals, like the advocates of trust, believed in natural progress along a hierarchy of civilization, they regarded conversion as a moral imperative and a prerequisite for 'civilized' social justice.

Trusteeship would continue to inform British views on India, but it appears that this concept did not figure prominently in other aspects of British imperial politics during much of the Victorian era.[26] This apparent lapse in the tradition of trusteeship in Britain is probably attributable to two factors in the political environment. As suggested above, trusteeship gave way to a tradition of evangelical philanthropy, which justified British missionary and commercial expansion on the next imperial frontier: the 'Dark Continent' of Africa. Also, trusteeship was primarily associated with imperial administration, and British governments throughout most of the nineteenth century pursued 'free trade imperialism' and attempted to avoid the creation of new administrations outside of India. It is telling, in this regard, that British officials began to return to trusteeship in the era of the 'new imperialism' at the end of the century, when Britain began to establish administrative control over an increasing amount of territory, especially in Africa. Most importantly, British officials wanted to represent the expansion of industrial capitalism as a means to promote social justice among the 'savages' who laboured for the capitalist's profit. In 1896, the Colonial Secretary, Joseph Chamberlain, declared: 'We, in our Colonial policy, as fast as we acquire new territory and develop it, develop it as trustees of civilization for the commerce of the world.'[27] As discussed below, the British government would subsequently join the United States in invoking trusteeship as the dominant principle of imperial administration and international government after World War I.

US officials would bring distinctive beliefs about trusteeship and empire to the Peace Conference at Versailles. The US government had looked to the British Empire in creating its own ethic of imperial expansion, but the US ethic had developed along different lines over the course of the nineteenth century. Whereas Britain most often asserted its imperial trust over South Asians and, subsequently, Africans, the US primarily asserted its trust over native Americans and, subsequently, Filipinos, following the Spanish–American War of 1898. While US officials generally did not use the word 'trust' to describe their relations to native Americans until the General Allotment Act, or Dawes Act, of 1887, they emphasized the status of the native American as a 'ward' – a term common in the British tradition of trusteeship – and described the just role of the US government with words such as 'guardian'.

The United States would reconcile capitalism and social justice in its trust over native Americans, but this trust departed from the tenets of Whig trusteeship as promulgated by Locke and Burke, and as deployed in British imperial policy in North America. US colonial officials regarded Christian conversion and social reform as prerequisites of social justice, and they distinguished themselves from the British imperial regime by funding missionaries as agents of official policy after the early nineteenth century.[28] This evangelical reform programme was inextricably linked to capitalist development, primarily in commercial agriculture, in the belief that such development would promote social virtues of the same kind that Locke had envisioned in the seventeenth century. Under the terms of numerous treaties, the US government attempted to shift native American property ownership from a communal to an individual basis, and to push native Americans from hunting or mixed economies to yoemanry.[29]

Social justice in US relations with native Americans depended on assimilation and capitalist development. However, the presumed Christian duty of the US government to reform native Americans conflicted initially with US recognition of native sovereignty. In contrast to the British Crown, which had acknowledged the sovereignty of native Americans through numerous treaties after the seventeenth century, the US government would proceed to undermine and then reject native sovereignty, first in the courts, and then in Congress. At the outset, however, with no clear plans for colonial expansion and without the resources to wage wars against native American tribes, the US government followed British precedents in recognizing native American sovereignty. In 1789, Henry Knox, the Secretary of War, who had authority over native American affairs, stated that 'Indian tribes possess the right of the soil of all lands within their limits,' and that the ownership of these lands could only be transferred with the native Americans' consent, through purchase under the authority of the US government.[30] This official recognition of native sovereignty was subsequently ignored by white settlers and state governments, which seized lands and challenged native American property rights in the courts. While the federal government generally acquiesced to settler and state demands, initiating the policy of 'Indian removal' under President James Monroe in the 1820s, the US Senate continued to ratify treaties – over four hundred in all – until 1871.

Four Supreme Court decisions by Chief Justice John Marshall, issued from 1810 to 1832, undermined native sovereignty and laid the legal foundation for the US government's explicit declaration of trust over native Americans later in the century.[31] These decisions generally focused on the need to reconcile native American sovereignty with state assertions of dominion over native lands. Looking back to relevant British policies and laws, Marshall decided that the relationship between native Americans and the US government was fundamentally different, given that native Americans increasingly depended on the government for protection and the regulation of trade. In his majority opinion in *Cherokee Nation* v. *State of Georgia* (1831), Marshall observed that native Americans were 'in a state of pupilage. Their relation to the United States resembles that of a ward to his guardian.' Consequently, Marshall chose to qualify native American sovereignty, explaining, 'It may be doubted whether those tribes which reside within the acknowledged boundaries of the United States can, with strict accuracy, be denominated foreign nations. They may, more correctly, perhaps be denominated domestic dependent nations.'[32] This peculiar legal status was further weakened after the mid-nineteenth century, when US officials used their military and economic superiority to establish treaties that gave formidable, discretionary powers to the President and Congress.[33] Although these treaties were irregular in their terms, they uniformly reflected a shift in the balance of power to the native Americans' detriment. This shift further weakened native American claims to sovereignty, which had been already undermined by the Marshall court, and prompted the Senate to cease ratifying treaties after 1871 on the grounds that native peoples no longer constituted sovereign nations in relation to the US.[34]

Having successfully challenged native American sovereignty, the US government simultaneously expanded its authority and asserted the justice of its rule on the bases of Christian reform and capitalist development. These policies came together most prominently in the Dawes Act of 1887, which made the government the trustee over vast tracts of land occupied by native peoples. This act was designed to facilitate the allotment of property to individual native Americans, in the hope of breaking down tribal control over lands and destroying the tribal cultures and economies that presumably kept many native Americans in a state of 'barbarism' – and beyond the reach of US capitalism. The mismanagement and exploitation of these 'trust lands' had calamitous affects upon the indigenous peoples, reducing native American land holdings from 138 million acres in 1887 to 48 million acres in 1934, when the allotment policy was ended.[35] Moreover, a landmark ruling on the government's trust policy destroyed the last vestiges of native American sovereignty under treaty. In the decision of *Lone Wolf* v. *Hitchcock* in 1903, the US government won unilateral authority to modify and terminate existing treaties.[36]

The Dawes Act advanced a larger government campaign to reform native American societies on a Christian, capitalist model. Between 1880 and 1930, for example, about 80 per cent of native American children were forced to attend boarding schools, away from their families and communities, where they were instructed in Euro-American culture, ranging from language to attire.[37] In an effort to induce native Americans to assilimate politically, the US government even began to impose citizenship upon them in the late nineteenth century, culminating in 1924, when Congress unilaterally conferred citizenship upon all native Americans. It is important to note that, while the US trust over native Americans was temporary, this trust was to conclude not with self-determination, but with complete acculturation and political assimilation. The social justice of this system derived from the firm belief of US officials and evangelical reformers that native Americans were better off 'civilized' than 'savage', whether they knew it or not.

The United States moved beyond colonialism in America to become an overseas imperial power during and after the Spanish-American War of 1898. This was not the first time that the US had projected its military power beyond the nation's borders, but it was the first time that the US was recognized as an imperial power comparable to the traditional Great Powers of Europe. Both US imperialists and anti-imperialists referred to US policies toward native Americans in major public debates over the annexation of the former Spanish colony of the Philippines.[38] Indeed, in declaring war on Spain, the US had defined its prospective relations with the Philippines as a trust. However, this trust proved to be different from the trust imposed on native Americans: it drew on the Whig tradition as opposed to the evangelical one. While the US government committed itself to the capitalist development of the Philippines, it also declared, through the first Philippine Commission in 1899, that it would enable the Philippine people to achieve democratic self-government.[39] Moreover, the US pursued a policy of relative toleration toward non-Christian tribes in the Philippines, in stark contrast to its treatment of native Americans.[40] These principles informed President William McKinley's statement on the Philippines to the US Congress on 3 December 1900: 'The fortunes of war have thrown upon this nation an unsought trust which should be unselfishly discharged and devolves upon this Government a moral as well as a material responsibility toward those millions we have freed from an oppressive yoke.'[41]

By the early twentieth century, the US had applied an evangelical tradition of political trusteeship to its domestic colonialism and a Whig tradition to its overseas imperialism. In the case of native Americans, the Dawes Act of 1887 and the decision in *Lone Wolf* in 1903 marked the erosion of native American sovereignty, and of any real hope for national self-determination. The justice of US trusteeship depended on native Americans conforming to the dominant Christian culture and capitalist economy of the United States. By contrast, the justice of the US trust over the Philippines depended on progress toward forms of political self-determination – however imperfect – official tolerance of cultural differences, and social improvement through capitalist development.

In the light of these incongruous evangelical and Whig traditions of trusteeship in the US, President Woodrow Wilson would apply the principle of trust to the settlement of international colonial issues after World War I. On 20 April 1915, two years before the entrance of the US into the war as an 'associate' power, Wilson anticipated the central role of the US as a mediator of the postwar settlement. The US was well suited to this role, he believed, because it could engage in just deliberation with 'no hampering ambitions as a world power'. With an eye toward the Philippines, and with no apparent reflection on the US trust over native Americans, Wilson declared:

> If we have been obliged by circumstances ... to take territory which we otherwise would not have thought of taking, I believe I am right in saying that we have considered it our duty to administer that territory, not for ourselves, but for the people living in it, and to put this burden upon our consciences – not to think that this thing is ours for our use, but to regard ourselves as trustees of the great business for those to whom it does really belong, trustees ready to hand it over to the *cestui que trust* at any time, when the business seems to make that possible and feasible.[42]

Trustees, wards and international government

World War I provoked debates in both Great Britain and the United States over capitalism, social justice and imperial rule. A growing number of British radicals and Labour Party leaders, in particular, questioned the established arrangements of the Empire, asking whether capitalism had actually promoted or undermined welfare and social justice among imperial subjects. One of the leading radical critics of imperialism, E. D. Morel, further argued that European capitalist competition in Africa had exacerbated tensions that had led to the war in the first place.[43] In order to reduce imperialist competition and ensure both welfare and social justice for imperial subjects, radicals proposed that a new system of international government, a 'league of nations', should oversee the redistribution of Europe's imperial possessions at the war's end.[44] This proposal immediately raised questions regarding sovereignty and the prospect of political self-determination for imperial subjects. After all, the war had involved millions of imperial subjects around the world, opening the door to numerous demands for self-government, if not independence, as just compensation for their labour, blood and treasure.

At the beginning of January 1918, the Prime Minister, David Lloyd George, informed his War Cabinet that he regarded Germany's colonies as the most difficult point in defining Britain's war aims.[45] Lloyd George and the Cabinet were determined to retain Germany's Empire if the allies won the war, but they had difficulty in justifying this seizure of territory in Britain's current political environment. Over the previous two years, radicals and Labour leaders had promoted public opposition to 'a war of conquest', asserting that there could be no justice in capitalist expansion at the expense of soldiers in the trenches.[46] This domestic pressure on Lloyd George was compounded on 8 January 1918, when President Woodrow Wilson made his famous Fourteen Points speech, in which he justified the war as a battle for the political self-determination of small nations. Since the US had entered the war in April 1917, Lloyd George had attempted to maintain at least the façade of consensus with Wilson, despite his personal frustration over the President's meddling in Britain's imperial affairs. On 5 January 1918, in his definitive speech on British war aims to trade union delegates at the Central Hall in Westminster, the Prime Minister had actually pre-empted Wilson in endorsing political self-determination for small nations, including the German colonies. Lloyd George explained that the political status of the colonies should be determined by a postwar conference 'whose decision must have primary regard to the wishes and interests of the native inhabitants'.[47] While Lloyd George made much of his support for national self-determination in public statements, he noted privately that 'precisely how the principle was to be applied need not now be discussed.'[48]

Lloyd George and Wilson were far from victory in January 1918, but they both hoped to achieve a peace settlement that would lay the foundation of a new era of Anglo-American cooperation and world leadership. Lloyd George tolerated Wilson's enthusiasm for a 'league of nations', despite his hostility to the idea that the league should function, in part, as a 'supernational' colonial authority. Wilson believed that the league could reduce future conflicts by managing the redistribution of European imperial territory after the war, and toward this end he attempted to conceive a new colonial system that would prove acceptable to the British. He found this acceptable alternative in the 'mandates system', an administrative system that he derived, in large part, from a treatise entitled, *The League of Nations: A Practical Suggestion*, by the Afrikaner war hero and politician, Jan Smuts, who was a member of the British Imperial War Cabinet.[49] Smuts modelled his own vision of the league on the British Commonwealth, stating: 'Today the British Commonwealth of Nations remains the only embryo League of Nations because it is based on the true principles of national freedom and political decentralization.'[50] In language reminiscent of Locke and Burke, Smuts asserted that a just international government, like a just imperial government, should resemble the relationship between a parent and a child. The colonial ward retained rights to his person, his labour and his land, but his property and affairs would be governed by a guardian for his benefit. The presumed immaturity of the colonial ward and the ward's incompetence to manage his own affairs were measured against a hierarchy of civilization. As Jan Smuts observed: 'The German colonies in the Pacific and Africa are inhabited by barbarians, who not only cannot possibly govern themselves, but to whom it would be impracticable to apply any ideas of political self-determination in the European sense.'[51] These wards would be raised as producers and consumers in the imperial capitalist economy until they achieved the level of civilization necessary to administrate social justice among themselves.

In seeking precedents for an international mandates system, Wilson, Smuts, and most other advocates of a league of nations, looked to the Berlin Act of 1885 and the Brussels Declaration of 1890, both of which had laid down ground rules of international administration in the Congo river basin.[52] In general terms, proponents of the mandates system pointed to these treaties as examples of a new spirit of international cooperation in imperial affairs. More specifically, they praised these treaties for promoting free commercial exchange and for transcending sovereignty in the interest of peaceful capitalist development. Granted, these treaties did nothing to halt the legendary brutalities of the Congo Free State, but proponents of the mandates system nonetheless saw them as important statements of principle that might finally be realized in practice.

The British War Cabinet embraced the prospective mandates system by the end of 1918, having calculated that Britain could acquire Germany's colonies through this experiment in international government. In November 1918, the Colonial Office noted that the Berlin Act and the Brussels Declaration, the most frequently cited precedents for the mandates system, carried no means of enforcement. In the end, the mandates system might prove to be only an ethical pretense. The particular phraseology of this ethical pretense had yet, however, to be determined, and so British officials remained wary of charges of territorial aggrandizement. Meanwhile, with a comparatively sincere interest in defining the justice of imperial governance under a new league of nations, President Wilson drew upon the work of a number of US, British and British imperial officials in drafting the Covenant of the League of Nations.[53] Again, Jan Smuts provided the means to reconcile US and British interests, this time through the concept of trusteeship. In a resolution of 30 January 1919, submitted to the Council of Ten, Smuts described the mandates system as a 'sacred trust'. Three days later, Wilson incorporated this specific language into his fourth draft of the League of Nations Covenant, and it would subsequently appear in the final Convenant under Article 22.[54]

The principle of trusteeship was ideally suited to British imperial ambitions under the League of Nations. In accepting responsibility for overseas territory and peoples 'in trust', British officials neither claimed sovereignty over the lands in question, nor did they completely deny the peoples' right to self-determination. Instead, they would ostensibly prepare their imperial 'wards' to determine their own political course in the future – and an indefinite future at that. The civilized hierarchy against which trustees evaluated their wards was manifested in the ranking of A, B and C mandates, ranging from those peoples who could be educated in the principles and skills of self-government in the foreseeable future to those peoples whose barbarism was irremediable. While there is no evidence that the Imperial War Cabinet made a concerted decision to deploy the tradition of trusteeship to support its aims, it is apparent that the themes of this tradition enabled them to navigate between domestic agitation against territorial aggrandizement and President Wilson's call for the self-determination of small nations.[55] The principle of self-determination resonated for years to come, but US pressure would dissipate after the US Congress refused to support the government's participation in the League, leaving the mandates system under strong British influence.

Apart from the League of Nations, there was a revival of the tradition of trusteeship in British imperial politics after World War I. Addressing the House of Lords on 13 May 1920, Viscount Milner, the former High Commissioner in South Africa and the current Colonial Secretary, stated:

> I may say ... that I accept – I have repeatedly stated it myself – the principle of trusteeship with regard to our position as a nation in all these dependent Crown Colonies and Protectorates. I consider that wherever we are obliged, owing to the backwardness of the population of these countries, to keep the ultimate authority in our own hands, we have to exercise that authority in the interests of the people of those countries and not for our own advantage.[56]

There is a significant difference between the concept of justice in the postwar revival of trusteeship and in the previous Whig and evangelical traditions. Considering the theological origins and strong Protestant connotations of trusteeship between the sixteenth and eighteenth centuries, it is noteworthy that Milner does not explicitly define trust as a Christian duty. It is remarkable, in fact, how little the advocates of 'trust' in the 1920s apparently knew of its theological origins.[57] Jan Smuts, who played an important role in presenting the British Commonwealth as a model for the 'sacred trust' of the mandates system, regarded trusteeship as a recent idea. In a speech in Cape Town, South Africa, in 1942, Smuts recalled: 'I remember from my young days that Cecil Rhodes used repeatedly to say that the proper relation between whites and blacks in this country was the relation between guardian and ward. This is the basis of trusteeship.'[58] Having cited Rhodes as the source of trusteeship, Smuts further observed that '(Trusteeship) is closely connected with our Christian ideals.'[59] Smuts, did not, however, elaborate upon the latter point.

This reference to Rhodes conveys the central importance of capitalism in defining the social justice of trusteeship in the twentieth century. British officials no longer articulated trusteeship as a Christian duty, but rather as a responsibility to maintain and improve 'native welfare' through capitalist development.[60] The most important postwar treatise on imperial administration, Sir Frederick Lugard's *The Dual Mandate in British Tropical Africa* (1922), makes virtually no mention of 'Christian duty' in defining Britain's 'dual mandate' as a colonial power. Lugard, the former Governor of Nigeria, argued that Britons should act 'as trustees to civilization for the adequate development of (the natives') resources and as trustees for the welfare of the native races.'[61] 'Let it be admitted,' declared Lugard, 'that Europe is in Africa for the mutual benefit of her own industrial classes and of the native races in their progress to a higher plane; that the benefit can be made reciprocal and that it is the aim and desire of civilised administration to fulfil this dual mandate.'[62] As a powerful member of the Permanent Mandates Commission of the League of Nations, Lugard saw to it that his dual mandate became the model upon which the principle of trusteeship took shape under international government.

Although the justice of trusteeship was no longer defined in elaborate Christian terms, there were other aspects of it that remained consistent with Whig themes. While government officials no longer characterized imperial governance as 'providential' – or in any respect theological – they nonetheless defined it as a 'sacred duty'. Like Burke, the latter-day advocates of trusteeship accepted cultural differences between peoples and preferred to avoid social reform projects. Imperial officials asserted that imperial subjects would benefit from capitalist development, with a view toward promoting liberal democracy and loyalty and, eventually, attaining self-government within the British Commonwealth. As in the Whig view of trusteeship, the ward retained his or her natural rights to property and sovereignty, and the trustee's authority to manage the ward's property was to expire at such time as the ward learned to emulate civilized society. The trustee, of course, possessed the ability to determine when the ward was ready for independence.

One might reasonably speculate that the shift away from the earlier religious connotations of trusteeship was a response to radicals who had propagated an economic critique of imperialism since the turn of the century. More importantly, imperial officials revived and reinvented the tradition of trusteeship after the war in ways that made ethical sense in view of their economic and political circumstances.[63] Britain emerged victorious, but in a weakened state, from the war, and it soon confronted uprisings in Ireland, India and Egypt by resurgent nationalist movements. At the same time, the Government was attempting to restore the home front through social reform and welfare initiatives under the gaze of a strengthening labour movement. In its efforts to stabilize the Empire and simultaneously recover at home, the Government sought to delegate political responsibilities when possible and avoid overseas social reform projects, which its saw as tangential to the business of Empire.

Yet there was more than one concept of trusteeship in postwar Britain. An alternative concept of trusteeship had developed since the turn of the century within a radical tradition that embraced Liberalism, the labour movement and Fabianism.[64] E. D. Morel, the most influential advocate of this radical tradition of trust during and immediately after the war, asserted that the justice of trusteeship depended on the trustee's positive support for native property rights and respect for cultural relativism. Moreover, he argued that in regions unsuited to white settlement, such as tropical Africa, trustees should be subject to international oversight.[65] Of these three factors, the preservation of land rights was clearly, in Morel's opinion, 'the acid test of trusteeship'.[66] Looking to the Berlin Act as a precedent for the mandates system, Morel emphasized that the act had 'made no attempt to define native tenure' or to forbid the expropriation of African lands.[67] Likewise, he faulted the mandates system for not providing positive guarantees of the land rights of indigenous peoples and he therefore condemned the mandates as 'an attempt ... to reconcile the altruistic pronouncements of President Wilson with what is substantially a policy of imperialistic grab at the expense of the beaten foe.'[68]

Morel believed that capitalism had to be combined with positive rights in order to achieve social justice, and in these terms he strongly supported capitalist development in Africa. Whereas Morel advocated development on the basis of native land rights and, in turn, a greater degree of freedom under colonial rule, Frederick Lugard and other imperial officials rejected positive rights as the seeds of discontent and political instability. Members of Britain's political left, and especially the Fabian Colonial Bureau, would continue to push Morel's radical agenda after his death in 1924, calling for the incorporation of native land rights and cultural relativism into the 'sacred trust' of the mandates system.[69] Leonard Woolf and Arthur Creech Jones, among others, would play important roles in incorporating this radical tradition of trust into official policy after the 1930s, presaging the terms of the United Nations Charter of 1945.

The proponents of this radical tradition of trusteeship, often couched in terms of rights, portrayed their agenda as an extension of lost imperial ideals. Specifically, they argued that capitalism had promoted injustice by destroying the social fabric of foreign nations, and they called for a return to policies of toleration, which had allegedly distinguished the British Empire until the late eighteenth century. Speaking of this earlier period, Leonard Woolf explained: 'There was ... no attempt to dominate or control or to force one civilization to adjust itself to the political or economic system of another. The adjustment of one civilization to the other was on a basis of tolerance – religious, racial, political, economic tolerance. The contract between the continents and the peoples remained mainly economic.'[70] This approach to Empire had allegedly ended in the nineteenth century, when industrialization provided Europe with the power of conquest. Woolf urged the League of Nations to return to imperial ideals and fulfil its trust by respecting natives' customary rights, thus enabling Europe's imperial wards to reclaim their freedom. He thus invoked the identification of trusteeship and cultural tolerance, as advocated from Locke to Burke, to advance the contemporary principle of cultural relativism.

By the 1930s, British advocates of trust on both the left and right acknowledged that capitalist development and nationalism were producing changes in African and Asian societies that they could not stop.

Nonetheless, they still hoped to manage these changes in a just manner under the terms of trusteeship. The Labour Party, like old guard imperialists, was committed to sustaining the Empire through improved welfare, and so it orchestrated passage of the Colonial Development Act of 1929, followed by the Colonial Development and Welfare Acts of 1940 and 1945.[71] At the same time, progressive colonial officials determined that they would have to expand upon their recognition of native rights to welfare by acknowledging native rights to eventual self-government under the principle of trust.[72] British Labour and progressive colonial officials were not calling for declarations of independence, but rather for a transition to a multinational, self-governing Commonwealth.

Colonial nationalism and the relatively weakened state of Britain's economy and military between the wars were the main reasons why British officials were prepared to begin laying the groundwork for political self-determination. Nationalists took different approaches to trusteeship, some choosing to adapt it to their own ends, while others rejected it altogether. Mohandas Gandhi took the former course, employing trusteeship to critique capitalism and define an alternative economic basis for social justice in India. While Gandhi subscribed to the concept of a hierarchy of civilizations, he criticized western nations for their self-serving materialism and their destruction of foreign societies to extract labour and wealth. As part of his campaign to establish economic autonomy for the Indian people, Gandhi advocated a distribution of wealth that would enable each man 'to supply all his natural needs'. This would not entail the violent seizure of money from the rich, because, Gandhi reasoned, 'society (would) be the poorer, for it (would) lose the gifts of a man who knows how to accumulate wealth'. Instead, he explained, 'The rich man will be left in possession of his wealth, of which he will use what he reasonably requires for his personal needs and will act as a trustee for the remainder to be used for the society. In this argument honesty on the part of the trustee is assumed.'[73]

Other nationalists rejected the justice of trusteeship altogether by invoking rights based on democratic principles and dissident concepts of culture and history. The rights claimed by these colonial nationalists were not contingent on an historical ascent of the imperialist's civilized hierarchy, but rather on their own cultural traditions. The Kenyan leader, Jomo Kenyatta, criticized 'those professional friends of the African who are prepared to maintain their friendship for eternity as a sacred duty, provided only that the African will continue to play the part of an ignorant savage so that they can monopolise the office of interpreting his mind and speaking for him.'[74] Trust was a waiting game, but rights empowered political claims in the present – political claims that the British government tried to accommodate more often after World War I, though not at the expense of ultimate political control.

Following the lead of nationalists, imperial officials increasingly recognized in the 1930s that the social justice of trusteeship depended on the recognition of political rights and on progress toward political self-determination. The Government in London was not ready, however, to construct a new, comprehensive political order – particularly not after Winston Churchill became Prime Minister during World War II in May 1940. Churchill wanted to turn back the clock on the progress of Britain's imperial subjects toward self-government, but his views were out of step with a general turn in Britain toward the fulfilment of trusteeship through the recognition of rights, as would become evident at the war's end. In the meantime, Churchill, like David Lloyd George, was forced to cater to the idealism of a US President.

President Franklin Roosevelt was by no means revolutionary in his approach to the British Empire, but he advocated a new political order that was less conventional or moderate than that proposed by Woodrow Wilson over 20 years earlier. In view of the war in Europe, Roosevelt declared in his State of the Union Address of 1941 that American freedoms hinged on 'the supremacy of human rights everywhere'. Building on Jeffersonian liberalism, Roosevelt identified 'human rights' with his famous 'Four Freedoms' – that is, the right to freedom of speech, freedom of religion, freedom from want and freedom from fear.[75] Churchill and other British officials regarded 'human rights' as a threat to the political legitimacy of the Empire, so they sought to reconcile US and British colonial policies, as in 1919, on the basis of the concept of trusteeship. To their dismay, however, US officials initially lacked a clear definition of trusteeship upon which to build consensus. In committee hearings and congressional debates, US officials commonly sought to clarify the meaning and origin of trust, with mixed results.[76] This uncertainty over the meaning of trust arguably suited the US government, as the idea of trusteeship could thus be manipulated to serve US interests in a new international order. By the end of the war, US and British officials had established conflicting policies on trusteeship, the postwar settlement and especially the construction of the United Nations on the shattered remains of the League of Nations. These differences informed negotiations over the creation of the United Nations at the San Francisco Conference in 1945, during which Churchill handed control over British imperial policy to Clement Attlee and the first majority Labour government.

By this time, most British officials felt compelled to endorse political rights for Britain's imperial subjects as the basis of social justice under trusteeship. This prevailing view probably reflected the common revulsion toward the Nazis' language of racial superiority, a respect for the crucial participation of imperial forces in the war and a realistic assessment of the power of colonial nationalists.[77] The politics of rights subsequently overcame the tradition of trusteeship in Britain. After the 1940s, trusteeship was actually replaced by new traditions of 'multi-racialism', 'non-racialism' and 'partnership' in a Commonwealth of nations.[78]

The radical tradition of trusteeship, typically articulated in terms of rights, had achieved currency in both British and US politics by 1945, but

Britain's commitment to the Empire could still not be easily reconciled with the US government's postwar policies. In addressing the proposal for a new International Trusteeship System under the United Nations, US officials wanted to make international peace and security the priorities of the system, with political oversight by a supervisory body under the UN Assembly.[79] By contrast, British officials argued that the Trusteeship System should prioritize welfare, and they opposed political oversight by any UN authority.[80] In the end, given the postwar balance of power, the UN International Trusteeship System was established as the US desired.

Conclusion

Building upon the League of Nations Covenant of 1919, the framers of the United Nations Charter of 1945 combined the League's 'sacred trust' with human rights in the new International Trusteeship System.[81] One might argue that this combination of trusteeship and human rights marked a political turning point from the era of European great powers and Empire to that of US and Soviet super powers and decolonization. After all, human rights are powerful bases of social justice, empowering claims to sustenance, relief from suffering and even political self-determination. Yet trust remained the dominant concept in UN colonial administration, displaying remarkable consistency with imperial traditions. Like earlier imperial trustees, UN trustees reconciled their commitments to the expansion of modern capitalism and social justice by making a social virtue of capitalist development under their authority. After 1945, as before, trustees acknowledged that their wards retained natural property rights, especially in the ownership of their land. Although the standards of 'civilized' hierarchy are more difficult to discern, a social hierarchy remained in place, given that the wards benefited from 'development' under their trustee's guidance. This development focused on integration into the global capitalist economy and the international community of nations, which entailed social reforms that finally rendered the wards capable of determining their own political course. Under international government, as in empire, the trustee acknowledged his political authority to be temporary. Indeed, the UN Trusteeship Council suspended its operation in 1994, after the independence of Palau, the last United Nations trust territory.

The experience of native Americans, by contrast, casts a different light upon the social justice of trust and the rights of colonized peoples under international government. In 1960 the United Nations issued the 'Declaration on the Granting of Independence to Colonial Countries and Peoples'. This declaration acknowledged that 'all peoples have the right to self-determination,' and it ordered that 'immediate steps shall be taken in Trust or Non-Self-Governing Territories or all other territories which have not yet attained independence, to transfer all powers to the peoples of those territories ... in accordance with their freely expressed will and desire.' This declaration might have provided native Americans, among other colonized peoples, with an international, legal basis upon which to build a case for a greater measure of autonomy. However, the UN General Assembly passed a follow-up provision, General Assembly Resolution 1541, which restricted the Declaration to peoples separated from colonizing powers by at least thirty miles of open ocean. Having unilaterally declared its trusteeship over native Americans, the US has thus been able to preclude any challenge to its colonial policies under international law. One might recall that native Americans were prominent subjects of John Locke's political philosophy, which was built upon trust, and so it is perhaps fitting to conclude this chapter with their experience. Unfortunately, the case of native Americans illustrates the problematic ethics of trust and self-determination under empire and international government in the twentieth century.

Notes

1. Wm. Roger Louis observed over 35 years ago that there was not an adequate history of trusteeship, empire and international government; an observation which remains true today. This chapter is a first attempt to construct a broad historical overview of trusteeship in comparative perspective. I gratefully acknowledge the critical assistance of Mark Bevir, Frank Trentmann, Caroline Cox and David Lieberman. See Wm. Roger Louis, 'Great Britain and International Trusteeship: The Mandate System', in Robin Winks (ed.), *The Historiography of the British Empire-Commonwealth* (Durham, NC: Duke University Press, 1966), p. 310.
2. Anthony Pagden, *Lords of all the World* (New Haven: Yale University Press, 1995); Wolfgang Mommsen, *Theories of Imperialism* (New York: Random House, 1980).
3. Valerie Braithwaite and Margaret Levi (eds), *Trust and Governance* (New York: Russell Sage Foundation, 1998).
4. Uday Mehta, 'Liberal Strategies of Exclusion', in Frederick Cooper and Ann Laura Stoler (eds), *Tensions of Empire* (Berkeley: University of California Press, 1997), p. 61.
5. Bernard Bailyn, *The Ideological Origins of the American Revolution* (Cambridge, MA: Belknap Press of Harvard University Press, 1967); Paul Nagel, *This Sacred Trust* (Oxford: Oxford University Press, 1971)
6. This genealogy of political trusteeship builds upon an important conceptual distinction which one finds in the fields of political philosophy and law. J. W. Gough suggests that political trusteeship can be divided into two forms: the idea of trust as a moral responsibility or duty, and the idea of trust as 'a metaphor for the private law of trusts' governing property. This study takes up Gough's suggestion 'that the idea [of political trusteeship] arose, independently at first of the legal trust, as an extension of the general meaning of trust or confidence ... ' I do not believe that the roots of trusteeship – at least in the Anglo-American imperial tradition – are to be found in the private law of trust governing property, as derived from the Roman law of trust. See J. W. Gough, *John Locke's Political Philosophy* (Oxford: Clarendon Press, 1973), pp. 154–6, 165. Regarding the history of the private law of trust and its political influences, see F. W. Maitland, *Equity* (Cambridge: Cambridge University Press, 1936); David Johnston, *The Roman Law of Trusts* (Oxford: Clarendon Press, 1988).

7. Luther's foremost advocate in England, William Tyndale, articulated the relationship of faith and trust in his interpolation of Luther's 'A Prologe to the Romayns'. See William Tyndale, *The New Testament translated by William Tyndale, 1534* (Cambridge: Cambridge University Press, 1938), p. 301.
8. Quentin Skinner, *The Foundations of Modern Political Thought, Vol. 2: The Age of Reformation* (Cambridge: Cambridge University Press, 1978), p. 18.
9. Ibid, pp. 236–8.
10. Peter Laslett observes that trust is the fundamental principle of Locke's political philosophy. See John Locke, *Two Treatises of Government*, ed. Peter Laslett (Cambridge: Cambridge University Press, 1996), p. 113.
11. James Tully, *An Approach to Political Philosophy: Locke in Contexts* (Cambridge: Cambridge University Press, 1993), pp. 137–76; Mehta, pp. 67–70.
12. Tully; Locke's acknowledgement of a right to own land must be distinguished from his related claim that Europeans had a right to claim particular lands in America that were presumably 'vacant'.
13. Tully, pp. 141–2; John Locke, *A Letter Concerning Toleration* (1685), ed. James Tully (Indianapolis: Hackett Publishing Co., 1983), p. 43.
14. Locke, *Two Treatises*, p. 381; Gough, p. 164.
15. Locke, *Two Treatises*, p. 381.
16. Ibid.
17. Ibid, pp. 287–8.
18. Locke did not extend this right to slaves on Britain's colonial plantations, who, he argued, had lost their freedom under the laws of 'just war'. See Ibid, pp. 284–5.
19. Ibid, pp. 109, 407–8.
20. P. J. Marshall (ed.), *Problems of Empire: Britain and India, 1757–1813* (London: George Allen & Unwin, Ltd., 1968), pp. 174–5.
21. Edmund Burke, *Reflections on the Revolution in France* (Indianapolis: Hackett Publishing Co., 1987), pp. 80–1; Edmund Burke, *The Works of the Right Honorable Edmund Burke (Revised Edition), Vol. IX* (Boston: Little Brown, and Co., 1867), p. 399.
22. Ibid, p. 340.
23. Ibid, p. 379.
24. C. B. Macpherson, *Burke* (New York: Hill and Wang, 1980), p. 59.
25. Historians have previously suggested that trusteeship was adapted to evangelicalism, but this is hard to reconcile with the fact that advocates of trust both before and after the Victorian era opposed an interventionist social reform programme. See G. R. Mellor, *British Imperial Trusteeship, 1783–1850* (London: Faber & Faber, Ltd, 1951).
26. See, for example, Thomas Macaulay, Speech in the House of Commons on the Government of India, 10 July 1833, in *Miscellaneous Works of Lord Macaulay, Vol. V* (New York: Harper, 1880), pp. 131–67.
27. Quoted by Lord Emmott in the House of Lords, 13 May 1920, *Parliamentary Debates*, Fifth Series, Vol. XL, House of Lords, (London, 1920), p. 317. Also see L. I. Izuakor, 'Colonial Challenges and Administrative Response: Sir Charles Eliot and "Native" Trusteeship in Kenya, 1901–1904', *Transafrican Journal of History*, 17 (1988), 34–49.
28. Robert F. Berkhofer, *The White Man's Indian* (New York: Vintage Books, 1979), p. 150.
29. Francis Paul Prucha, *American Indian Treaties* (Berkeley: University of California Press, 1994), p. 10.

30. Anthony F. C. Wallace, *Jefferson and the Indians* (Cambridge, MA: Belknap Press of Harvard University Press, 1999), p. 167.

31. The four cases were *Fletcher v. Peck* (1810), *Johnson v. McIntosh* (1823), *Cherokee Nation v. State of Georgia* (1831), and *Worcester v. State of Georgia* (1832). See J. Burke, 'The Cherokee Cases: A Study in Law, Politics, and Morality', *Stanford Law Review*, 21 (1969), 500–31.

32. Ward Churchill, 'The Tragedy and the Travesty: The Subversion of Indigenous Sovereignty in North America', *American Indian Culture and Research Journal* 22 (2)(1998), 28–9.

33. Prucha, pp. 7–9.

34. John R. Wunder, *Retained by the People* (Oxford: Oxford University Press, 1994), p. 29.

35. Ibid, p. 33.

36. Blue Clark, *Lone Wolf v. Hitchcock* (Lincoln, Nebraska: University of Nebraska Press, 1994).

37. Churchill, 'The Tragedy and the Travesty', 23.

38. Walter Williams, 'United States Indian Policy and the Debate over Philippine Annexation', *Journal of American History* 66(4)(March 1980), 810–1.

39. Alpheus Snow, *The Question of Aborigines* (New York: G. P. Putnam's Sons, 1921), pp. 327–30.

40. Ibid, pp. 62–3.

41. M. F. Lindley, *The Acquisition and Government of Backward Territory in International Law* (Longmans, Green and Co., Ltd, London, 1926), p. 331.

42. *The Papers of Woodrow Wilson, Vol. 33*, ed. Arthur Link (Princeton University Press, Princeton, 1980), p. 39.

43. E. D. Morel, 'The African Problem and the Peace Settlement' (London: UDC. Pamphlet, No. 22a, July 1917), p. 5

44. George Egerton, *Great Britain and the Creation of the League of Nations* (Chapel Hill, NC: University of North Carolina Press, 1978).

45. Minutes of the War Cabinet, 3 January 1918, Public Records Office, Kew (hereafter PRO), CAB 23/5

46. Arthur Henderson, *The Aims of Labour* (London: Headley Bros Publishers, Ltd , 1918), pp. 85–7.

47. *The Times*, 7 January 1918

48. Minutes of the War Cabinet, 3 January 1918, PRO, CAB 23/5.

49. Jan Smuts, *The League of Nations: A Practical Suggestion* (London: Hodder and Stoughton, 1918); Lloyd E. Ambrosius, *Woodrow Wilson and the American Diplomatic Tradition* (Cambridge: Cambridge University Press, 1987); Michael D. Callahan, *Mandates and Empire: The League of Nations and Africa, 1914–1931* (Brighton: Sussex Academic Press, 1999).

50. Smuts, *The League of Nations*, p. 9

51. Ibid, p. 15.

52. Wm. Roger Louis, 'African Origins of the Mandates Idea', *International Organization* (Winter 1965).

53. David Hunter Miller, *The Drafting of the Convenant, Vol. 1* (New York: G. P. Putnam's Sons, 1928), especially Ch. 1.

54. Ibid, pp. 101, 105, 109; David Hunter Miller, *The Drafting of the Covenant, Vol. 2* (New York: G. P. Putnam's Sons, 1928), pp. 28, 103, 152.

55. Wm. Roger Louis, 'Great Britain and International Trusteeship: The Mandate System'.

56. House of Lords Debate, 13 May 1920, *The Parliamentary Debates*, Fifth Series, Vol. XL, House of Lords, (London, 1920), p. 319.
57. On the contrary, Ronald Robinson observes with reference to imperial officials of this era: 'If the men of the empire made a habit of moralizing their mundane purposes, it is reasonable to suppose that this was because theology was as vital to the imperial process as surplus capital or high velocity guns.' See Ronald Robinson, 'Andrew Cohen and the Transfer of Power in Tropical Africa, 1940–1951', in W. H. Morris-Jones and Georges Fischer (eds), *Decolonisation and After: The British and French Experience* (London: Frank Cass, 1980), p. 57.
58. Jan Smuts, 'The Basis of Trusteeship in African Native Policy', a speech delivered in Cape Town on 21 January 1942 (Cape Town: South African Institute of Race Relations, 1942), p. 7.
59. Ibid, p. 12.
60. Nicholas Owen, 'Critics of Empire in Britain', in Judith M. Brown and Wm. Roger Louis (eds), *The Oxford History of the British Empire, Vol. IV* (Oxford: Oxford University Press, 1999), pp. 194–95.
61. Lord Lugard, *The Dual Mandate in British Tropical Africa* (Hamden, CT.: Archon Books, 1965), p. 391.
62. Ibid, p. 617
63. Owen, p. 193.
64. Paul Rich, *Race and Empire in British Politics* (Cambridge: Cambridge University Press, 1986); Stephen Howe, *Anticolonialism in British Politics* (Oxford: Oxford University Press, 1993).
65. E. D. Morel, *The Black Man's Burden* (London: The National Labour Press, Ltd, 1920), pp. 224–5, 228.
66. Ibid, p. 170.
67. Ibid.
68. Ibid, p. 228
69. Leonard Woolf, *Imperialism and Civilization* (New York: Harcourt Brace and Co., 1928), pp. 116, 175–82.
70. Ibid, p. 60.
71. Wm. Roger Louis, *Imperialism at Bay* (Oxford: Oxford University Press, 1978), p. 100.
72. Robinson, 'Andrew Cohen and the Transfer of Power'.
73. *The Collected Works of Mahatma Gandhi, Vol. LXXII* (Ahmedabad: Navajivan Trust, 1994), pp. 399–401.
74. Jomo Kenyatta, *Facing Mt. Kenya* (New York: Vintage Books, 1965), p. xviii.
75. M. Glenn Johnson, 'The Contributions of Eleanor and Franklin Roosevelt to the Development of International Protection for Human Rights', *Human Rights Quarterly* 9(1) (1987), 19–48.
76. See, for example, Minutes of the First Meeting of the US Delegation to the San Francisco Conference, 13 March 1945, *Foreign Relations of the United States, Diplomatic Papers, 1945, Vol. 1* (Washington: U. S. Government Printing Office, 1967), p. 117.
77. Howe, *Anticolonialism*, pp. 325–6.
78. Ronald Hyam, 'Bureaucracy and "Trusteeship" in the Colonial Empire', in Judith Brown and Wm. Roger Louis (eds), *The Oxford History of the British Empire, Vol. IV* (Oxford: Oxford University Press, 1999), p. 265, 274.

79. The US policy on trusteeship was largely determined by the State Department's Committee on Dependent Areas. For a definitive account of Anglo-American policy making and negotiations, see Louis, *Imperialism at Bay*.
80. Memorandum by Mr Leo Pasvolsky, Special Assistant to the Secretary of State, for the President, 13 January 1945, *Foreign Relations of the United States, Diplomatic Papers, 1945, Vol. 1.*, p. 19.
81. See the Charter of the United Nations (1945), Ch. XII, Articles 73 and 76.

8
Cosmopolitanism, Rawls and the English School

Simon Caney

This chapter seeks to compare British and American treatments of internationalism, distributive justice and the market in the second half of the twentieth century. To do this, it outlines and compares two traditions on international justice and the market (one British and one American) before then examining how two alternative perspectives (again one British and one American) have emerged from reflection on the dilemmas faced by these two traditions. Section I examines the tradition of the 'English school' where this refers to a number of scholars working in British universities in the second half of the twentieth century who sought to defend a society of states. Section II turns to the Kantian tradition personified in the work of the leading American political philosopher, John Rawls, analysing his account of internationalism, justice and the market both in his early work *A Theory of Justice* and in his later work *The Law of Peoples*.[1] It argues that notwithstanding their different intellectual backgrounds, these two traditions share a number of common points in their account of international justice and in their relation to capitalism. The Westphalian ideals affirmed by Rawls and the English school have been subjected to much criticism. Section III analyses the critique of Rawls's treatment of international justice developed by American Rawlsian scholars including, most prominently, Charles Beitz. What Beitz, among others, has argued is that a consistent application of Rawls's international theory combined with a proper appreciation of the nature of international markets leads us to a radically revised, more cosmopolitan, theory of distributive justice.[2] The chapter then turns to recent British work on internationalism, namely the ideal of cosmopolitan democracy defended by British thinkers like David Held and Andrew Linklater.[3] The latter, like the cosmopolitan critics of Rawls's theory, invoke the existence of global markets, but they do so to show that democratic self-government requires democratic transnational political organizations. Both brands of cosmopolitanism, thus, argue that existing traditions presuppose a world containing economically independent political communities and that they need to be revised in a more cosmopolitan direction if they are to accommodate the dilemmas posed by global markets.[4] Equally important, however, this comparative analysis makes clear the diversity of cosmopolitan responses to the dilemmas issued by modern capitalism.

I

Let us begin then with the tradition of the English school. This term refers to an approach developed by a number of scholars, almost all of whom are based in British universities, normally in departments of international relations. Although identifying the members of a school of thought is not straightforward, the English school is normally taken to include figures such as Herbert Butterfield, Hedley Bull, Martin Wight, John Vincent and later writers like Robert Jackson, Barry Buzan, Andrew Hurrell, Tim Dunne and Nicholas Wheeler. One of the most significant contributions is Wight and Butterfield's edited volume on *Diplomatic Investigations*. This includes Wight's famous two essays 'Why is there no International Theory?' and 'Western Values in International Relations'.[5] Wight's thought is also represented in his posthumously published lectures *International Theory: The Three Traditions*.[6] Bull's major works include his influential book, *The Anarchical Society*, as well two early essays – 'Society and Anarchy in International Relations' and 'The Grotian Conception of International Society' – both of which were first published in *Diplomatic Investigations*.[7] More recently, the English School has enjoyed a considerable renaissance. Current defenders include Timothy Dunne, whose *Inventing International Society* is a sympathetic history of the English school, and Nicholas Wheeler, who has written a number of works exploring the approach of the English school to nonintervention.[8] Other contributions have been made by Barry Buzan and Andrew Hurrell.[9] Perhaps the most significant recent statement and defence of the ideals of the English school, however, is Robert Jackson's impressive *The Global Covenant*.[10]

Members of the English School tend to affirm two distinct, but related, claims.[11] First, they maintain, as a descriptive claim, that the international order is best understood as a society of states where '[a] *society of states* (or international society) exists when a group of states, conscious of certain common interests and common values, form a society in the sense that they conceive themselves to be bound by a common set of rules in their relations with one another, and share in the working of common institutions.'[12] For members of the English school, such as Bull and Wight, the 'society of states' is an accurate description of international politics.[13] They tend to contrast this factual position with two others. On the one hand, they reject certain realist conceptions of the international order. Bull, for example, distinguishes between an international system and international society. Realists see the international order as a 'system' in which units interact but they fail to see that the international order is a 'society' in which the members, states, see themselves as socially constituted and bound by the norms, values and rules of the international arena.[14] To develop the point somewhat, members of the English school contend that states internalize norms and see themselves as members of a society. As such purely mechanical accounts, such as that provided by structural realists like the American thinker Kenneth Waltz, are inadequate.[15] To use H. L. A. Hart's terms, the complaint against realists is that they do not capture the 'internal point of view'.[16] It is interesting to note here that when characterizing the society of states Bull ascribes mental states to states: they are described as '*recognising* certain common interests and perhaps some common values' and are said to '*regard* themselves as bound by certain rules' (my emphasis).[17] In other words, what a purely systemic account leaves out, and what the international society approach includes, is the first person perspective. Systemic accounts give a purely third person description of the international order but this omits the subjective experiences (the internal mental life) of the participants.

To recognize this point does not, however, lead them to overlook the central importance of power. Members of the English school thus often criticize what they see as utopian projects for ignoring power politics and as such they have much in common with realists. This points to a second contrast for as well as contrasting their view with realist depictions of the international arena, members of the English school contrast their position with a second position, which they term Kantianism, according to which there is a global community of persons.[18] In proposing the concept of an international society (or society of states) as a model by which to understand international relations, members of the English school thus explicitly locate themselves between two extremes, a Hobbesian realism and a Kantian world community.[19]

In addition to this descriptive claim, members of the English school affirm a second claim, arguing that the society of states represents an attractive ideal. The society of states is thus not simply an accurate account of international relations: it is also a desirable ethical vision that should be preserved and protected.[20] The society of states is defended primarily on the grounds that it protects liberty best in a plural and multicultural world. This, for example, is a key claim in Jackson's *The Global Covenant*.[21] This normative commitment is evident in the English school's endorsement of a strong norm of nonintervention. Indeed, the normative research agenda of the English school has traditionally focused primarily on the issues surrounding nonintervention. Bull edited a volume on the subject and John Vincent's first work, *Nonintervention and International Order*, is a major treatise on the role of nonintervention in international society and a vindication of nonintervention on the grounds that intervention would issue in international instability.[22] Again the argumentative strategy adopted by English school writers is to counterpose their position with two extremes, again, one realist and Hobbesian and the other cosmopolitan and Kantian, and to maintain that it is a promising middle way between two unacceptable extremes.[23] As a corollary of their commitment to preserving international society and the sovereignty of states, they tend to reject global schemes of distributive justice. Social justice, for members of the English school, should generally be implemented within the state and not at a transnational or global level. At the global level, what are of paramount importance are order and the integrity of states and consequently members of the English school have tended to be highly sceptical of global schemes of social justice.

The extent of this scepticism varies among members of the English School. To see this it is useful to bear in mind Bull's distinction, in 'The Grotian Conception of International Society', between 'pluralist' and 'solidarist' conceptions of international society.[24] According to the former, the international order is highly diverse and calls for states simply to respect one another. According to the latter, there is room for states to work together to promote common goals, including some minimal transnational ideals of distributive justice. As a number of scholars make clear, Bull's earliest work is emphatically pluralist but towards the end of his life he had moved towards the solidarist position.[25] The clearest illustration of this is his 1983 Hagey Lectures, which recognize the importance of international principles of distributive justice and record that there is an increasing recognition of people's entitlements.[26] Bull goes on to advance six propositions about international norms of economic justice. These are, first, that concepts of distributive justice are now a part of the international agenda and second that the participants in the debate continue to emphasize the entitlements of states rather than individuals. Third, and most significantly, he advances for the first time a substantive principle of international justice, one that requires the satisfaction of all persons' basic needs. He adds, however, in his fourth statement that there is no consensus on any principle above this bare minimum. He further maintains that while there is agreement that an outcome is unjust if it is generated by an unlawful process there is no agreement on the implications of this for colonialism and the issues of justice arising from that. There is, moreover, controversy about attempts to equalize the material resources of states.[27] Bull's Hagey Lectures do emphasize, then, the existence of diversity and he remains committed to order, arguing that the pursuit of justice can subvert international society.[28] Thus, even at the high point of his solidarism, Bull's principles of economic justice are minimal and heavily qualified and his pluralism is still evident.

Other members of the English school have also adopted a solidarist stance, expressing a concern about international distributive justice and criticizing earlier, more pluralist, strands in English school thinking. One prominent contemporary representative of the English school, for example, has written that '[i]t is hard to escape the conclusion that the international society tradition [which he equates with the English school] is vulnerable for its silences (or should it be silencing?) on the exploitative nature of global capitalist relations.'[29] Another contemporary English school thinker, Andrew Hurrell, has explored the nature of globalization and its impact on inequality.[30] Others have embraced some modest cosmopolitan conceptions of distributive justice. Most notably John Vincent defended a right to subsistence in his last work, *Human Rights and International Relations*. Vincent's treatment of international distributive justice is, however, rather limited. It does not explain why justice requires merely subsistence rights. In addition, it does not deal with the question of who is duty bound to protect these rights or what it would involve.[31] Furthermore, it is highly questionable whether the society of states is capable of resolving these distributive questions successfully because by dispersing power it precludes the sort of concerted action which is required to control global markets and promote a fair distribution of resources.[32] Nonetheless the solidarist members of the English school show a far greater willingness to entertain the possibility of global principles of distributive justice than do pluralist members.

II

We may now turn to the Kantian tradition associated with Rawls's work. As we shall see, his thought and that of the English school have some aspects in common. As is well known, Rawls employs the idea of a hypothetical social contract and locates himself in the contractarian tradition, drawing in particular on Immanuel Kant. His highly influential *A Theory of Justice* outlines and defends two principles of distributive justice, the first requiring the protection of each person's basic liberties and the second requiring both fair equality of opportunity and that social and economic institutions be structured to maximize the condition of the least well-off (the difference principle).[33] These principles apply to what Rawls terms the 'basic structure', by which he means the social economic and political institutions that determine people's lives.[34]

Two key features of Rawls's theory are worth noting. First, Rawls is often assumed to be defending a capitalist economy with a welfare state. This interpretation, while understandable, is nonetheless mistaken. In *A Theory of Justice* Rawls includes a few suggestive remarks on the market and makes clear that his two principles do not necessarily require the private ownership of the means of production. They are, Rawls argues, compatible both with liberal socialism and with what, following James Meade, he terms 'a property-owning democracy'.[35] In his preface to the French edition of *A Theory of Justice* Rawls elaborates further on the nature of a property-owning democracy, describing it as an economic regime in which the ownership of wealth and productive skills is widely dispersed, arguing that this is preferable to a system that combines capitalism with a welfare state.[36] The most extensive elaboration of his position is, however, in his recently published *Justice as Fairness: A Restatement* where Rawls discusses five different types of economic regime, which he terms, 'laissez-faire capitalism', 'welfare-state capitalism', 'state socialism with a command economy', 'property-owning democracy' and 'liberal (democratic) socialism'.[37] He argues that none of the first three are adequate. Laissez faire capitalism fails to secure the fair value of the political liberties, does not ensure people fair equality of opportunity and shows insufficient concern for the least well-off. Welfare state capitalism fares better but it, too, is inadequate. It also does not ensure that people have the material resources necessary for them to employ their basic liberties. Furthermore, although it aims at fair equality of opportunity it does not make sufficient headway. In addition to this, it is compatible with wealth being concentrated in the hands of a small minority and as such it fails to embody the value of 'reciprocity'. The latter, for Rawls, is an important failing for an integral part of his theory of justice is that it is a system of cooperation. State socialism, the third regime Rawls considers, is rejected on the grounds that it is undemocratic and does not protect the basic liberties.[38] This leaves two possibilities – liberal democratic socialism (by which Rawls means a democratic brand of market socialism)[39] and a property-owning democracy. The latter, Rawls stresses, by ensuring 'the widespread ownership of productive assets and human capital' enables 'all citizens in a position to manage their own affairs on a footing of a suitable degree of social and economic equality'.[40] The aim in doing so is to enable everyone to participate in social and economic life as a free and equal citizen.[41] Rawls's view (expressed both in *A Theory of Justice* and his recent *Justice as Fairness*) is that the choice between these two systems (liberal socialism and a property-owning democracy) is finely balanced and which is preferable depends on the history of a country, its traditions and its culture.[42]

The second pertinent feature of Rawls's theory in the context of this chapter is his claim that principles such as the difference principle should be implemented within the state. He disavows more cosmopolitan schemes of distributive justice which call for global liberal egalitarian principles of distributive justice. Rather, what Rawls favours is a step-by-step approach, according to which one first constructs principles of justice for a society (asking what people in a hypothetical contract who are unaware of their talents and conception of the good would choose). Once one has selected the principles of justice to apply within the state one can then turn to the question of what principles of justice should apply between states. To settle the latter question Rawls again employs the concept of a hypothetical contract but asks which principles would be selected by representatives of states who are unaware of what states they represent. Such representatives, claims Rawls, would adopt some traditional principles of international justice, including the principle of nonintervention, the right of states to defend themselves, the principle that states should comply with their treaties and some orthodox principles of *ius in bello*.[43]

Rawls's treatment of international justice in *A Theory of Justice* is succinct. He provides a much fuller treatment in his 1993 Amnesty Lecture and a yet fuller account in his subsequent book *The Law of Peoples*.[44] In the latter work, Rawls maintains that liberal peoples are not entitled to apply their views on the rest of the world and accordingly must tolerate societies that, although not liberal, are morally satisfactory ('decent peoples').[45] Hence it is important to identify principles that both liberal and decent non-liberal peoples find fair. They will endorse principles affirming the equality and freedom of peoples, their independence, their right to self-defence, rules of *ius in bello*, some minimal human rights and a duty to assist peoples who face unpropitious socioeconomic circumstances.[46]

Having outlined Rawls's international theory we can note some interesting comparisons between it and the English school. First, the ethical ideal defended by Rawls has some similarities with that canvassed by members of the English school. Both defend a world of separate political regimes, governed by international law. Both, moreover, reject realist perspectives on international political morality. They both also reject cosmopolitan conceptions of international distributive justice.[47] Rawls has most in common with solidarist members of the English school for, like them, he maintains some very minimal principles of economic justice. Indeed, like John Vincent (whom he cites), he argues that persons have a right to subsistence.[48] He argues, in addition, that liberal and decent peoples are under 'duties of assistance' to enable other societies to evolve into decent societies.[49]

A second aspect that Rawls's theory and the English school have in common is that both employ the value of toleration to ground their international theories. Rawls, for example, reasons that '[i]f all societies were required to be liberal, then the idea of political liberalism would fail to express due toleration for other acceptable ways (if such there are, as I assume) of ordering society.'[50] In a similar spirit, members of the English school maintain that diversity is best protected by the Westphalian system.[51] Furthermore, both reject the concept of a world state on the grounds that it would prove tyrannical.[52]

For a third commonality, we should note that both the English school and Rawls draw on international law and on the work of international lawyers. For example, in both *A Theory of Justice* and *The Law of Peoples*, Rawls follows the principles of international law provided by J. L. Brierly, and he makes clear in *The Law of Peoples* that he derives his eight principles 'from the history and usages of international law and practice'.[53] Alderson and Hurrell rightly stress the importance of international law for thinkers like Bull and its significance is evident in his early work, which focused on the work of the international lawyers Hersch Lauterpacht and Lassa Oppenheim.[54] Furthermore, contemporary international lawyers like Michael Byers have also noted the similarity between international law and the English school.[55]

A final feature common to both Rawls and the English school is their belief that the impotence of states stemming from globalization and the rise of transnational markets has been much exaggerated. Bull, for example, argued in this way against critics of a state-centric model of international politics.[56] Rawls has not explicitly addressed the issue of international economic interdependence but it is implicit in his analysis for his belief that principles of distributive justice should be adopted within (liberal) states is predicated on the assumption that the latter comprise fairly autonomous systems of interaction. Members of the English school and Rawls are, thus, joined in their denial that international economic trade is so profound that it vitiates a state-centric political morality. As we shall see shortly, this assumption represents one of the main sources of conflict between Rawls's theory and the English school, on the one hand, and their cosmopolitan critics, on the other.

These commonalities between Rawls's theory and the English school should not obscure some considerable differences. One complicating factor is that Rawls invokes a distinction between 'states' and 'peoples' and he emphasizes that he is defending a society of well-ordered peoples (not states).[57] Rawls's distinction is, however, opaque. It takes two forms. On some occasions, the distinction concerns the legal rights of peoples and states: Rawls argues that states have the legal 'right to go to war in pursuit of state policies' and 'unrestricted internal autonomy'.[58] Peoples, however, lack these legal rights and powers. On other occasions, the difference between states and peoples concerns not their legal rights but their dispositions. His claim here is that states are inclined to seek their own power and glory whereas peoples are mindful of the interests of other peoples.[59] This difference between Rawls and the English school should not, however, be exaggerated since both versions of Rawls's distinction rely on a dubious notion of the state. The first version fails because the concept of a state need not be defined in terms of unlimited legal rights to engage in war or to treat subjects as they wish.[60] The second version fails because the concept of a state does not, as a matter of logic, entail a disposition to expand military and economic power. It might empirically often be the case that states seek only their own gain but we have no reason to make this part of the very definition of a state. In any event, the properties he ascribes to peoples are the standard ones ascribed to a state.[61] Moreover, revealingly, in *Justice as Fairness*, Rawls describes *The Law of Peoples* as outlining 'the just relations between nation-*states*' (my emphasis), thereby equating peoples with nation-states.[62] Rawls's disavowal of the term 'the state' should not mislead one into overlooking the commonality between his ideal and that of Bull, Wight and other members of the English school.

There are, however, some important differences between the English school and Rawls's theory. One important contrast concerns the broader intellectual traditions on which they draw. As noted above, Rawls draws heavily on Kant's moral and political philosophy. This is also true of his treatment of international justice and in *The Law of Peoples* he draws on Kant's essay on 'Perpetual Peace' and in particular on Kant's idea of a *foedus pacificum*.[63] Members of the English school, however, look more to the work of Hugo Grotius and his work *de Jure Belli ac Pacis*.[64] This is reflected in a number of ways. Wight, and Bull after him, simply define their preferred descriptive and normative vision as Grotian. Bull's commitment to, and interest in, Grotius is evident in his first major contribution, namely the two essays in *Diplomatic Investigations*, and is still very much in evidence in *The Anarchical Society*.[65] Finally, we might note that Bull co-edited a volume on Grotius with Benedict Kingsbury and Adam Roberts, and that both Bull and Vincent addressed, respectively, Grotius' contribution to international relations and his position on nonintervention.[66] In the light of Kant's dismissal of Grotius' views – Grotius, like Samuel Pufendorf and Emmerich de Vattel, is described by Kant as a 'sorry comforter' – this difference in their intellectual backgrounds is significant.[67]

We should also note that these two traditions have developed in relative isolation from each other. Rawls, as mentioned above, cites John Vincent but he does not engage with the work of Bull or Wight or Butterfield. For their part, members of the English school do not draw on Rawls's work. Indeed, they tend to be sceptical of the value of philosophical theorizing of the type embodied by Rawls.[68] This in part reflects a disciplinary divide between analytical philosophy, on the one hand, and the historical approach practised by international relations scholars, on the other.

III

Having outlined and compared two traditions of thought on internationalism and justice, I now want, in the following two sections, to trace attempts to argue that these traditions can not deal adequately with dilemmas posed by global capitalism and so must be revised in a more cosmopolitan direction if they are to have contemporary relevance. This section begins this task by examining the ways that several contemporary political philosophers, based in America, who work in the Rawlsian tradition have argued that a coherent application of Rawls's Kantian theory requires the adoption of cosmopolitan principles of distributive justice. This critique has come in two waves, the first directed against *A Theory of Justice* and the second against *The Law of Peoples*. Let us consider each in turn.

After the publication of *A Theory of Justice*, a number of philosophers argued that the internal logic of Rawls's own theory of 'justice as fairness', once conjoined with a proper appreciation of the importance of global markets, entails that one should accept a global difference principle. Since the most sustained version of this argument is given by Charles Beitz, first in his article 'Justice and International Relations' and second in his book *Political Theory and International Relations*, I shall concentrate on his version of the critique.[69] Beitz advances two distinct claims, both of which work within the terms of Rawls's own theory. First, he maintains that representatives of states would choose more radical principles than the ones Rawls proposes. In particular, Beitz reasons, the parties would deem natural resources to be morally arbitrary and hence available for redistribution. Parties, not knowing which society they represent, would thus agree to an equal distribution of natural resources.[70] His second critique focuses on Rawls's claim that principles of distributive justice should operate within schemes of economic interaction. Justice, as Rawls defines it, concerns how to distribute the advantages and disadvantages that result from cooperation. Beitz then notes that one can sustain a purely domestic theory of distributive justice only if one maintains that economies are contained within states. The latter, however, is not credible given the tremendous importance and effects of transnational and global markets. Given the facts of modern political economy an adherent to 'justice as fairness' can not coherently maintain that principles of fairness should be implemented within states. Rawls must, therefore, abandon his claim that the difference principle should be implemented within a state and embrace a global difference principle.[71]

Let us turn now to the second wave of criticism, namely that directed against *The Law of Peoples*. Cosmopolitan Rawlsians challenge the latter on (at least) two grounds, both of which work within Rawls's own theory. One powerful line of reasoning maintains that Rawls has misapplied the concept of 'toleration' and that he is wrong to argue that toleration requires one to show respect to the illiberal practices of non-liberal societies. If one is persuaded by the concept of toleration and the ideal of a neutral state then, the critique runs, this requires that one apply egalitarian liberal principles of civil, political and distributive justice across the world. Rawls's scheme thus is not tolerant: rather, it acquiesces in injustice for it withholds equal individual rights from some (members of decent non-liberal societies) that it ascribes to others (members of liberal societies). In a manner quite alien to the individualism apparent in *A Theory of Justice* and *Political Liberalism* it allows peoples' economic entitlements and political rights to be determined by their cultural identity.[72] A second, distinct, internal critique maintains that, even if one employs Rawls's hypothetical contractarian device, more radical principles of international distributive justice would emerge than Rawls countenances for both liberal and decent peoples would consent to principles demanding a greater global redistribution of wealth. Both liberal and decent peoples would, for example, select global principles of distributive justice to ensure the economic independence and equal standing of peoples. Rawls's own scheme is therefore unacceptable to liberal and decent peoples for it sanctions unlimited international inequalities, inequalities that can subvert the idea of equal peoples.[73] Furthermore, as Thomas Pogge points out, poor political regimes are vulnerable to corruption and hence a society of 'decent' political regimes is possible only if there are global principles of distributive justice regulating the global economy.[74]

Both waves of criticism, then, explicitly operate within the Rawlsian tradition but maintain that the latter needs revision if it is to cohere with facts

about the world (such as, the presence of significant international economic interdependence) and with other aspects of Rawls's theory (such as
his individualistic conception of rights in *Political Liberalism* and his commitment to free and equal peoples in *The Law of Peoples*).

IV

Having sketched the cosmopolitan response to Rawls's accounts of international justice developed by American theorists such as Beitz, we may now
turn to a second, distinct, strand of cosmopolitan thinking, namely that
approach developed by a number of British theorists centred around the
ideal of a 'cosmopolitan democracy'. The pioneering work in this regard is
David Held's seminal *Democracy and the Global Order: From the Modern State
to Cosmopolitan Governance*, published in 1995. A second significant contribution to this approach was published three years later, namely Andrew
Linklater's *The Transformation of Political Community: Ethical Foundations of
the Post-Westphalian Era*.

In his theoretical and historical *tour de force* Held argues that a commitment
to democracy should lead us to move from a Westphalian model of a society
of states to a world in which there are supra-state, state, and sub-state democratic institutions. Held begins by tracing the origin of the state and the evolution of the system of states. He then argues that there are what he terms
'disjunctures' between sovereign states and modern political and economic
reality, where these disjunctures refer to those ways in which the notion of
self-governing states is not in keeping with the existing social, economic and
political reality. Held notes five such 'disjunctures'. These are, first, the enormous growth of international law.[75] Second, is what Held terms the 'internationalization of political decision-making', by which he means the
importance of institutions like the International Monetary Fund, World Bank,
United Nations, European Union and UNESCO.[76] A third important international factor is the presence of 'hegemonic powers and international security
structures' – where this refers to institutions like NATO.[77] A fourth disjuncture
between the idea of a sovereign state and the global reality is the increasing
'globalization of culture'.[78] Finally, and perhaps most crucially, is the development of a world economy and 'the internationalization of production and the
internationalization of financial transactions'.[79] Held's central empirical claim
is that the globalization of legal norms, political power, economy, culture and
military power fundamentally invalidate a state-centric account of world politics.[80] Given this radical transformation, Held argues, we have to rethink the
traditional account of democracy. To do this Held begins by articulating what
he sees as the key principle underpinning democratic theory, namely a principle of autonomy that stipulates that people have equal rights to enjoy
autonomous action. A just world is, according to this principle, one that free
and equal persons would agree to.[81] Such agents, Held maintains, would reject

a system of unequal life chances and would agree to the protection of their autonomy in seven key areas (which Held refers to as the body, welfare, economy, culture, civic associations, violence and the legal system) and thus agree to seven types of rights corresponding to each of these areas.[82] Three of these areas (and the three corresponding types of rights) are particularly important from the point of view of social justice. First, the body: to be autonomous persons need to enjoy good health. This in turn entails rights to physical health, a healthy environment and to have a family.[83] Second, what Held terms 'welfare': the ideal of autonomy requires the ability to play a role in one's community and this generates rights to 'universal childcare', 'universal education' and support for parents.[84] Third, what Held terms the 'economy': autonomy in this realm requires the capacity to participate in the economy. This entails rights to a 'minimum income', choice of both goods and vocations and the resources necessary for economic independence.[85]

Drawing on this account of social justice, Held evaluates the market. It is clear that, on his scheme, untrammelled markets are highly unjust since they suffer from market imperfections, subvert political equality and limit the autonomy of democratic institutions. Held dismisses, however, the total rejection of markets and calls instead for the global regulation of markets. Drawing on seven core rights he proposes a 'basic income', 'minimum wages' and the internal democracy of economic institutions and suggests that economic benefits should be withheld from those who violate the cosmopolitan law affirming his seven types of rights. He further calls for development areas and the creation of a transnational economic authority.[86]

Held makes additional institutional proposals and, having outlined his programme of distributive justice and its relation to the market, the final stage of Held's argument is then devoted to outlining the ways in which the world order must be reformed to meet this ideal of autonomy. These include, in the long term, a number of highly ambitious proposals such as a 'Global Parliament (with limited revenue-raising capacity)' and the '[p]ermanent shift of a growing proportion of a nation-state's coercive capability to regional and global institutions'.[87]

A second highly significant defence of cosmopolitan democracy is developed by Andrew Linklater in his *The Transformation of Political Community*. Linklater's powerfully argued work has two distinct features. The first is methodological. Linklater argues that a global political theory should combine normative argument, sociology and what he terms 'praxeology' (where the latter refers to the study of the existing potential within the current system for moral change).[88] *The Transformation of Political Community* thus seeks to establish what is right and to argue that it is viable and attainable from the current world order. The second important feature of Linklater's programme concerns his normative ideal. Building on his earlier work, Linklater develops a cosmopolitan normative programme committed to three specific ideals: the need for universal principles, the importance of respecting cultural diversity, and the case for a broadly egalitarian distribution of resources.[89] There are several aspects to Linklater's account of economic justice. First, he makes clear that any special obligations that people may have to their fellow citizens or fellow nationals must be weighed against the cosmopolitan duties of distributive justice they have to all human beings.[90] When he turns to the case for cosmopolitan principles of distributive justice, Linklater argues that global economic distribution follows from his ideal of cosmopolitan citizenship. He maintains that people can participate in global dialogic frameworks only if they have sufficient economic resources. Global citizenship thus requires global redistribution.[91] In addition to this, however, Linklater criticizes what he terms transnational harm on the grounds that the latter fails to treat non-citizens as equals.[92] Cosmopolitan justice thus precludes inflicting economic and environmental harm on foreigners and requires that each have sufficient resources to participate in a cosmopolitan dialogic process. The latter concept – dialogue – is of pivotal importance for Linklater. In *The Transformation of Political Community* he defends universalism against postmodernist critiques, arguing that the latter are in themselves universalistic and that their insights can be accommodated by universalists.[93] To do this, he defends a 'dialogic cosmopolitanism', which requires that all concerned be enabled to affect political decisions.[94] Drawing on this he outlines ways in which the current order should be restructured to bring about his three-fold normative cosmopolitan vision of universality, diversity and equality.[95]

Held and Linklater, it should be noted, both draw on the work of Jürgen Habermas. His 'discourse ethics' is central to their dialogic conception of politics and their overriding commitment to ensuring a political order that secures the consent of free and equal persons.[96] This leads directly to their repudiation of exclusionary concepts of citizenship which tie citizenship to states. Given this, it is important to recognize that their work forms part of a more general move by Habermas and Habermassians to trace the implications of his discourse ethics for international politics. Habermas has himself developed his account of international politics both in his essay on 'Kant's Idea of Perpetual Peace, with the Benefit of Two Hundred Years' Hindsight' and in *The Postnational Constellation*.[97] Held's cosmopolitan democratic vision can also be fruitfully compared and contrasted with the recent calls for a democratic global civil society made by Habermassian political theorists such as James Bohman and John Dryzek and by the international lawyer Richard Falk.[98]

Having outlined Held and Linklater's defences of 'cosmopolitan democracy', it is worth noting that, although sharing a common vision, they do differ in some respects. One relevant difference, for example, is that Linklater, unlike Held, is keen to relate his project closely to the English school. Linklater writes favourably, for example, of the solidarist tendencies of the English school and is, moreover, keen to emphasize the continuity between his post-Westphalian vision and Bull's observations about neo-medieval political orders.[99]

With this in mind we may now turn to comparing Held and Linklater's 'cosmopolitan democracy' with Beitz's 'cosmopolitan Rawlsianism'. The first, and most obvious point to make, is that, by contrast with Beitz, British cosmopolitans like Held and Linklater prioritize democracy over distributive justice. Of course, as the above analysis shows, Held and Linklater also propose principles of distributive justice. There is, nonetheless, a clear difference of emphasis and they tend to defend their distributive ideals in terms of their relationship to democratic dialogue.

This difference notwithstanding, there are a number of commonalities. First, both cosmopolitan programmes reject the emphasis on the value of sovereignty common among English school theorists. Second, and crucially, both cosmopolitan critiques of earlier state-centric or people-centric moralities are predicated on factual claims about economic interdependence and the significance of global capitalism. Held and Linklater's proposals are, as we have just seen, driven by a belief that increased global interdependence requires broadening the borders of democratic politics beyond the borders of states. Furthermore, as we saw earlier, Beitz's critique is *in part* based on his view that economic interaction transcends state borders. Both thus reject the state-centric models proposed by Rawls and Bull for their inattention to global economic factors and, in particular, global markets. A third common feature concerns the intellectual traditions within which both types of cosmopolitanism locate themselves. Both Linklater and Held, on the one hand, and American cosmopolitans, like Beitz, on the other, emphasize their indebtedness to Kant. Held, for example, grounds his ideal of cosmopolitan democracy in part on the Kantian claim that justice within the political community presupposes a stable and fair international environment. Linklater's theory draws on both Kant's moral universalism (for his normative vision) and his philosophy of history (for his praxeology).[100] Turning now to Beitz, we can see that Beitz draws on Kant for both of his two arguments against Rawls. Thus, when arguing that natural resources should be distributed to all persons he cites Kant's discussion of this in 'Perpetual Peace'; and he traces the idea that economic interaction generates duties and rights of economic justice to Kant's 'Perpetual Peace' and *The Metaphysical Elements of Justice*.[101] This latter Kantian principle, combined with Beitz's empirical contentions about the extent of global capitalism, underpin his commitment to a cosmopolitan difference principle.

V

In *Diplomatic Investigations*, Martin Wight famously argued that there was no international theory.[102] Such a conclusion is no longer sustainable. In both Britain and America a considerable literature has developed on internationalism, justice and the market. Reflection on this recent history prompts two conclusions. First, as we have seen, there has been a common pattern in both Britain and America. In both orthodox political thinking, represented by Rawls' Kantian tradition and by the English school, has eschewed global principles of justice, arguing that justice requires a society of states honouring the norm of non-intervention. Furthermore, in both, this Westphalian vision has been challenged by cosmopolitan critics who maintain that it fails to respond to the dilemmas raised by contemporary global capitalism.

Second, the preceding analysis brings out the diverse nature of cosmopolitan responses to contemporary capitalism. Whereas Held and Linklater have argued for a cosmopolitan democracy, the emphasis of cosmopolitan Rawlsians like Beitz has been for cosmopolitan principles of distributive justice. Both approaches have generated a rich and extensive literature.[103] What remains to be seen, however, is how these two divergent traditions of cosmopolitan political morality relate to each other. Given the Habermassian origins of the cosmopolitan democratic approach (with its emphasis on procedure rather than outcomes) and the emphasis of cosmopolitan Rawlsians on the priority of distributive justice, it is far from clear that the two traditions will converge. In the light of this, one pressing task for contemporary cosmopolitan thought is to address the issue of the compatibility of these two traditions – both of which articulate powerful moral visions – and to explore how tensions between them are to be negotiated.[104]

Notes

1. See John Rawls, *A Theory of Justice* Revised Edition (Oxford: Oxford University Press, 1999) and Rawls, *The Law of Peoples with 'The Idea of Public Reason Revisited'* (Cambridge, MA: Harvard University Press, 1999).
2. See Charles Beitz, *Political Theory and International Relations* (Princeton: Princeton University Press, 1999) with a new afterword by the author.
3. See David Held, *Democracy and the Global Order: From the Modern State to Cosmopolitan Governance* (Cambridge: Polity, 1995) and Andrew Linklater, *The Transformation of Political Community: Ethical Foundations of the Post-Westphalian Era* (Cambridge: Polity, 1998).
4. On traditions and on change see: Mark Bevir and Frank Trentmann, ch. 1, this volume, and Bevir, *The Logic of the History of Ideas* (Cambridge: Cambridge University Press, 1999), especially chs 5 and 6.
5. See Herbert Butterfield and Martin Wight, eds, *Diplomatic Investigations: Essays in the Theory of International Politics* (London: George Allen and Unwin, 1966).
6. See Gabriele Wight and Brian Porter, eds, *Martin Wight International Theory: The Three Traditions* (London: Leicester University Press, 1991), with an introductory essay by Hedley Bull.
7. See *The Anarchical Society: A Study of Order in World Politics* (Basingstoke: Macmillan, now Palgrave Macmillan, 1977). The two essays are also reprinted in Kai Alderson and Andrew Hurrell's useful volume, *Hedley Bull on International Society* (Basingstoke: Macmillan, now Palgrave Macmillan, 2000). Subsequent page references will be to Alderson and Hurrell's edited volume. The latter includes nine of Bull's papers on international relations theory.

8. See Tim Dunne, *Inventing International Society: A History of the English School* (Basingstoke: Macmillan, now Palgrave Macmillan, 1998); Dunne, 'The Social Construction of International Society', *European Journal of International Relations* I (3) (1995), 367–89; Dunne, 'New Thinking on International Society', *The British Journal of Politics and International Relations* III (2) (2001), 223–44; Nicholas Wheeler, 'Pluralist or Solidarist Conceptions of International Society: Bull and Vincent on Humanitarian Intervention', *Millennium* XXI (3) (1992), 463–87; Wheeler, 'Guardian Angel or Global Gangster: a Review of the Ethical Claims of International Society', *Political Studies* XLIV (1) (1996), 123–35; Wheeler, *Saving Strangers: Humanitarian Intervention in International Society* (Oxford: Oxford University Press, 2000); and Wheeler and Dunne, 'Hedley Bull's Pluralism of the Intellect and Solidarism of the Will', *International Affairs* LXXII (1) (1996), 91–107.

9. For some of Buzan's writings see Buzan, 'From International System to International Society: Structural Realism and Regime Theory meet the English School', *International Organization* XLVII (3) (1993), 327–52; Buzan, 'The English School: An Underexploited Resource in IR', *Review of International Studies* XXVII (3) (2001), 471–88; and Barry Buzan and Richard Little, 'The "English Patient" Strikes Back: A Response to Hall's Mis-diagnosis', *International Affairs* LXXVII (3) (2001), 943–6. Buzan's paper 'The English School: An Underexploited Resource in IR' is the lead article in a 'Forum on the English School', *Review of International Studies* XXVII (3) (2001), 465–513. Buzan has recently played an active role in promoting the English school, including setting up a website: www.ukc.ac.uk/politics/englishschool/. For some of Hurrell's writings see: Hurrell, 'International Society and the Study of Regimes: A Reflective Approach', in Volker Rittberger, ed., *Regime Theory and International Relations* (Oxford: Oxford University Press, 1993), pp. 49–72; Kai Alderson and Andrew Hurrell 'Part 1' in Kai Alderson and Andrew Hurrell, eds, *Hedley Bull on International Society*; Hurrell, 'Keeping History, Law and Political Philosophy firmly within the English School', *Review of International Studies* XXVII (3) (2001), 489–94; and Hurrell, 'Global Inequality and International Institutions', *Metaphilosophy* XXXII (1/2) (2001), 34–57. For another recent contribution see Richard Little, 'The English School's Contribution to the Study of International Relations', *European Journal of International Relations* VI (3) (2000), 395–422.

10. See Robert Jackson, *The Global Covenant: Human Conduct in a World of States* (Oxford: Oxford University Press, 2000). As is frequently noted, the term 'the *English* school' is problematic for many of its members are not English. Hedley Bull was an Australian and Robert Jackson is a Canadian. The term is appropriate, however, in the sense that the members taught and/or were educated in England. They tended to be members of the British Committee for the Theory of International Politics, an institutional forum set up by Herbert Butterfield in 1958. For a good history of this committee see Dunne *Inventing International Society*, pp. 89–135.

11. For a different account see Ibid, pp. 5–11.

12. The definition is Bull's. See *The Anarchical Society*, p. 13: cf further pp. 13–16.

13. See Bull, 'Society and Anarchy in International Relations', p. 82; Bull, *The Anarchical Society*, 26–7, 40–51; and Wight, 'Western Values in International Relations', pp. 92–8, especially 95–8.

14. Ibid, pp. 9–16. See further Andrew Hurrell, 'International Society and the Study of Regimes', 49–72.

15. See Kenneth Waltz, *Theory of International Politics* (Reading, MA: Addison Wesley, 1979). For Bull's assessment of Waltz's influential book see Kai Alderson and Andrew Hurrell, 'International Society and the Academic Study of International Relations', in *Hedley Bull on International Society*, p. 25. Cf also Bull's critique of E. H. Carr, 'The Twenty Years' Crisis Thirty Years On', in *Hedley Bull on International Society*, pp. 125–38.

16. See H. L. A. Hart, *The Concept of Law* (Oxford: Oxford University Press, 1997) second edition, pp. 89–91, 102–4, 242–3.

17. *The Anarchical Society*, p. 13. Cf also on this point: Dunne, 'The Social Construction of International Society'.

18. See Bull, *The Anarchical Society*, pp. 25–6 and Wight, 'Western Values in International Relations', pp. 93–5.

19. For the tripartite distinction between Hobbesians, Kantians and Grotians (the latter being the preferred position of the English School) see Bull, 'Society and Anarchy in International Relations', pp. 79–94; Bull, 'Martin Wight and the Theory of International Relations' in Wight *International Theory*, pp. xi–xix; Bull, *The Anarchical Society*, pp. 24–7; Wight, 'Western Values in International Relations'; and Wight, *International Theory*, especially pp. 7–24. Bull credits this distinction to Wight (particularly his 'Western Values in International Relations'): cf Bull, *The Anarchical Society*, p. 322 footnote 1.

20. See, for example, Bull, 'Society and Anarchy in International Relations', p. 82 and Bull, *The Anarchical Society*, p. 27.

21. See *The Global Covenant*.

22. See Bull, ed., *Intervention in World Politics* (Oxford: Clarendon Press, 1984) and R. J. Vincent, *Nonintervention and International Order* (Princeton: Princeton University Press, 1974). See, however, Vincent's later work *Human Rights and International Relations* (Cambridge: Cambridge University Press, 1986).

23. See, for example, Wheeler, 'Pluralist or Solidarist Conceptions of International Society' and Wheeler and Dunne, 'Hedley Bull's Pluralism of the Intellect and Solidarism of the Will'.

24. Alderson and Hurrell, *Hedley Bull on International Society*.

25. See Alderson and Hurrell, 'Bull's Conception of International Society', in *Hedley Bull on International Society*, pp. 7–15 and Dunne, *Inventing International Society*, pp. 142, 146–55. See also Wheeler, 'Pluralist or Solidarist Conceptions of International Society'; and Wheeler and Dunne, 'Hedley Bull's Pluralism of the Intellect and Solidarism of the Will'.

26. 'Justice in International Relations', especially pp. 219–26.

27. Ibid, pp. 225–6.

28. Ibid, pp. 216–17, 221, 226–7.

29. Wheeler, 'Guardian Angel or Global Gangster', 132: see further, 131–2.

30. Andrew Hurrell and Ngaire Woods, 'Globalisation and Inequality', *Millennium* XXIV (3) (1995), 447–70; Hurrell and Woods, eds, *Inequality, Globalization, and World Politics* (Oxford: Oxford University Press, 1999). See also Hurrell's illuminating and suggestive 'Global Inequality and International Institutions'.

31. For Vincent's discussion see *Human Rights and International Relations*, especially pp. 143–50. For the criticisms see Dunne's diagnosis of the limitations of Vincent's cosmopolitan proposals, *Inventing International Society*, p. 171 and Wheeler, 'Guardian Angel or Global Gangster', 132. For Dunne's analysis of Vincent in general see Dunne, *Inventing International Society*, ch. 8 esp pp. 169–74.

32. See Susan Strange, 'The Westfailure System', *Review of International Studies* XXV (3) (1999), 345–54; Booth, 'Human Wrongs and International Relations', *International Affairs*, LXXI (1) (1995), 122–4; and Thomas Pogge, 'Cosmopolitanism and Sovereignty', *Ethics* CIII (1) (1992), 48–75 especially 61–3.
33. *A Theory of Justice*, p. 266.
34. *Ibid*, p. 6: cf also pp. 6–10.
35. *Ibid*, pp. 239–42, 248. Rawls draws on J. E. Meade, *Efficiency, Equality and the Ownership of Property* (London: George Allen & Unwin, 1964), ch. V: cf Rawls, *A Theory of Justice*, p. 242, footnote 13.
36. See Rawls, 'Preface for the French Edition of *A Theory of Justice*', in Samuel Freeman, ed., *Collected Papers* (Cambridge, MA: Harvard University Press, 1999), pp. 419–20.
37. *Justice as Fairness: A Restatement* (Cambridge, MA: Harvard University Press, 2001) edited by Erin Kelly, pp. 136–40. For further discussion of the idea of a property owning democracy see *Justice as Fairness*, part IV (especially sections 41, 42, 49 and 52).
38. For Rawls's arguments against the first three models see *Justice as Fairness*, pp. 137–8. See also Rawls's critique of welfare state capitalism in 'Preface for the French Edition of *A Theory of Justice*', pp. 419–20.
39. *Justice as Fairness*, p. 138.
40. Ibid, p. 139.
41. Ibid, pp. 139–40.
42. *A Theory of Justice*, pp. 239, 242, 248 and *Justice as Fairness*, p. 139.
43. *A Theory of Justice*, pp. 331–3.
44. See Rawls, 'The Law of Peoples', in Stephen Shute and Susan Hurley, eds, *On Human Rights: The Oxford Amnesty Lectures 1993* (New York: Basic Books, 1993), pp. 41–82, and Rawls, *The Law of Peoples*.
45. Rawls distinguishes between five distinct categories of political system. These include the two mentioned in the text ('liberal peoples' and 'decent peoples') and 'outlaw states', 'societies burdened by unfavorable conditions' and 'benevolent absolutisms', *The Law of Peoples*, p. 4.
46. Ibid, p. 37. For a fuller description, and analysis of, *The Law of Peoples* see Caney, 'Survey Article: Cosmopolitanism and the Law of Peoples' *Journal of Political Philosophy* X (1) (2002), 95–123; and 'Review Article: International Distributive Justice', *Political Studies* XLIX (5) (2001), 983–6.
47. See, for example, *The Law of Peoples*, pp. 119–20.
48. See ibid, p. 65 (and footnote 1 on that page for the reference to Vincent, *Human Rights and International Relations*).
49. *The Law of Peoples*, pp. 106–12.
50. Ibid, p. 59.
51. This receives its clearest and more sophisticated statement in Jackson, *The Global Covenant*.
52. See Bull, *The Anarchical Society*, pp. 353–4; Rawls, *The Law of Peoples*, p. 36; and Rawls *Justice as Fairness*, p. 13. See also Alderson and Hurrell, 'Bull's Conception of International Society', p. 8. Rawls makes clear that he is here following Kant's lead in his essay 'Perpetual Peace'. See Kant, 'Perpetual Peace: A Philosophical Sketch', in Hans Reiss, ed., *Kant's Political Writings* (Cambridge: Cambridge University Press, 1989), pp. 113–14.
53. *The Law of Peoples*, p. 41. For Rawls' references to J. L., Brierly, *The Law of Nations: An Introduction to the Law of Peace*, (Oxford: Clarendon Press, 1963)

sixth edition see *A Theory of Justice*, p. 332 footnote 27 and *The Law of Peoples*, p. 37 footnote 42.

54. See Alderson and Hurrell, 'International Society and the Academic Study of International Relations', pp. 29–34 and Hurrell, 'International Society and the Study of Regimes', pp. 49–72. See also Bull's essay 'The Grotian Conception of International Society', pp. 96–118. Hersch Lauterpacht is the author of the distinguished paper 'The Grotian Tradition in International Law', *British Yearbook of International Law*, XXIII (1946), pp. 1–53.

55. Byers, *Custom, Power and the Power of Rules: International Relations and Customary International Law* (Cambridge: Cambridge University Press, 1999), pp. 31–4. Barry Buzan has also argued that relations between the English school and international law represent a fertile area for future research: 'The English School: An Underexploited resource in IR', 486.

56. See, for example, Bull, 'The State's Positive Role in World Affairs', in *Hedley Bull on International Society*, pp. 140–3.

57. Chris Brown cautions against equating the English school and Rawls's theory, in part for this reason: see Brown 'John Rawls, "The Law of Peoples", and International Political Theory', *Ethics and International Affairs* XIV (2000), 132; 'The Construction of a "Realistic Utopia": John Rawls and International Political Theory', *Review of International Studies* XXVIII (1) (2002), 16.

58. *The Law of Peoples*, pp. 25, 27. Cf *The Law of Peoples*, pp. 25–7.

59. Ibid, pp. 17, 27–9.

60. Curiously Rawls appears to recognize this for he observes that since World War II international law has evolved in such a way as to deny states these two rights, *The Law of Peoples*, p. 27.

61. For likeminded criticism of Rawls on these points: see Allen Buchanan, 'Rawls's Law of Peoples: Rules for a Vanished Westphalian World', *Ethics* CX (4) (2000), 698–700; Onora O'Neill, 'Agents of Justice', *Metaphilosophy* XXXII (1/2) (2001), 186–8; and O'Neill, 'Bounded and Cosmopolitan Justice', *Review of International Studies* XXVI (5) (2000), 50–1. See also Caney, 'Review Article: International Distributive Justice', 983–4.

62. *Justice as Fairness*, p. 183.

63. *The Law of Peoples*, pp. 10, 19, 21, 36, 54, 86.

64. Hugo Grotius, *de Jure Belli ac Pacis* (Oxford: Clarendon Press, 1925) translated by Francis W. Kelsey.

65. See 'Society and Anarchy in International Relations', 'The Grotian Conception of International Society', and *The Anarchical Society*, pp. 28–32, 39, 45, 185, 198.

66. See Bull, 'The Importance of Grotius in the Study of International Relations' and R. J. Vincent, 'Grotius, Human Rights, and Intervention', both in Hedley Bull, Benedict Kingsbury, Adam Roberts, (eds), *Hugo Grotius and International Relations* (Oxford: Clarendon Press, 1990).

67. Kant, 'Perpetual Peace', p. 103.

68. Jackson, *The Global Covenant*, pp. 87–8 esp p. 88 footnote 17. On the lack of interaction between Rawls and the English school cf also Brown, 'The Construction of a "Realistic Utopia"', 16–17.

69. Charles Beitz, 'Justice and International Relations', *Philosophy and Public Affairs* IV (4) (1975), 360–89 and *Political Theory and International Relations*, part III. Others have also argued that, given the facts of economic interdependence, Rawls's own theory entails the global application of the difference principle.

See, for example, Thomas Scanlon, 'Rawls' Theory of Justice', in Norman Daniels, ed., *Reading Rawls: Critical Studies of A Theory of Justice* (Oxford: Blackwell, 1975), p. 202 and Thomas Pogge, *Realizing Rawls* (Ithaca: Cornell University Press, 1989) part III.

70. *Political Theory and International Relations*, pp. 136–43.
71. Ibid, pp. 144–52.
72. These lines of reasoning can be found in, among others: Bruce Ackerman, 'Political Liberalisms', *Journal of Philosophy* XCIX (7) (1994), 364–86; Buchanan, 'Rawls's Law of Peoples', 697–721; Andrew Kuper, 'Rawlsian Global Justice: Beyond *The Law of Peoples* to a Cosmopolitan Law of Persons', *Political Theory* XXVIII (5) (2000), esp 648–53; Darrel Moellendorf, 'Constructing the Law of Peoples', *Pacific Philosophical Quarterly* LXXVII (1996), 132–54; Thomas Pogge, 'An Egalitarian Law of Peoples', *Philosophy and Public Affairs*, XXIII (3) (1994), 216–18; Pogge, 'Rawls on International Justice', *The Philosophical Quarterly* LI (203) (2001), 247–9; Kok-Chor Tan, *Toleration, Diversity, and Global Justice* (Pennsylvania: Pennsylvania State University Press, 2000), esp ch. 2; Fernando R. Tesón, 'The Rawlsian Theory of International Law', *Ethics and International Affairs* IX (1995), 79–99; and Tesón, *A Philosophy of International Law* (Oxford: Westview Press, 1998), ch. 4. For a fuller discussion see Caney, 'Cosmopolitanism and the Law of Peoples', 95–114.
73. For a fuller exploration see Caney, 'Review Article: International Distributive Justice', 985–6 and the references contained therein. Cf also Beitz, 'Rawls's Law of Peoples', *Ethics* CX (4) (2000), 693–4; Buchanan, 'Rawls's Law of Peoples', 708–15; Pogge, 'An Egalitarian Law of Peoples', 208–11; and Leif Wenar, 'Contractualism and Global Economic Justice', *Metaphilosophy* XXXII (1/2) (2001), 88.
74. Pogge, 'An Egalitarian Law of Peoples', 213–14.
75. *Democracy and the Global Order*, pp. 101–7.
76. Ibid, pp. 107–13.
77. Ibid, pp. 113–20.
78. Ibid, pp. 121–7.
79. Ibid, p. 127 and, more generally, pp. 127–34.
80. Ibid, p. 135. See, more generally, ch. 5 and 6 for the five disjunctures.
81. Ibid, pp. 145–56, 159–67.
82. Ibid, pp. 167–72, 176–86, 191–201, esp 192–4.
83. Ibid, pp. 176–8, 192, 194–5.
84. Ibid, pp. 178–80, 192, 195.
85. Ibid, pp. 182–3, 193, 197–8.
86. For all the proposals listed in this paragraph see ibid, ch. 11 esp, pp. 245–60 and 264.
87. Ibid, p. 279.
88. *The Transformation of Political Community*, pp. 3–6, 10–11.
89. Ibid, pp. 3, 6–7. Of his earlier work see, in particular, Linklater, *Men and Citizens in the Theory of International Relations* (Basingstoke: Macmillan, now Palgrave Macmillan 1982, second edition 1990).
90. *The Transformation of Political Community*, pp. 49–50, 61, 105.
91. Ibid, pp. 192, 203, 205–6, 212, 220, 239 (footnote 19).
92. Ibid, pp. 84, 105, 203. Linklater here draws on Henry Shue's work on exporting hazards: Shue, 'Exporting Hazards', in Peter G. Brown and Henry Shue, (eds), *Boundaries: National Autonomy and its Limits* (Totowa, NJ: Rowman and Littlefield,

1981). See also Andrew Linklater, 'Citizenship, Humanity, and Cosmopolitan Harm Conventions', *International Political Science Review* XXII (3) (2001), 261–77.

93. *The Transformation of Political Community*, pp. 48, 67–73.
94. Ibid, pp. 77–108.
95. Ibid, pp. 193–204. For a fuller statement of his approach to global distributive justice see Linklater, 'The Evolving Spheres of International Justice', *International Affairs* LXXV (3) (1999), 473–82.
96. See Held, *Democracy and the Global Order*, pp. 159–60, 162–6 and Linklater, *The Transformation of Political Community*, pp. 90–3. For Habermas's discourse ethics see, inter alia, Habermas, *Moral Consciousness and Communicative Action* (Cambridge: Polity, 1992).
97. See Jürgen Habermas, 'Kant's Idea of Perpetual Peace, with the Benefit of Two Hundred Years' Hindsight', in James Bohman and Matthias Lutz-Bachmann, (eds), *Perpetual Peace: Essays on Kant's Cosmopolitan Ideal* (Cambridge, MA: MIT Press, 1997), pp. 113–53; and Habermas, *The Postnational Constellation: Political Essays* (Cambridge: Polity, 2001).
98. See, Bohman, 'The Public Spheres of the World Citizen', in *Perpetual Peace: Essays on Kant's Cosmopolitan Ideal*, pp. 179–200; Dryzek, *Deliberative Democracy and Beyond: Liberals, Critics, Contestations* (Oxford: Oxford University Press, 2000), esp ch. 5; and Falk, 'Global Civil Society and the Democratic Prospect', in Barry Holden, ed., *Global Democracy: Key Debates* (London: Routledge, 2000), pp. 162–78.
99. *The Transformation of Political Community*, pp. 59–60, 193–5. See also 'Citizenship, Humanity, and Cosmopolitan Harm Conventions', esp pp. 267–9. It is also striking that Dunne thinks of Linklater as a member of the English school: *Inventing International Society*, pp. 15, 22 (footnote 56), 190.
100. See respectively Held, *Democracy and the Global Order*, pp. 221–2, 226–30 and Linklater, *The Transformation of Political Community*, pp. 35–43.
101. See, respectively, *Political Theory and International Relations*, pp. 138 footnote 26 and 144 footnote 34.
102. 'Why is there no International Theory?'.
103. For additional work on cosmopolitan distributive justice see the special issue of *Metaphilosophy* XXXII (1/2) (2001) edited by Thomas Pogge. For additional work on cosmopolitan democracy see Daniele Archibugi and David Held, (eds), *Cosmopolitan Democracy: An Agenda for a New World Order* (Cambridge: Polity, 1995) and Daniele Archibugi, David Held and Martin Köhler, (eds), *Re-imagining Political Community: Studies in Cosmopolitan Democracy* (Cambridge: Polity, 1998).
104. For an insightful discussion see Pogge, 'Cosmopolitanism and Sovereignty', esp 65–9. Some of the material in this chapter was published in 'Review: British Perspectives on Internationalism, Justice and Sovereignty: From the English School to Cosmopolitan Democracy', *The European Legacy* VI (2) (2001), 265–75. I thank Mark Bevir and Frank Trentmann for their helpful comments on an earlier draft of this chapter.

9
New Labour and 'Third Way' Political Economy: Paving the European Road to Washington?

Colin Hay

No single concept is more closely associated with the 'modernization' of the British Labour Party and, now, the European social democratic tradition more broadly than that of globalization.* The notion of a qualitative and epochal shift in the contours of contemporary capitalism, marking the transition from an era of closed national economies to a single global market, has come to dominate Labour's understanding of the context in which it now finds itself. It lies at the heart of the conception of the 'third way' New Labour now seeks to export to Europe and more broadly.[1] As the following discussion will hopefully demonstrate, it is a very particular – and distinctly Anglo-US – conception of globalization that has come to inform Labour's radical and increasingly infectious reassessment of the parameters of political possibility.[2] Globalization has come to be invoked by New Labour, in opposition and now in government, as a largely non-negotiable external economic constraint necessitating market-conforming social and economic reform.[3] Consequently, the 'harsh economic realities' of 'new times' are held to compromise not only the Keynesianism, corporatism and traditional social democracy of the postwar period, but also the 'over-regulated' 'European social model' which was developed and consolidated throughout Northern Europe over this period of time. The casualties of globalization are, on the basis of this account, considerable; the stakes of New Labour's understanding of the challenges and constraints it imposes significant indeed.

Yet Labour's programmatic transformation and subsequent proselytizing for a rejuvenated and somewhat 'leaner and fitter' European social model is not merely a story of the translation of the constraints of globalization into a series of non-negotiable economic imperatives. That, as we shall see, is crucial. However, at least as important has been the promotion of the (presumed) comparative institutional advantage, under such conditions, of the US model. That model owes its comparative and competitive strength, for proponents of the third way, to its virtuous and mutually reinforcing combination of a deregulated labour-market and a more residual and labour-market oriented welfare–workfare state. It is this, in particular, that Labour has increasingly promoted as, if not the template for a 'modernized' European social model, then certainly the standard against which it should be judged.[4]

In this chapter I review the role of ideas about globalization in the process of Labour's 'modernization', emphasizing, in particular, the significance of the trans-Atlantic axis established between the New Democrats and New Labour in the 1990s. I evaluate critically the assumptions upon which Labour's modernization and its promotion of the comparative and competitive advantage of an 'Anglo-US model' has been predicated publicly. I conclude by considering the contradictions inherent in this new political economy for new times and the prospects for its export to continental Europe (and beyond). Before turning to the genealogy of external economic constraint in the political economy of Labour's modernization, however, it is important to establish some preliminaries on the complex relationship between the discourse, rhetoric and reality of globalization.

The discourse, rhetoric and reality of globalization

It is all too tempting to reduce issues relating to the discourse of globalization to the question of the degree of accuracy of the ideas actors hold about the environment in which they find themselves – in short, to the extent of globalization itself and to the degree of fit between 'real' globalization and perceptions of globalization. The result has been a profusion of academic literature trading claim and counter-claim and seeking to establish empirically the objective reality or mythical status (depending on one's view) of globalization through extensive appeal to the 'material' evidence.[5] Important though systematic empirical scrutiny of the substantive evidence for (and against) the globalization thesis is, it cannot exhaust our interest in the discourse and rhetoric of globalization. For, quite simply, whether accurate or otherwise it is the ideas political subjects hold about the context in which they find themselves rather than the material reality of the context itself which informs their conduct. Consequently, as argued elsewhere, 'whether the globalisation thesis is "true" or not may matter far less than whether it is deemed to be true (*or, quite possibly, just useful*) by those employing it.'[6] For present purposes, the parentheses are particularly significant. We are rarely privy to political actors' direct conceptions of economic constraints. What we are more frequently subjected to, however, are political subjects' rhetorics of economic constraint, rhetorics in which in recent years the notion of globalization has come to feature ever more prominently. We should, then, be careful not simply to assume that such rhetorics reflect accurately political actors' internalized understandings of the constraints they face (as distinct from the constraints they may benefit from acknowledging). Political actors are reflexive and strategic. Consequently, at least equally plausible is that the deployment of political discourses of globalization reflects less an assessment of material economic constraints than of the rhetorical strategies deemed most conducive to secure continued political legitimacy.[7]

Three points perhaps reinforce such a suggestion in the British context. First, the political deployment of the discourse of globalization significantly post-dates the qualitative epochal shift it purportedly describes. Second, while globalization has tended to be associated, at least in Anglophone debate, with neoliberalism and, indeed, neoliberalization as a perceived economic imperative, it is the centre-left and not the right that has most consistently made appeal to globalization as a non-negotiable external economic constraint necessitating (an accommodation to) neoliberal reforms. Finally, that globalization is less an inexorable process which must simply be accommodated and rather more a conscious political strategy has effectively been acknowledged by a succession of prominent New Labour spokesmen (not, as it happens, spokeswomen) in international fora in the wake of the Asian financial crisis. This has nowhere been more clearly articulated than by Stephen Byers in his address to the WTO ministerial meeting in Seattle in November 1999.

> There are those who say that globalization and trade liberalization are innately harmful, bringing benefits only to a handful of multinational corporations, widening the gap between the richest and poorest, threatening the environment and undermining social structures. Such people can be found at all stages of human history, casting doubt on progress and pointing to the ills it allegedly brings while ignoring the benefits ... By working together we can confound the critics and show that globalization and liberalization together can be a decisive force for good. But in our countries we need to work at convincing our people that this is to be welcomed rather than feared.[8]

What this extract suggests, again, is the strategic use made of ideas about globalization. In a context in which parties of the centre-left have increasingly become agents of unpalatable social and economic reforms (such as the introduction of ever more punitive welfare conditionalities), this is a not insignificant point. It reminds us of the political capital to be gained or, more likely, retained by disclaiming responsibility for otherwise unpopular reforms. These might be rendered more acceptable if presented as the very condition of continued economic growth in a harsh new economic environment.

Towards a genealogy of economic constraint in postwar Britain

The invocation of globalization as a non-negotiable external – principally economic – constraint has become a familiar aspect of the political discourse of contemporary liberal democracy, especially in the Anglophone world. The competitive imperatives of a borderless and global economy characterized by the near perfect mobility of the factors of production, we are frequently entreated, reveal the welfare state of the postwar period to be an indulgent luxury of a bygone era. Along with Keynesianism, social democracy and encompassing labour-market institutions (now cursorily dismissed as 'supply-side rigidities') it must now be sacrificed, if it has not already been sacrificed, on the altar of the competitive imperative – a further casualty of the 'harsh economic realities' summoned by globalization. This discourse has its origins in the US and, within the Clinton administration, came to be embodied in Labour Secretary Robert Reich.[9]

In all this it is perhaps tempting to forget that the political invocation of economic constraints is by no means a qualitatively novel phenomenon, confined to the present and to the appeal to transnational economic processes (such as globalization). The logic of economic constraint and implied social and political imperative has played, as it will surely continue to play, a crucial role in the legitimation of often unpopular social and political reform throughout the history of capitalism. Moreover, as many of the chapters in this volume attest, it has also played a crucial role in the history of opposition to capitalist social relations. Given this, it is surely instructive to compare this contemporary manifestation of the (discursive) logic of economic constraint with those that preceded it. In the pages that follow I present an (albeit) highly stylized genealogy of the discourse of economic constraint in postwar Britain.

At the risk of some inevitable simplification, I split the period into three distinct phases – the so-called 'golden age' from the initial postwar years to the early 1970s; the crisis period during the 1970s; and the contemporary period, from the mid 1980s to the present day. In so doing, it is important to note, I am not seeking to advance a periodization of political and economic development in postwar Britain so much as a periodization of dominant *discourses* of economic constraint over this time frame.

The postwar 'golden age'

The postwar period until the 1970s is generally characterized as one in which political and economic imperatives were brought back into harmony after the persistent economic pathologies of the 1930s. The problem throughout the 1930s was one of a demand shortfall brought about by rapid technological innovation which generated for the first time the prospect of mass production for a (still largely hypothetical) mass market.

The postwar extension and development of the welfare state, it is widely argued, served to generalize levels of demand sufficient to ensure both high and stable growth rates throughout the early postwar years. Such measures were counter-cyclical, injecting demand when it was most needed. They were also targeted on the most needy who were, in turn, most likely to spend (rather than save) such transfer payments as they received and to do so by purchasing domestic products as opposed to luxury imports. This served to ensure high levels of effective demand on the basis of comparatively modest rates of redistribution, helping in turn to establish a fortuitous synergy between economic imperatives and political expediency. More specifically, the state was able to deliver for its citizens the promise made during the war of a universal welfare state in return for the sacrifice of war while at the same time serving to secure demand sufficient to sustain the growth in supply facilitated by the introduction of Fordist mass production techniques. In this stylized and popularized Keynesian account, economic imperatives were almost exclusively endogenous and were largely satisfied by social and political reforms (such as the extension of the welfare state) which were popular and which could be legitimated without appeal to a logic of economic compulsion.

From virtuous cycle to vicious circle: the crisis of the 1970s

This fortuitous situation, in which economic imperatives (relating to demand management) were satisfied as a by-product of political goods and political imperatives (relating to legitimation) were satisfied from economic externalities, would not survive the 1970s.[10] Moreover, the Keynesian paradigm that had provided an intellectual rationale for the postwar growth phase was seen to offer no diagnosis or explanation of the dilemma which now beset the European economies. The problem was one of 'stagflation' – a condition of high and rising inflation combined with high and rising unemployment in a welfare state society premised upon full employment. In the context of widely perceived crisis (associated in the public's imagination first with the negotiation of the IMF loan in 1976 and, subsequently, with the long 'Winter of Discontent' of 1978–9) dominant economic understandings changed as the intellectual pendulum swung from left to right, from Keynesianism to neoliberalism.[11]

The new right's diagnosis was elegant in its simplicity and in its simplicity lay its persuasive capacity. The pathology arose in the trade-off between the short-term political expediency of elected officials on the one hand and longer-term economic rationality on the other, with the former dominating the latter. Thinking merely of narrow electoral advantage, politicians would seek to accommodate themselves to the (ill-educated) preferences of the electorate for material gain by sanctioning ever spiralling and ever more costly expectations. Consequently, in the run up to a general election the parties would seek to outbid one another in terms of the generosity of their electoral pledges. This served to establish a political market for votes, yet one lacking the disciplining price mechanism of a genuine market. Since the cost of each vote could effectively be discounted by politicians motivated only by short-term electoral advantage, the price would spiral, with demand increasing to the point of political 'overload'. The result was a fiscal crisis of the state born of political irresponsibility.[12]

Though the overload thesis is premised upon an economic analogy, it depicts an essentially political constraint. For it is the domination of parochial political concerns over ultimately more fundamental economic imperatives which precipitates the condition of overload, ungovernability and stagflation. Yet although the constraint is this time political, it is again endogenous – overload is a condition of irresponsible domestic political actors' own making. As such it demands a domestic response. That response was to reassert the primacy of economic imperatives in the name of neoliberal (initially, monetarist) economics, imposing a new financial discipline and, in time, launching a shift from discretionary (political) to rules-bounded (economic and technical) monetary policy.

The contemporary situation: The invocation of external economic constraint

It is only from the mid 1980s, in the wake of the crisis of the 1970s, that we witness the sustained and systematic appeal to globalization as an external economic constraint. Here the economic reclaims precedence over political factors as, it is argued, heightened capital mobility serves to tilt the balance of power from immobile government and comparatively immobile labour to fluid capital. Under this qualitatively novel constellation of circumstances, the state (as fiscal authority) must adapt and accommodate itself to the perceived interest of capital (for labour market flexibility, a 'competitive' taxation environment and so forth) if it is not to precipitate a haemorrhaging of invested funds.[13] The judgement of mobile assets (whether of invested or still liquid funds) is assumed to be both harsh and immediate, selecting for fiscal responsibility, prudence and a rules-bounded economic policy (as guarantor of credibility and competence). The appeal to globalization thus conjures a logic of economic compulsion which reaffirms the dominance of the economic in the first, last and every intervening instance. In contrast to the overload thesis, the economic is conceptualized as an external or exogenous imperative passing judgement on domestic institutions and policies.

What is remarkable about this hyperglobalization thesis is that, despite the profound differences in the form of analysis, its policy implications are remarkably similar to those associated with the overload thesis – namely market-conforming economic and social reform. Moreover, in the (increasingly hegemonic) view of globalists, the late 1970s/early 1980s is also identified as the point of transition – only this time from closed national economies to an open international market in which national economies and sectors compete. Here the debacle of the 'Mitterrand experiment' has come to acquire a particular significance, marking symbolically the point of no return for 'Keynesianism in one country'. Whether this account is accurate or otherwise – and there is now a considerable body of evidence pointing to the dominance of domestic political factors in bringing to an abrupt end the Parti Socialiste's redistributivist developmental statism – its symbolic status as the line in the sand demarcating the old and new social democracy is clear.[14]

These three rather different discourses of economic and political constraint are summarised in Table 9.1. On the basis of this somewhat stylized genealogy, a number of general points might be made about the appeal to economic and political constraints in political discourse in postwar Britain and about the invocation of external economic constraint associated with transnational processes more specifically.

First, the identification of previously unacknowledged political and economic constraints, whether endogenous or exogenous in origin, is frequently associated with moments of significant institutional and ideational change (what, in Kuhnian terms, Peter Hall has elsewhere labelled 'paradigm shifts').[15] Moreover, in such widely identified crisis scenarios, the ideational change invariably predates institutional change. The 'crisis' of the 1970s is an obvious example, though it is by no means unprecedented in modern British history.[16] Arguably, the ability of the new right to offer a popular, compelling and simple narrative to account for the observed pathologies of Keynesian social democracy (and to attribute responsibility for such contradictions), was crucial to its ability to enact significant institutional change in the subsequent decade(s).[17] Yet this sense of rapid ideational change as a precursor to cumulative yet iterative institutional change is by no means confined to the crisis phase of the 1970s.[18] We see something similar with respect to the appeal to globalization as an external economic constraint, with parties of the centre-left – notably Labour in Britain – revising significantly their agendas for office as they have come to internalize the (perceived) imperatives globalization summons.[19] What this suggests, in keeping with the theme of the relative autonomy of beliefs and traditions running throughout this volume, is the key role that ideational change may play in establishing the trajectory of subsequent institutional evolution.[20]

What the above paragraphs also demonstrate is the way in which both the overload thesis and the invocation of globalization's 'logic of no alternative' have been appealed to in order to provide justification, in terms of observed constraint, for a paradigm shift to neoliberal economic policies. Yet they could scarcely be more different in the manner in which they do this. The former takes the form of a voluntarist and politicist tirade against the brazen self-interest and irresponsibility of politicians, making the normative and political case for a decisive shift in the governing paradigm. The latter, by contrast, appeals to the 'harsh realities' of new economic times in a (superficially) dispassionate, almost technocratic, manner. It points, in a highly deterministic way, to processes beyond the control of political actors which must simply be accommodated and hence to a dull logic of economic compulsion which is non-negotiable.

Table 9.1 Discourses of political and economic constraint

	Economy–politics relationship	Conditions of economic growth/pathology	Proponents
'Golden age' (1940s–1960s)	Economic–political synergy	Endogenous. Political imperatives (legitimation) met by economic externalities; economic imperatives (demand management) met by political externalities. Possible danger of wage-push inflationary pressures arising from strength of labour.	Keynesians, social democrats
Fiscal crisis; political 'overload' (1970s)	Economic imperatives subordinated to narrow political interests leading to fiscal crisis of the state	Endogenous. Political-induced logic of economic pathology. Electoral gain bought at an ever escalating cost to the exchequer as expectations spiral precipitating a condition of fiscal and political 'overload'.	New right – neoliberals and neoconservatives
Globalization (1980s – present)	Economic imperatives externally imposed. Political autonomy subordinated to external economic constraints.	Exogenous. Heightened mobility of capital exposes the welfare state, encompassing labour market institutions and other 'supply-side rigidities' as luxuries of a bygone era. The state must internalize the perceived interest of capital if it is not to precipitate capital flight.	Beleaguered social democrats; proponents of the 'third way'

Hegemonic though both discourses in turn have become, there is in fact precious little evidence for either. It is not my aim to review in detail the now well-trodden terrain. Suffice it to note that the overload thesis contains a series of glaring internal contradictions and inconsistencies while the hyperglobalization thesis has been subjected to devastating empirical and theoretical challenge (as outlined in Table 9.2). Yet, important though this observation may be, it is equally important that we resist the temptation to suspend the analysis at this point (as many have). For, whether accurate or otherwise, the effects of such discourses of internal and external constraint have been considerable.

While the overload thesis provided popular legitimation for the conversion of the right to neoliberalism in the 1970s, the hyperglobalization thesis has come to justify a similar conversion (though one born more of perceived necessity than of enthusiastic endorsement) for broad sections of the left and centre-left. It is ironic to note that although the current situation is frequently identified as one of global neoliberalism or neoliberal globalism, the notion of globalization itself was invariably not appealed to in the initial transition to neoliberalism. Thus, in public policy, the invocation of globalization post-dates that which it is now used to explain by at least a decade and has been deployed principally as a means to legitimate the left's conversion to the tenets of neoliberal economic policies already enshrined within the governing economic paradigm.

This final point is perhaps particularly significant and begs the question of how transnational economic constraints have come to be invoked as, in effect, a *post hoc* rationalization for the accommodation to a neoliberal economic paradigm already in the ascendancy. Two answers present themselves fairly naturally. There is something in each. First, it is plausible to suggest that where the right was the immediate agent of the initial transition to neoliberalism (as in Britain), its tenure in office served to unleash globalization's logic of inevitability and external constraint. This, it might be argued, served to throw open the lid of a Pandora's box for social democrats as legislation was enacted which imposed a regime of free capital mobility through the liberalization of capital controls. Yet such an argument is really only credible, at least in Europe, for the British case and even here it was not the sole – nor perhaps even the major – factor at work.[21] Altogether more significant is that the appeal to transnational economic constraints displaced responsibility from those who might otherwise be held responsible for reneging on previously hallowed social democratic commitments. Though the argument might now be generalized to (nominally) socialist and social democratic governments across Europe, the case of the British Labour Party is particularly significant.[22] For, arguably, the British Labour Party was a very early mover. So long as it remained wedded to a reversal of much of the policy change initiated by the Thatcher administration, the party's assessment of ongoing political and economic dynam-

204

Table 9.2 The anomalies, contradictions, inconsistencies of the overload and hyperglobalization theses

Overload thesis	Hyperglobalization thesis
1. Were the thesis true, neoliberal economic policies could never be chosen at the polls – the 'responsible' right would be confined to the electoral margins as long as it resisted the logic of political expediency and fiscal irresponsibility. A radical curtailment of democratic electoral freedoms would seem the only means to halt the crisis of ungovernability. Ironically, the election of Thatcher in Britain in 1979 represented a most effective refutation of the overload thesis.	1. The observed positive correlation between state expenditure (as a percentage of GDP) and openness (imports plus exports as a percentage of GDP) challenges the notion that globalization necessitates a minimal state.
2. The suggestion that governments were elected with minimal consideration of their likely economic consequences is flatly contradicted by the available empirical evidence – the principal factor determining success at the polls throughout the 1960s and 1970s was the perceived state of the economy.	2. Claims as to the hypermobility of foreign direct investors and of productive capital more generally have been grossly exaggerated.
3. The conception of the elector as too stupid to appreciate the economic consequences of exaggerated political promises, yet presumably sharp enough to be woken from such delusions by the persuasive rhetoric of the new right, is both inconsistent and opportunistic.	3. Domestic consumption demands continue to be satisfied overwhelmingly via the domestic circuit of capital (a tendency reinforced by the growth of the service sector); production tends to remain predominantly domestically owned.
	4. International flows of capital are ever more highly concentrated within the 'triad' economies of Europe, North America and Pacific Asia and, when expressed as a percentage of GDP are merely comparable to those immediately prior to World War I.
	5. Statistical evidence continues to demonstrate the endogenous determinants of economic growth.

ics was one which emphasized the agency of Thatcherism as a political project. Yet, as it came gradually to accommodate itself to the mounting legacy of Thatcherite neoliberalism, its analysis shifted markedly. What had previously been attributed to an essentially domestic political project which might be overturned was now increasingly put down to the dawning of a new phase of economic accumulation (post-Fordism or 'new times') which had circumscribed the parameters of political and economic choice. However desirable a return to postwar social democracy might have seemed, this no longer fell within the field of political possibility. As such, the party's accommodation to the harsh economic realities of 'new times' – a synonym for labour-market flexibility and welfare conditionality (in short, neoliberalism) – was purely pragmatic. No blame could thus be apportioned for what amounted to a fundamental dilution of the left's normative agenda. This begs a final question and one which is seldom asked. Where did the discourse of globalization come from in the first place?

As the above brief discussion amply demonstrates, highly stylized and often crudely simplified caricatures of regulation theory have proved extremely influential in establishing the need for the 'modernization' of the Labour Party. They have invariably been used to draw a rigid (and arguably artificial) demarcation between the closed and national economies which (supposedly) characterized Fordism and the (equally constructed) open, integrated and global economy of post-Fordism. This distinction between old times and new times, then and now, was popularized in perhaps its most vulgarized form in the highly influential pages of *Marxism Today* (the theoretical discussion journal of the, then, Communist Party of Great Britain).[23] This has, in turn, created something of a space into which a revisionist and distinctly post-social democratic blend of communitarian and market-conforming themes has been inserted in the name of the 'third way'.[24] Yet, ultimately, it was *Marxism Today*'s new times thesis rather than Giddens' invocation of 'late modernity' that provided the source of New Labour's much-vaunted 'modernization' and re-launch as a paragon of all things novel.[25] That modernization has been associated, variously, with significant concessions to neoliberal economic policies (and the legacy of Thatcherism) and an open acceptance of welfare conditionality. Yet it is also distinguished by a range of more neo-Schumpeterian themes – an emphasis upon the 'new economy', on investment in human capital and on permanent innovation as a condition of continued international competitiveness.

At this point it is perhaps worth briefly considering the reasons for the British left's sympathy, particularly in its academic neo-Marxist guise, for the New Times thesis and with it, arguably a capitulation to neoliberalism. Two points might here be noted. First, broad sections of anglo-Marxist informed political debate were always extremely hostile to what they saw as the voluntarism and revisionist politicism of Hall and Jacques' Gramscian analysis of

Thatcherism. This, they suggested, failed adequately to reflect the determinism in the last instance (and in some variants, the first, the last and every intervening instance) by the economic. Consequently, when an alternative narrative was offered, couched in more familiarly deterministic terms, appealing to the harsh economic realities of the present juncture, it was always more likely to attract the attention and support of those who had cut their teeth on Althusserian structuralist Marxism. Second, by the late 1980s it was fairly clear that the writing was on the wall for any last lingering vestiges of the Keynesianism and (aspirational) social democracy of the postwar period. The legacy of Thatcherism was to be considerable for any incoming Labour administration. Consequently, if journals like *Marxism Today* were to pride themselves on their ability to influence public debate and, in time, political practice, they would have to have to embrace the 'new times' any Labour administration would inevitably face. This was impossible while Thatcherism remained a hegemonic political/economic project rather than an albeit politicized and problematic response to a genuine crisis in – if not of – British capitalism. In short, economic determinism made the, by this stage largely inevitable,[26] capitulation more palatable than an emphasis upon political voluntarism.

The trans-Atlantic axis: The third way as the road to Washington

Yet, while the 'new times' thesis was crucial, the distinctive 'third way' political economy which New Labour came subsequently to embrace and, more recently still, to promote internationally, did not flow in any simple manner from the pages of *Marxism Today*. What Labour came increasingly to accept in the late 1980s and early 1990s was the *need for* a new political economy for new times. It was here that the new times thesis was decisive. Yet, if we are to understand the *content* of that new political economy we need to cast our net rather more widely. As I have elsewhere argued, it was not really until the mid 1990s that what might now be regarded as New, Labour's distinctive 'third way' political economy took shape.[27] This suggests, first, that it is difficult to suggest that its content owes much to Anthony Giddens' conception of the third way which appears little more than a *post hoc* rationalization for a trajectory already well-established by the time his ideas came to attract attention in the party. But it also suggests that such a political economy cannot be attributed to the new times thesis either, for its central message had been internalized long before the significant changes in economic policy which occurred in the mid 1990s. This leaves us with something of a conundrum: for if the content of New Labour's new political economy can be attributed neither to the new times thesis nor Giddens' attempt to pave a path 'beyond left and right', then to what can it be attributed? In what follows I attempt to provide an, albeit brief and perhaps no more than suggestive, answer.

If the significant changes in Labour's political economy did occur between 1994 and 1996, as I have argued, then it is perhaps important to consider where Labour's Shadow Treasury team was looking for ideas in the period immediately following the 1992 General Election debacle. Even the briefest of surveys of the biographies of Labour's key figures and advisors makes that very clear. They were looking across the Atlantic to the self-styled New Democrats.[28] Yet it was the Democrats who, surprisingly perhaps, first made overtures to the Labour Party. Georges Stephanopoulos, in particular, had been most impressed if not by the 1987 campaign itself then certainly by Hugh Hudson's inspirational party political broadcast, during the campaign, of the Kinnocks walking along windswept cliffs. This served to re-establish high-level communications between the parties. For although Joe Napolitan, a Democratic Party electoral consultant had been seconded to London for the duration of the 1987 campaign, his role had been a modest one. Between 1987 and 1992, however, the extent of the dialogue and the degree of strategic learning and policy transfer between the parties grew significantly. Thus, following Labour's defeat in 1992 David Hill, Head of Communications during the campaign, was now seconded to the Clinton team. He took Peter Mandelson with him. Philip Gould, Labour's 'sultan of spin', was approached directly by the Democrats and spent the last four weeks of the campaign in Clinton's election team in Little Rock.[29] Yet up until this point the degree of substantive policy dialogue and transfer was relatively modest with the exchange between the parties principally concentrated on more narrowly electoral and presentational matters.

This was to change from 1993 with Bill Clinton now the new incumbent of the oval office. Washington was now a key destination for Labour's young modernizers, particularly those associated with economic policy, and they racked up the air miles. As David Dolowitz, Stephen Greenwold and David Marsh note, 'Gordon Brown ... and his key adviser Ed Balls ... were frequent visitors to Washington between 1993 and 1997.'[30] What is more, as Desmond King and Mark Wickham-Jones make very clear, they spent most of their time with Clinton's *economic* advisers.[31] Notable among these were Robert Reich, Labour Secretary and chief translator of the globalization thesis into policy proposals for the New Democrat administration, Larry Summers, deputy secretary at the US Treasury (with whom Balls had co-authored an academic paper, while at Harvard, on unemployment in Britain), Larry Katz, chief economist to Reich, and, although somewhat later, Alan Greenspan himself, chairman of the Federal Reserve.

Though largely overlooked in the existing literature, these contacts are potentially very significant. Dolowitz *et al.*, King and Wickham-Jones are principally concerned with welfare reform and, as a consequence emphasize and document the (unquestionable) significance of these trips for the party's conversion to 'welfare-to-work', the New Deal for the unemployed and the adoption of a scarcely disguised version of Clinton's Earned Income Tax Credit proposals in the form of the Working Families Tax Credit. Yet, key those these reforms to New Labour's social policy agenda were, it is surely no less plausible to suggest that this was not all that was going on in these visits.

For, as I have already argued, key aspects of the party's new political economy emerged at about this time. That Labour came to embrace an economic policy which resonated very closely with Reich's understanding of the competitive pressures associated with globalization is surely no coincidence. Indeed, one might plausibly suggest that Reich had rather more influence on New Labour's political economy than he did on that of the New Democrats.[32] Likewise, that the party came to internalize, if not at this point to proclaim externally, the desirability of a more independent regime for the setting of monetary policy is surely not unrelated to the influence of Greenspan on Brown and Balls from 1997.

It is at this point worth examining the economic ideas which Labour may have drawn from its New Democratic counterparts in more detail and to situate them with respect to the party's evolving political economic tradition. In the years immediately prior to its landslide electoral triumph in 1997 Labour came to embrace a very similar set of assumptions about the nature of the global economy and the constraints it imposed to those which had already come to characterize the first Clinton administration. The diagnosis of the condition afflicting contemporary social democracy which it implied was, at the time, fundamentally at odds with that of its geographically more proximate neighbours in Europe. It provided the basis for what was later to become the 'third way'.

In economic policy terms, five themes clearly emerge. Each became an article of faith for New Labour; each reflected a significant shift in economic policy; and each had an enduring pedigree within the Clinton administration. Stated most simply they were: central bank independence; human capital formation; welfare conditionality; labour-market flexibility; and, internationally, a wholesale endorsement of a global regime of free trade and free capital mobility. Here I confine myself to brief comments on the extent of the US influence on the emergent *domestic* agenda.[33] A fuller discussion of the character of New Labour's political economy is presented in the next section.

1. *Central bank independence.* The influence here of Alan Greenspan and Lawrence Summers is unmistakable. It is no secret that Brown and Balls visited Washington many times, and with ever greater frequency, in the years and months prior to the 1997 General Election. High on their agenda were profound reforms to Britain's monetary policy regime. Indeed, it was Greenspan who suggested to the Chancellor-in-waiting (in February 1997) that the decision to cede operational independence to the Bank of England not be announced until after the election, to

maximize the potential boost to the government's monetary policy cred-ibility.[34] Clear though the personal connections are, however, some caution is still required is seeing this as unambiguous evidence of policy transfer. For although New Labour clearly sought guidance from its allies in the Clinton administration and the Fed, it seems unlikely that the origins of and inspiration for operational independence for the Bank of England can be traced to conversations in Washington. Moreover, the model of central bank independence which Labour came to propose for the Bank of England was not that of the Fed, but a combination of ele-ments from New Zealand, Germany and the US.[35] Here, as elsewhere, transatlantic communications were rather more strategic and theoreti-cal. This is not a simple story of policy transfer. What Labour in fact came to embrace was the view, with its origins in the rational expecta-tions revolution of the mid-1970s, that governments could not be trusted with monetary policy. Here the schooling of key Labour strate-gists (notably Balls and Miliband) in US economics departments was as, if not more important, than the idea that the Fed provided a template for sound monetary policy which Labour could usefully emulate.

2. *Human capital formation.* Here a similar story can be told, though the key external influence on New Labour's thinking is now Robert Reich, whose contribution for the New Democrats and New Labour alike, was effec-tively to translate (post-neoclassical) endogenous growth theory into simple policy-relevant mantras. As I shall argue in the next section, New Labour's emphasis upon the need for human capital formation is one of the more distinctive aspects of its 'third way' political economy. Moreover, in replacing a more traditional emphasis upon industrial policy and investment in physical capital in particular, it represents a significant departure from the industrial modernization strategy the party had been developing since 1992.

3. *Welfare conditionality.* A consistent theme both of New Democrat and New Labour rhetoric under Clinton and Blair has been the need to 'make welfare work'; in short, to render welfare expenditure accountable in economic terms. This reflects a common diagnosis of the non-negotiable external economic constraints elected officials face under conditions of globalization. In an era of heightened capital mobility, the competitive imperative identified by authors like Lester Thurow, Ira Magaziner and, again, the ubiquitous Robert Reich, renders welfare for welfare's sake an indulgent luxury. Consequently, welfare must be held to account in terms of its contribution to the competitiveness of the economy. This entails ever greater elements of welfare conditionality and, in particular, the development of an elaborate system of 'welfare-to-work'. The degree of policy transfer is here well-documented.

4. *Labour-market flexibility.* Yet welfare conditionality should not be seen as an isolated aspect of 'third way' political economy. For it reflects a more

fundamental set of assumptions about the operation of the labour-market which are, again, considerably at odds with the European tradition of social democracy – a tradition which Labour, in the early 1990s, seemed keen to embrace.[36] During Kinnock's leadership – under the influence of economists like John Eatwell – Labour came to regard the encompassing labour-market institutions of its Northern European neighbours, characterized as they were by nationally coordinated wage bargaining regimes, as the key to keeping down inflation without driving up interest rates. In this sense, the future that was being projected for the party was one of continental European social democracy. Yet by the mid 1990s, under the influence now of more orthodox economics, New Labour came enthusiastically to proclaim the superiority of a deregulated Anglo-US model of capitalism over that of its more regulated Northern European counterparts. The influence of New Labour's new breed of young, US-trained economic advisors should not be underemphasized. In 'third way' political economy, encompassing labour-market institutions are now re-presented as supply-side rigidities impeding the efficient operation of the labour-market and producing a series of negative externalities for competitiveness, attractiveness to foreign direct investors, the volume of economic activity and employment.

It is important to be careful about what can be concluded on the basis of the above paragraphs. What they present is an argument that is, I think, suggestive of the extent of the trans-Atlantic influence on the content of New Labour's new political economy. There are clear parallels between the ideas New Labour came to embrace and that of its allies in Clinton's New Democrat administration. Those ideas were developed first in the US. And there is clear evidence of close contact between the parties in the period in which Labour's political economy was significantly revised. Authors like Dolowitz *et al*, King and Wickham-Jones have made a compelling *and empirical* case for the transfer of welfare to work from the US to the UK. It remains to be seen whether a similarly convincing empirical case can be made for the transfer of economic policy.

The 'Third Way': The European road from social democracy?

This brings us eventually to the political economy to which New Labour has been drawn and, in particular, to its advocacy of the 'third way' as a pan-European solution to the problems of social democracy in an era of globalization.

Perhaps the defining feature of the political economy of the third way (under conditions of globalization) is the simultaneous pursuit of economic credibility and international competitiveness. There is a directional dependence, in third way political economy, between these twin imperatives, with the former seen as the very condition of the latter. The specification of such goals serves to situate the British (and, potentially, the European) economy internationally in that both credibility and competitiveness entail an essentially external judgement (on the part of mobile asset holders and international consumers respectively).

The credibility imperative has come to be associated with Labour's fiscal moderation and, above all, its radical reform of the institutional architecture of monetary policy; that of competitiveness with a three-fold strategy of labour-market flexibilization, welfare conditionality and human capital formation. Yet far from credibility serving as the condition of the competitiveness, even the most cursory analysis of the political economy of New Labour reveals a series of clear tensions and contradictions *within and between* each set of seemingly laudable objectives. Taken together they constitute a significant challenge to the notion that the third way can serve to pave the British, far less the European, road beyond left and right towards a revitalized and modernized social democratic regime of sustainable economic growth.[37] I consider each aspect in turn.

Credibility

The key to Labour's attempt to bolster the credibility of economic policy-making in Britain was its decision to cede operational autonomy for the setting of interest rates to the Bank of England. The radicalism of such a gesture should not be understated, especially given the proximity to the election of the announcement and the lack of even a hint at such a measure in the manifesto itself. Thus, while the ostensible aim of such a measure may well have been to increase accountability and transparency (to the international financial markets), scarcely could the introduction of a reform of this significance have been delivered in a less accountable or transparent manner. Clearly, however, its real aim was somewhat different – to temper, at a stroke, any residual anxieties of holders of mobile assets about the extent of Labour's conversion in opposition to macroeconomic orthodoxy. It served, moreover, thoroughly to depoliticize monetary policy (again, in the name of transnational economic imperatives beyond the government's control).

Here is not the place for a detailed exposition of the rationale behind this reform nor of the full implications for the setting of monetary policy. Suffice it to note that its consequences can only serve to compromise significantly other aspects of Labour's economic strategy, in particular its articulated aim to boost the competitiveness of the British economy (however understood).[38] A number of points might briefly be noted.

1. Under the new macroeconomic policy regime, monetary policy is now restricted to adjustments in interest rates by an independent monetary authority. Yet interest rate rises are an extremely blunt instrument of

monetary policy, imposing deflationary pressures across the entire economy. In an economy characterized by regional and sectoral segregation (a stubborn manufacturing recession at the same time as a housing and service-sector boom in certain parts of England), this can only serve to institutionalize a deflationary bias in the most disadvantaged sectors and regions of the economy (further exacerbating existing regional and sectoral inequalities and threatening to establish a vicious circle).

2. The British economy has been characterized for some time by chronically low levels of productive investment, reflective of a high cost of capital and the endemic short-termism, risk aversion and overseas orientation of Britain's financial institutions.[39] The result has been significant capacity constraints. Consequently, modest rates of economic growth see the economy operating in excess of full capacity, generating inflationary pressures (and, in anticipation of this, inflationary expectations). The response of an independent central bank in such a scenario is inevitable: interest rates rises. Yet such interest rates hikes can only serve further to increase the cost of capital, thereby lowering productive investment and exacerbating the original structural pathology of the British economy (pervasive capacity constraints). The result, again, is a vicious circle which effectively guarantees an interest rates premium over Britain's competitors which is set to escalate while economic growth exceeds 2 to 2.5 per cent per annum (by the Treasury's own figures).

3. No less significant is the (more widely noted) effect of this on Britain's exchange rates. Consistent interest rate premiums over competitor economies will tend to be associated with an over-valued currency, further penalizing exporters, decreasing their investment incentives and hence exacerbating existing capacity constraints. For a government committed to competitiveness it is strange that its first economic intervention in office should be to impose institutionally its impotence with respect to an exchange rate which is fundamentally and unambiguously corrosive of Britain's ability to compete for market share on the basis of cost.

Competitiveness

New Labour's attempts to guarantee for itself a reputation for credibility may come at a considerable price in terms of its simultaneous goal of competitiveness, but they do not in and of themselves entail a rejection of the 'third way' as a potential model for beleaguered European social democrats. That this is so is for one rather obvious reason: given the exceptional status of the Bank of England prior to Labour's election in 1997 in comparison to its European counterparts (and now in comparison to the ECB) it would make little difference. Third way monetary policy had, in short, been orthodox in continental Europe (as, indeed, in the US) for a while. Yet this is not the end of the story. For even a brief analysis of Labour's 'third way' agenda for labour-market and welfare reform rapidly reveals the dangers for (genuine) social democrats of the projection of Labour's 'third way adventism' onto a European stage.[40]

As noted above, Labour's agenda for labour-market and welfare reform is characterized by a three-fold emphasis upon labour-market flexibility, welfare conditionality and investment in human capital. Each of these dimensions pulls in a different direction. Yet they are unified by a common concern – to render welfare answerable to (perceived) economic imperatives (imperatives again associated with globalization). A number of tensions and internal contradictions can nonetheless be identified which together challenge the notion that the third way might provide a sustainable growth strategy for contemporary European social democrats.

First, Labour's advocacy of labour-market flexibilization arguably owes more to the competitive advantage of the British economy bequeathed from the Thatcher/Major years than it does any more dispassionate assessment of the condition of contemporary Europe or of the imperatives summoned by globalization. Quite simply, given Britain's persistently low levels of productive investment, its resulting capacity constraints and its enduring skills deficit, the Thatcherite accumulation strategy was, unremarkably, premised upon a relatively low-wage, low-skill, deregulated labour-market. Whether it is desirable for Labour to continue to seek a competitive advantage for Britain within Europe on this basis is a debatable point. Suffice it to note the obvious difficulties in re-branding Britain a high-wage, high-skill economy with the significant investment in both human and, first, physical capital that such a transformation would entail. Nonetheless, what is surely clear is that labour-market flexibilization is hardly a plausible, let alone desirable, strategy for Northern European economies (such as the Swedish, Finnish, Danish, Dutch or German) which have traditionally sought competitive advantage on the basis of quality not cost.

Second, the high rates of labour turnover which already characterize the British (and certain sections of the North American) labour market(s), and which are only likely to be exacerbated by further labour market flexibilization, militate severely against human capital formation. As elsewhere noted, 'if labour turnover is high and labour shedding is simple, why invest in the skills of your workers when you can poach those skilled by others and when any investment in human capital you do make will only enhance the mobility in the labour market of those in whom you invest?.'[41]

Third, and relatedly, Labour's emphasis upon human capital formation, while in one sense laudable, is surely misplaced in the absence of a strategy to reverse Britain's poor record of investment in physical capital. Indeed, it would seem to be based on a (convenient?) misreading of the new and much-vaunted endogenous growth theory which, in fact, emphasizes more forcefully investment in physical capital, research and development and new product development and gives relatively little attention to human capital formation.[42] Put simply, given Britain's pathological capacity constraints, to prioritize human capital formation is to put the cart before the horse. It is to invest in human capital at a time when Britain suffers from a distinct lack of investment in the physical capital which a highly trained workforce might deploy. It may also be to assume that a supply of skills generates its own demand. As the empirical evidence suggests, however, the problem is the not so much the supply of skills but the under-utilization of extant skills.[43]

Finally, while New Labour's rhetorical commitment to full employment is to be welcomed, it must surely be taken with a considerable dose of salt. For since last it was invoked by the Labour Party its meaning has changed significantly, such that what now passes for full employment is in fact far closer to what most neoclassical economists term the natural or equilibrium rate of unemployment (in which there is a rough parity of vacancies and benefit claimants). Such a definition serves to render unemployment an inertial supply-side phenomenon. This, in turn, justifies an emphasis upon employability and the obligations of benefit recipients to match their skills to the needs of the economy.[44] Such a strategy may work well with the economy operating in excess of full capacity, but it leaves no space for counter-cyclical measures which might respond to the demand-side characteristics of unemployment especially in times of recession. In short, while it may deal relatively successfully with inertial unemployment it offers no solution to structural or cyclical unemployment. It is, as such, no solution to the pathologies of European labour markets.

The road *from* Washington: the search for alternatives

The lesson of the above analysis is essentially a simple one. It may well be convenient for parties of the centre-left to invoke globalization as a non-negotiable external economic constraint in justifying otherwise unpalatable social and economic reforms – or, indeed, their accommodation to the legacy of such reforms enacted by others. Yet there is no particular reason to assume that the 'third way' represents a feasible path beyond left and right towards a revitalized and modernized social democratic regime of sustainable economic growth in Britain or elsewhere, far less that it represents the *only* alternative to neoliberalism in the context of a genuinely global political economy. If we are to improve the quality of public debate and to regain the capacity to hold political actors accountable for their conduct, then we must acquire a far greater scepticism as to the invocation of globalization as a non-negotiable external economic constraint. We can no longer afford – if ever we could – to confuse political expediency for economic necessity.

This is perhaps suggestive of a more general and theoretical point, a theme of much of the present volume. If we are to move beyond the structural determinism that dominates discussion of the contemporary political economic environment, it is necessary that we recognize the constructed and hence contestable nature of 'globalization' and the constraints it is held to impose. Discourses of globalization are the constructions of agents, often advanced for (perceived) strategic purpose. It is only if they remain unchallenged that the imperatives of globalization appear inevitable. Moreover, as I have sought to demonstrate, if they appear inevitable they may serve to become self-fulfilling prophecies.

It is my argument that there is, in fact, nothing inevitable about the imperatives of globalization in whose image 'third way' political economy has been constructed. It is, then, important to conclude with the outline of one potential alternative.[45] As a strategy, it derives fairly directly from the above analysis. The problem with much of the third way's tacit accommodation to neoliberal economics is the impotence of the state, specifically in its ability to intervene in the economic sphere, that this entails. Were the British economy characterized by comparative advantage, high productivity growth, a surfeit of human capital and persistently impressive levels of investment in physical capital this would present less of a problem (at least, for a while). But, in each respect, we know this not to be the case. What this suggests, is that what Britain requires is the return to a rather older tradition in leftist economic and political analysis – one that acknowledges the specificity of both British capitalism and its distinctive pathologies and retains (or seeks to reinstil) a confidence in the state's capacity to intervene to (re)regulate economic relations. The irony in this is that precisely such ideas – whose lineage can be traced from Anderson and Nairn to Hutton[46] – had considerable purchase amongst many modernizers within the Labour Party until the mid 1990s (marked, perhaps by Bryan Gould's self-inflicted antipodean exile and Robin Cook's 'promotion' beyond the sphere of economic influence). What such an emphasis upon the distinctive pathologies of British capitalism would also suggest is the inherent danger of exporting the third way to continental European economies whose institutional and cultural traditions exhibit different and diverse developmental trajectories. For if it is unlikely to provide much of a solution to the 'the state we're in', then it is even less likely to present a universal panacea for the state of European social democracy.

Notes

* The author would like to acknowledge the help and advice of Mark Bevir, David Coates, Chris Howell, Ben Rosamond, Vivien Schmidt, Frank Trentmann, Helen Wallace and Matthew Watson in developing the argument presented here and the support of the UK's Economic and Social Research Council for ongoing research on 'Globalization, European Integration and the European Social Model' (L213252043).
1. For evidence of the projected global reach of the 'third way', see Anthony Giddens, (ed.), *The Global Third Way Debate* (Cambridge: Polity, 2001).

2. On alternative conceptions of globalization, see Colin Hay and Ben Rosamond, 'Globalization, European and the Discursive Construction of Economic Imperatives', *Journal of European Public Policy* 9(2) (2002), 147–67.

3. Colin Hay, *The Political Economy of New Labour: Labouring Under False Pretences?* (Manchester: Manchester University Press, 1999); Mark Wickham-Jones, 'New Labour in the Global Economy: Partisan Politics and the Social Democratic Model', *British Journal of Politics and International Relations* 2(1) (2000), 1–25.

4. This is in fact most clearly expressed not in any statement by the British government itself, but in the Presidential papers for the Lisbon Special European Council of May 2000 which addressed directly the future of the 'European social model' and whose agenda the British government was extremely influential in shaping. Interviews, Cabinet Office and Number 10 Downing Street, April 2001. See also Tony Blair and Gerhard Schröder, 'The Third Way/Die Neue Mitte', reprinted in Otto Hombach, *The Politics of the New Centre* (Cambridge: Polity, 1999).

5. See, for instance, David Held *et al*, *Global Transformations* (Cambridge: Polity, 1999); Paul Hirst and Grahame Thompson, *Globalization in Question*, Second Edition (Cambridge: Polity, 1999); A. Kleinknecht and J. ter Wengel, 'The Myth of Globalization', *Cambridge Journal of Economics* 22 (1998), 637–47.

6. Hay and Rosamond, 'Globalization, European Integration ... ', p. 148; emphasis added.

7. For a more theoretical treatment of the duplicitous appeal to political and economic constraints, see, Mark Bevir, *The Logic of the History of Ideas* (Cambridge: Cambridge University Press, 1999), pp. 267–70.

8. Stephen Byers, plenary address, World Trade Organization ministerial meeting, Seattle, 30 November 1999.

9. See, for instance, Robert Reich, *The Work of Nations* (New York: Vintage Books, 1992); *Education and the Next Economy* (Washington DC: National Education Association, 1988); *Locked In the Cabinet* (New York: Alfred A. Knopf, 1997).

10. Andrew Glyn *et al*, 'The Rise and Fall of the Golden Age', in Scott Marglin and Juliet Schor, (eds), *The Golden Age of Capitalism: Reinterpreting the Postwar Experience* (Oxford: Clarendon Press, 1990), pp. 39–125; Peter A. Hall, *Governing the Economy: The Politics of State Intervention in Britain and France* (New York: Oxford University Press, 1986).

11. For more detailed elaboration of the unfolding and narration of the moment of crisis itself, see Colin Hay, 'The Crisis of Keynesianism and the Rise of Neoliberalism in Britain: An Ideational institutionalist Approach', in John L. Campbell and Ove K. Pedersen, (eds), *The Rise of Neoliberalism and Institutional Analysis* (Princeton: Princeton University Press, 2001), pp. 192–218; 'Narrating Crisis: The Discursive Construction of the Winter of Discontent', *Sociology* 30(2) (1996), 253–77.

12. Sam Brittan, The Economic Contradictions of Democracy, *British Journal of Political Science* 5(2)(1975), 129–59; Michel Crozier *et al*, *Crisis of Democracy* (New York: New York University Press, 1975); J. Douglas, 'The Overloaded Crown', *British Journal of Political Science* 6(4)(1976), 483–505; Anthony King, 'Overload: Problems of Governing Britain in the 1970s', *Political Studies* 23(2/3) (1975), 284–96.

13. Adam Przeworksi and Michael Wallerstein, 'Structural Dependence of the State on Capital', *American Political Science Review* 82(1)(1988), 11–30; Dani Rodrik, *Has Globalization Gone Too Far?* (Washington, DC: Institute for International

Economics, 1997); Fritz Scharpf, *Crisis and Choice in European Social Democracy* (Ithaca, NY: Cornell University Press, 1991); Mark Wickham-Jones, 'Anticipating Social Democracy, Preempting Anticipations: Economic Policy-Making in the British Labour Party, 1987–1992', *Politics and Society* 23(4) (1995), 465–94.

14. For revisionist accounts of the 'Mitterrand experiment' see, especially, David Cameron, *The Colours of a Rose: On the Ambiguous Record of French Socialism*, Center for European Studies Working Paper (Cambridge, MA: Harvard University, 1988); 'Exchange Rate Policies in France, 1981–1983: The Regime-Defining Choices of the Mitterrand Presidency', in A. Daley, (ed.), *The Mitterrand Era: Policy Alternatives and Political Mobilisation in France* (Basingstoke: Macmillan, now Palgrave Macmillan 1996), pp. 56–82; Serge Halmi *et al*, 'The Mitterrand Experience, in Jonathan Michie and John Grieve Smith, (eds), *Unemployment in Europe'* (London: Academic Press, 1994), pp. 97–115.

15. See, especially, Peter A. Hall, 'Policy Paradigms, Social Learning and the State: The Case of Economic Policy-Making in Britain', *Comparative Politics* 25(3) (1993), 175–96.

16. One might, for instance, think of the 1832 Reform Act as the culmination of a period, following the French Revolution, in which the mobilization within the political elite of a sense of revolutionary crisis (however unrealistic the perception) prepared the way for institutional reform. Yet, as Thomis and Holt perceptively note, 'like many threats it [revolution] remained most potent when not carried out and its employment in politics, the art of the possible, was to some extent a matter of elaborate bluff.' Malcolm I. Thomis and Peter Holt, *Threats of Revolution in Britain, 1789–1848* (London: Archon, 1977), p. 83. See also John Belchem, *Popular Radicalism in Nineteenth Century Britain* (New York: St Martin's Press, now Palgrave Macmillan 1996); Charles Tilly, *Popular Contention in Great Britain, 1758–1834* (Cambridge, MA: Harvard University Press), esp. pp. 308 ff.; Dror Wahrman, *Imaging the Middle Class: The Political Representation of Class in Britain, c. 1870–1840* (Cambridge: Cambridge University Press, 1995). A similar process of crisis narration has been identified over the issue of tariff reform and free trade in the period following World War. See, in particular, Frank Trentmann, 'Political Culture and Political Economy: Interest, Ideology and Free Trade', *Review of International Political Economy* 5(2)(1998), 217–51; Susan Pedersen, 'From National Crisis to National Crisis: British Politics, 1914–1931', *Journal of British Studies* 33(3)(1994), 322–35. On the crisis of 'overload' of the 1970s, see Mark Bevir and R. A. W. Rhodes, 'Narratives of Thatcherism', *West European Politics* 21(1)(1999), 97–119; Colin Hay, Crisis and Political Development in Postwar Britain, in David Marsh *et al*, *Postwar British Politics in Perspective* (Cambridge: Polity, 1999), pp. 87–106, esp. pp. 93–7.

17. Hay, 'The Crisis of Keynesianism'.

18. See note 15 above.

19. Colin Hay and Matthew Watson, *Rendering the Contingent Necessary: New Labour's Neoliberal Conversion and the Discourse of Globalization*, Center for European Studies Working Paper #8.4 (Cambridge, MA: Harvard University, 1998); Hay, *The Political Economy of New Labour*.

20. On the significance of ideational legacies, see Mark Bevir, *The Logic of the History of Ideas* Cambridge: Cambridge University Press; 'New Labour: A Study in Ideology', *British Journal of Politics and International Relations*, 2 (2000), 277–301.

21. It might be noted that the liberalization of capital controls in both France and Germany occurred under Socialist or Social Democratic administrations.

218 New Labour and the 'Third Way'

22. Here the specificity of British political dynamics is perhaps worth emphasizing again. Although it is certainly the case that discourses of globalization have come to play a key role in the downsizing of social democratic aspirations across Western Europe (and elsewhere besides), this revisioning of the parameters of political possibility has tended to occur more gradually and somewhat later than in the British case. Indeed, in recent years the British Labour Party has acted as an agent for the dissemination of a 'third way' (post) social democratic accommodation to the perceived economic imperatives of globalization. In both the rise of neoliberalism and the invocation of globalization as a non-negotiable external economic constraint, Britain has been an early mover. The adversarial and bipartisan character of British political competition renders it particularly prone to the narration of crisis and this, in turn, tends to lend itself to a more discontinuous, punctuated and abrupt transition between policy paradigms – whether those paradigms are governmental or internal to a particular political party.

23. See, for instance, Stuart Hall and Martin Jacques, (eds), *The Changing Face of Politics in the 1990s* (London: Lawrence and Wishart, 1989).

24. See, for a flavour of this heady cocktail, Anthony Giddens, *The Third Way: The Renewal of Social Democracy* (Cambridge: Polity, 1998).

25. For a contrite admission of culpability and guilt by intellectual association see Stuart Hall's comments in Les Terry, 'Travelling the Hard Road to Renewal: A Continuing Conversation with Stuart Hall', *Renewal* 8 (1997), 39–58.

26. Inevitable only in the sense that by this stage the British Labour Party clearly lacked the motivation for a genuinely counter-hegemonic attempt to narrate the crisis of Thatcherite neoliberalism.

27. Colin Hay, 'Anticipating Accommodations, Accommodating Anticipations: The Appeasement of Capital in the Modernisation of the British Labour Party, 1987–1992', *Politics and Society* 25 (1997), 234–56.

28. See, for instance, Paul Anderson and Nyta Mann, *Safety First: The Making of New Labour* (London: Granta Books, 1998); Philip Gould, *Unfinished Revolution* (London: Little, Brown, 1998); John Rentoul, *Tony Blair* (London: Little Brown, 1995); Paul Routledge, *Gordon Brown: The Biography* (London: Simon and Schuster, 1998); for more academic treatments see also Desmond King and Mark Wickham-Jones, 'From Clinton to Blair: The Democratic (Party) Origins of Welfare to Work', *Political Quarterly* 68 (1999), 62–74; Bill Jordon, *The New Politics of Welfare: Social Justice in a Global Context* (London: Sage, 1998); David Dolowitz, Stephen Greenwold and David Marsh, 'Policy Transfer: Something Old, Something New, Something Borrowed, But Why Red, White and Blue?', *Parliamentary Affairs* 52(4) (1999), 719–30.

29. See Gould, *Unfinished Revolution*, 162–71.

30. Dolowitz *et al*, 'Policy Transfer', 723.

31. King and Wickham-Jones, 'From Clinton to Blair', 68–9.

32. As Douglas Jänicke points out, Reich was rapidly marginalized within the first Clinton administration by economic policy analysts – like Leon Panetta and Alan Greenspan – who gave rather more importance to cutting budget deficits than human capital formation. Jänicke, 'New Labour and the Clinton Presidency', in David Coates and Peter Lawler, (eds), *New Labour in Power* (Manchester: Manchester University Press, 2001), pp. 34–48; Margaret Weir, 'The Collapse of Bill Clinton's Third Way', in Stuart White, (ed.), *New Labour: The Progressive Future?* (Basingstoke: Palgrave Macmillan, 2001), pp. 137–48.

33. Though on the relationship between the internal and external dimensions of New Labour's economic policy, see David Coates and Colin Hay, 'The Internal and External Face of New Labour's Political Economy', *Government and Opposition* 36(4) (2001), 447–72.

34. Geoffrey Robinson, *The Unconventional Minister* (London: Michael Joseph, 2000); Philip Stevens, 'The Treasury Under Labour', in Anthony Seldon, (ed), *The Blair Effect: The Blair Government 1997–2001* (London: Little Brown, 2001), pp. 185–208.

35. HM Treasury, *Reforming Britain's Economic and Financial Policy: Towards Greater Economic Stability* (Basingstoke: Palgrave Macmillan, 2002), ch. 6.

36. See, for instance, John Eatwell, 'The Development of Labour Policy, 1987–92', in Jonathan Michie, (ed.), *The Economic Legacy, 1987–92* (London: Academic Press, 1992); Wickham-Jones, 'New Labour in the Global Economy'.

37. For a much more detailed elaboration of this argument see Coates and Hay, 'The Internal and External Face of New Labour's Political Economy'.

38. On the contested meaning of competitiveness, see D. P. Rapkin and J. R. Strand, 'Competitiveness: Useful Concept, Political Slogan or Dangerous Obsession?', in D. P. Rapkin and W. P. Avery, (eds), *National Competitiveness in a Global Economy* (Boulder, CO: Lynne Rienner, 1995).

39. Matthew Watson and Colin Hay, 'In the Dedicated Pursuit of Dedicated Capital: Restoring an Indigenous Investment to British Capitalism', *New Political Economy* 3(3)(1998), 407–26.

40. On the evangelism of New Labour's 'third way adventism', see Colin Hay and Matthew Watson, 'Neither Here Nor There? New Labour's Third Way Adventism', in Lothar Funk, (ed), *The Economics and the Politics of the Third Way* (Münster: Lit Verlag, 1999), pp. 171–80.

41. Coates and Hay, 'The Internal and External Face of New Labour's Political Economy'.

42. It is perhaps interesting to note here that Reich is, again, a key figure in the promotion of the rather denuded variant of the new growth theory – with its emphasis upon human capital formation – with which third way political economy has come to be associated. See, especially, his *Locked in the Cabinet*.

43. Ewart Keep and Ken Mayhew, 'Vocational Education and Training and Economic Performance', in Tony Buxton *et al*, (eds), *Britain's Economic Performance*, Second Edition (London: Routledge, 1998), pp. 165–86.

44. A consistent theme, it might again be noted, of Reich's variant of the new growth theory.

45. The argument is outlined in more detail elsewhere. See Hay, *Political Economy of New Labour*; Watson and Hay, 'In the Dedicated Pursuit … '.

46. See, in particular, Perry Anderson, *English Questions* (London: Verso, 1992); Will Hutton, *The State We're In* (London: Viking, 1996, revised edition).

Index

Printed and bound by CPI Group (UK) Ltd, Croydon, CR0 4YY